Praise for
The High-Performing Real Estate Team

"Read this book and learn from the best in the industry. Brian Icenhower unlocks the five components of team growth and provides you with the tools to do the same on your own real estate team."

> —Rick Fuller, Team Leader of the Rick Fuller Team, San Francisco, California: $123 million in annual sales volume with 256 units sold per year

"Brian Icenhower and Icenhower Coaching gave Edie Waters Network the path for explosive growth over the last seven years. As I started my career, meeting with Brian, I was at $30 million in real estate volume. Last year in 2020 we topped $150 million in volume. For those willing to do the work, and follow the guide and path in this book, the future is in your hands."

> —Edie Waters, Team Leader of the Edie Waters Network, Kansas City, Missouri: $152 million in annual sales volume with 605 units sold per year

"Before we started implementing the team dashboard, everyone on my team was running around like a chicken with its head cut off. Now, thanks to this book, the team dashboard is a part of our everyday life and keeps us on track with the specific activities we need to do to achieve our goals. This book has changed our whole business. Before, we didn't know how we should be spending our time and what we should be focusing on. It has revolutionized our real estate team. This is the bible for real estate teams."

> —Cynthia Ostos, Broker & Team Leader of the Cynthia Ostos Real Estate Team, Toronto, Canada: $28 million in annual sales volume with 42 units sold per year

"I went from a solo agent to owning and operating the highest producing team in our area in just five years by utilizing the tools, structures, and systems outlined in this amazing book by Brian Icenhower! It's the operations manual that everyone in real estate should be reading."

> —Eric Craig, Team Leader of the Eric Craig Real Estate Team, Smithville, Missouri: $100 million in annual sales volume with 400 units sold per year

"Within a year of implementing the systems and techniques explained in this book, we instantly tripled the size and sales production of our team. Our team's culture and sales volume have steadily improved every year thereafter, as well. I would highly recommend this book to anyone looking to take their real estate business to the next level."

—Noah Bailey, Team Leader of the Noah Bailey Group, Jacksonville, Florida: $68 million in annual sales volume with 178 units sold per year

"The concepts and processes revealed in this book make complete sense and the dashboard makes it possible to see if we are doing the things we deemed necessary as a team to hit our viral goal. Understanding what activities have the best return and focusing on those activities has had a big impact on the team and the team members' success."

—Chad and Tami Aronson, Team Leaders of Team Tami, Los Angeles, California: $60 million in annual sales volume with 43 units sold per year

the
High-
performing
real estate team

BRIAN ICENHOWER

the High-performing real estate team

FIVE KEYS TO DRAMATICALLY INCREASING
SALES & COMMISSIONS

WILEY

Published by John Wiley & Sons, Inc., Hoboken, New Jersey.
Published simultaneously in Canada.

For general information on our other products and services or for technical support, please contact our Customer Care Department within the United States at (800) 762-2974, outside the United States at (317) 572-3993 or fax (317) 572-4002.

Wiley publishes in a variety of print and electronic formats and by print-on-demand. Some material included with standard print versions of this book may not be included in e-books or in print-on-demand. If this book refers to media such as a CD or DVD that is not included in the version you purchased, you may download this material at **http://booksupport.wiley.com**. For more information about Wiley products, visit **www.wiley.com**.

Library of Congress Cataloging-in-Publication Data:

Names: Icenhower, Brian, author.
Title: The high-performing real estate team : Five keys to dramatically increasing sales & commissions / Brian Icenhower.
Description: Hoboken, New Jersey : Wiley, [2022] | Includes index.
Identifiers: LCCN 2021031037 (print) | LCCN 2021031038 (ebook) | ISBN 9781119801856 (paperback) | ISBN 9781119801863 (ePDF) | ISBN 9781119801870 (ePub)
Subjects: LCSH: Real estate business. | Real estate agents. | Success in business.
Classification: LCC HD1375 .I43 2022 (print) | LCC HD1375 (ebook) | DDC 333.33—dc23
LC record available at https://lccn.loc.gov/2021031037
LC ebook record available at https://lccn.loc.gov/2021031038

Cover Design: Rachel Varner
Cover Images: Roof: ©lyovajan/Shutterstock
Team: ©Pushkarevskyy/Shutterstock

SKY10028913_080921

For Robyn, Carson, and Landon

Contents

Part 4   Powerful Team Tools to Drive Growth   163

Part 5   Huddle Up and Make a Plan   199

Preface: How to Use This Book to Grow Your Teams' Sales

Traditional approaches to organizational change-implementation are dictatorial, undemocratic, exclusionary, and alienating. A single individual or small group of people makes unilateral decisions designed around their own wants and needs and without consideration for how this affects their team members.

While the principles we speak about have been proven again and again across countless real estate teams, they are only as effective as their application.

Naturally, we want you to be excited and energized by this book, but if you rush through the process and apply sweeping changes without warning or sincere collaboration, you risk alienating and overwhelming the people you most need to persuade and reach with our message. Instead, we invite you to view this book and its component principles as a manual for a slow, steady, seamless – and successful – team metamorphosis that abandons outdated methods of implementation and embraces an entirely different mode of transformation.

A Manual for Metamorphosis

Metamorphosis stresses the necessity of action and participation coupled with patient persistence. A metamorphosis is a *process*. Growing a real estate team is not a change that happens suddenly and dramatically overnight. Rather, it is a transformation that takes time and occurs in evolving, incremental, yet seamless stages.

In our many years of coaching and consulting real estate teams and brokerages to greater success, we have discovered that it's far more effective to implement radical changes gradually and collaboratively. As well as providing you with insights and practical guidance that you can begin to apply right away, our goal is to provide you and your team members with an *experiential* and immersive guide to the key components of organizational growth.

The best way to connect to the five components of team growth is to process and internalize the principles and information for yourself. To do this, we suggest a simple and modest – but highly effective – approach to change-implementation: Team leaders and team members participate in a book club in which they read, discuss, and process this book as a community.

The Team Book Club

We have seen this implementation model work with wonderful results. Introducing the Team Book Club!

FIGURE P.1   The Team Book Club Logo

To conduct your book club, the team leader should read through the book first. Once the leader has finished reading this book and digested its principles, everyone on the real estate team should also receive a copy. At that point, your team will embark on a five-week journey through the book together. Each week, for five consecutive weeks, team members will read one section of the book and meet to discuss it. At the end of the five weeks, your real estate team will have a clear understanding of each of the five components of team growth, and will be ready to take what you have learned and apply it directly to your team.

Once the book club part of the process is over, you will spend the next week "huddling up" to create an Annual Business Plan. In all, the implementation process will actually take place over a six-week period, piloted and facilitated by the crucial Team Book Club gatherings. In the final week, your team will synthesize each of the five components of growth, and execute on the principles you have read, discussed, and internalized over the preceding five weeks.

If you are the leader of a larger real estate team or brokerage, we recommend that you first hold a book club with your organization's leadership team. The exact same reading schedule and book club process will occur, but among your organization's leaders/managers. After the leadership team has read this book and conducted their own book club, they will then branch out to conduct *simultaneous* book clubs within different departments or divisions.

Navigating the book as a group and assimilating each component in turn allows you to transform your team in incremental yet seamless stages. Week by week, your team will consolidate and synthesize critical growth goals while bonding together and maturing as a team at the same time.

What's more, we have found that being exposed to ideas from an *authoritative, experienced*, and *neutral third party* results in higher levels of receptivity and acceptance. Our book, and its accompanying book club, eliminates the traditional hierarchical relationship where the real estate team leaders simply tell their team members what to do without any warning or demonstrable rationale or reasoning. Instead, team leaders and team members are on the *same side*, reading, discussing, and collaborating on the ideas and principles set forth in this book together and, for the most part, at the same time. Together, you will follow the same journey toward realizing, "*this* is what we need to do if we're going to succeed and grow."

THE TEAM BOOK CLUB

WEEK ① Part One: What's Your Viral Goal? Commissions Earned, Volume Closed, or Units Sold?

WEEK ② Part Two: The Sales Team Activities That Will Grow Your Pipeline

WEEK ③ Part Three: Cultivate Personal Responsibility Through Team Accountability

WEEK ④ Part Four: Powerful Team Tools to Drive Growth

WEEK ⑤ Part Five: Huddle Up and Make a Plan

WEEK ⑥ Business Planning Week

FIGURE P.2   The Team Book Club Outline

The five components of team growth presented in this book are well-established and proven concepts that are completely in line with the dominant discourse on real estate business management and transformational team leadership.

Together, you will follow the _same_ journey.

FIGURE P.3   Together

This book, and the ideas set forth within it, differs primarily in its engaging, *experiential*, and effective implementation process. By the end of the Team Book Club process we are certain that you'll agree, and be more than ready to huddle up and put the five components of team growth into action on your real estate team.

Too Many People? Short on Time and Space? How to Host a Digital Book Club

Now, we know what some team leaders have been thinking. How on earth can I possibly implement a book club on *my* real estate team? While gathering and conversing face to face in the same physical space is a great way for team members who share an office to bond as a group, an online/digital book club is a smart solution for:

- Larger teams or brokerages with multiple locations;
- Teams with agents that work remotely;
- Teams that are short on physical space, or where it's highly impractical or impossible for everyone to meet together at the same time;
- Meeting with your team during a pandemic.

Count Us In! But How Do We Do It?

If a digital book club is right for you, all of the standard book club rules will still apply. You will need to:

- Establish clear expectations about the purpose and goal of the book club.
- Set a regular schedule or time to (virtually) meet and talk about each chapter.
- Distribute a prepared chapter summary and/or discussion questions before every meeting (more about that in the next chapter).
- Hold team members accountable to attending and actively participating in each book club session.

Choose a Facilitator/Moderator for Discussions

If you've ever been to a book club in real life, you know that too many book lovers can get out of control quickly. But if you think in-person discussions can get out of hand or derailed, just wait until you try to hold a productive discussion online.

It's important that your online book club is organized and managed by a chosen facilitator who is responsible for moderating discussion, posting "meeting" dates and times, posting the weekly chapter summary, getting the discussion going with prepared questions, and who has the rights and ability to remove wholly irrelevant or unnecessarily argumentative comments, in the unlikely event that the issue arises.

Onward!

After explaining how to use this book to grow your teams' sales, we now provide you with an introduction to give you a glimpse into the transformation that is to come.

Introduction

Welcome to *The High-Performing Real Estate Team* – a practical and experiential guide to the fundamental components of team growth for real estate teams. This book has been designed to help your team realize greater success and profitability and to serve more people, while bonding and growing as a team at the same time. We're really glad you're here.

We're assuming you picked up this book because, like so many others, your real estate team is stuck in the status quo, has reached a point of stasis, or is at a significant turning point.

Perhaps you are the member of a real estate team. You see the sales targets, but you don't understand what you should be doing to reach those targets. You feel stuck, and not very motivated to work hard because you don't see how being on the team is really helping your business improve. In fact, you may even be considering jumping ship and going solo. You are frustrated and you are looking for answers.

You may be the leader of your real estate team. You know that sales targets need to be established and written down and you've done just that, but you're still not growing. You're tracking results and outcomes, but you're still not growing. You're driving your team members to work harder, faster, and longer, but still you're not growing. Try as you might, you just can't seem to move the needle and hit your target revenue.

Maybe your agents are simply not producing. Or, maybe you are experiencing a high amount of personnel turnover. Perhaps you are stuck at your current production level. You might not know how to grow your team to take yourself, as well as your team, to the next level. Or, it could be that you just feel it's time to up your leadership game.

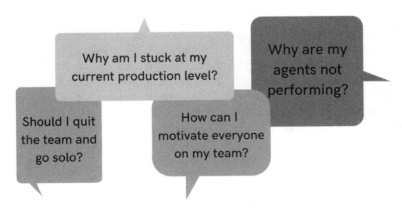

FIGURE I.1 Common Questions

Congratulations – whether you are the team leader or the team member, you're in the right place. Whatever your criteria of growth, this book has been designed to help you achieve your real estate team's definition and vision of growth.

This book helps you understand and implement the fundamental, non-negotiable components necessary for real estate team growth and success. We are here to help you every step of the way.

The Status Quo

Before we look at where you are headed and how you hope to grow, let's take a look at where you are now and examine the status quo.

Maybe you were drawn to this book because, like so many others, your team is stuck in an *unsatisfactory* status quo. This isn't to say that your team is failing. In fact, to other people you may seem to be ticking along quite nicely, and there are days when you may even feel this way yourself. Yet, deep down, you're not content with the current state of affairs and you know that your real estate team is nowhere near where it could and should be.

Let's take a look at the existing state or condition of the majority of real estate teams today. An abundance of academic research and anecdotal accounts confirms what we have seen in our decades of coaching and consulting with team and brokerage leaders across North America: apathy, fear, a resistance to change, and a futile focus on day-to-day operations is the unfortunate status quo for a great many people.

Apathy

In the coming pages, you will hear us talking about creating a goal that energizes your team members and spreads like wildfire around your real estate team. We call it having a "viral goal," and it is the first and most important component for initiating growth and creating buy-in with those around you.

Nowadays, when people hear the word "viral" they probably think of an adorable, hilarious, or poignant video that's been shared many millions of times by email and social media. As you'll soon see, this is the positive, beneficial, and exponentially sharable vision that we have in mind when we urge you to create a viral goal for your team.

However, the word viral also brings to mind the flu or some other undesirable illness. Recently, this analogy hits even harder with the recent COVID-19 pandemic. Nevertheless, the analogy of a virus seems to serve us well when we consider the mechanics of a virus. Without boring you with all the microscopic details about how a virus works, at Icenhower Coaching and Consulting (ICC) when we think about the apathy that occurs within real estate teams, we see many similarities between biological viruses and the lack of interest, enthusiasm, and concern that affects so many groups, institutions, and workplaces across the country and beyond.

For example, oftentimes a virus works its way through someone's system before they notice any symptoms or obvious signs of illness. One minute you feel fine, perhaps a little more tired than usual, and the next minute you're barely able to function. Likewise, apathy can slowly and silently work its way through a real estate team and remain largely undetected until the most pronounced and damaging symptoms are impossible to ignore, and the culture and environment has become dangerously dysfunctional.

Apathy is contagious. It enters a team unnoticed and spreads from person to person. It seems to come out of nowhere and yet, when you look back, you can see that the signs have been there all along. Like the person who just feels "a little more tired than usual," a real estate team that's been infected with apathy is filled with team members who are listless and lacking in energy each and every day. They're certainly not happy but neither are they disgruntled or particularly resentful or discontented. Rather, they're just there – going through the motions, watching the clock, or engrossed in social media, completing only the tasks absolutely required of them in any given day, disconnected from their peers and leaders, channeling their energy into petty dramas with coworkers or group members, and counting down the seconds till the weekend.

No real estate team is immune to apathy. While the leaders and team members of a given real estate team might be dissatisfied and discontented with the existing state of affairs, when apathy seeps in it dulls people's desire and motivation, and heightens a human fear of and resistance to the change that may end up curing apathy, which then presents further challenges for achieving team growth and success.

Fear and Resistance to Change

Research from McKinsey & Company shows that 70% of all organizational transformations fail, largely due to employee resistance and a lack of support from those in positions of leadership. Whether the statistic is quite as high as that is subject to some debate, but in our experience a resistance to change goes hand in hand with apathy and is a key reason why so many real estate teams get stuck in a stagnant and precarious status quo.

Change is difficult for everyone. While there are some people who are less risk-averse and open to change than others, there are few people who don't feel somewhat anxious at the prospect of a major upheaval in their lives and routines, particularly if that upheaval means a heavier workload or increased responsibilities.

Salaried or hourly employees are not motivated by growth because growth means change and change means more work for them with, typically, no commensurate change in pay (at least until the team achieves its growth goals). Their existing routine represents stability, order, and calmness. Apathy coupled with resistance to change provides little incentive to push people out of their comfort zone.

And while you might think that commission-based employees, like most real estate team members, would be more than inclined to embrace the changes required to achieve success and growth, the fact is that they, too, are resistant to change. To be more precise, they are resistant to the *activities* that drive growth. While team members want more listings and more sales, it can be enormously difficult for them to perform the activities they need to, day in day out.

Knocking on a stranger's door, calling people who aren't expecting you, or contacting people who do not want to be contacted is extremely uncomfortable, no matter how talented and persuasive you are. Even with good training and a good script, it's not a "fun" activity. On top of that, the level and frequency of rejection that comes with a sales-oriented job is very difficult to deal with, especially for ambitious people who don't want to risk failure, or for team leaders who don't want to take risks.

We fear change because we can't anticipate or guarantee the outcome.

A Futile Focus on the Day-to-Day

Generally speaking, it should be abundantly clear to anyone that, when your people are disconnected, demotivated, or despairing, it shows in their productivity, performance, and participation.

Because of this, real estate team leaders become entangled and lost in a futile focus on the day-to-day. As we explain further later, 80% of what we do on a daily and yearly basis represents a very small minority of the results we achieve. The 80% is the daily issues and other duties that take up most people's time and gives rise to the biggest excuse for not performing impactful, growth-building activities. People tend to practice "crisis management" all day long by always handling every problem or task as it arises. This is practicing "business by default" by handling each task as it comes along, as opposed to blocking out time to practice "business by design," and focusing on activities that will tangibly and exponentially take you toward your goal.

Whether it's managing existing business and daily tasks and to-do lists, putting out various smaller and bigger fires, or intervening in interpersonal drama among your people, expending all your energy on the 80% day-to-day operations, demands, concerns, and activities leaves you with no space to breathe let alone thrive, evolve, and grow.

If your real estate team isn't _growing_, then it's dying.

FIGURE I.2   If Your Real Estate Team Isn't Growing

If you focus all your time and energy on the 80%, you won't get very far toward reaching your most important and most impactful goals. At best you may experience periodic yo-yo growth and occasional signs of success, but more likely you will simply break even, drifting along on dangerously tight margins and presiding over a team that is stagnant and devoid of vitality and purpose. Simply put: if your real estate team isn't growing, then it's dying. It may be a slow and incremental death by a thousand tiny paper cuts, but we assure you that if you don't shift your focus away from the day-to-day and prioritize growth-building activities then organizational death is certain.

The Solution

If some or all of what you just read sounds like your team, then please do not fear. In the pages to follow, we show you the solution to the spread of apathy, fear, resistance to change, and a futile focus on the day-to-day.

Researchers have discovered that you can fight biological viruses with other viruses. We prove that this approach is effective when challenging the spread of apathy throughout your team. Beginning with a "viral goal" in which the goals and ambitions of individuals on your team are intrinsically linked to the team's overall growth goals, the five components of organizational growth will:

- Defeat team apathy.
- Shift your focus away from trivial 80% tasks and demands, toward 20% activities that result in expansion and growth.
- Motivate your team members with renewed enthusiasm, productivity, engagement, and a desire to grow and change.

The Five Components of Growth for Your Team

Through the five parts of this book, we explore each component of team growth in turn and in much more detail. For now, we tell you simply what the five components of team growth are: (1) devise a viral goal; (2) focus on activities first; (3) cultivate personal responsibility Through public accountability; (4) drive growth with a dashboard; and (5) huddle up.

FIGURE I.3   Five Components

We firmly believe that these five components of team growth offer a proven and practical solution for any real estate team leader or team member, in so far as you are willing to apply and commit to each and every element of the process.

However, the *manner* in which you apply this process matters as much as your desire and dedication to implementing meaningful change. Remember that most people are resistant to change not because they don't want it but because they're afraid of failure and unnerved by the unknown. When applying the five components of team growth to your real estate team, it's essential that you move beyond traditional and outmoded forms of change-implementation. In the Preface, we talked in greater detail about our implementation method of choice: the Team Book Club.

Next Steps

We trust that you are excited and eager to begin the process of team transformation.

For now, the team leader's next step is simply to read through the rest of this book and begin to internalize each of the five components of team growth for a real estate team. As the leader (or one of the leaders) of your real estate team, it's crucial that you are highly familiar with and deeply invested in these five components before you introduce your people to the changes and challenges ahead of them.

And as for team members reading this – it's time to dive in and embrace the idea of change. Yes, there are challenges ahead, but this book is set up to help you succeed. With the help of your team leader's guidance, you and your team members will work through this together.

At the end of each chapter, we provide you with more strategies and techniques for structuring the Team Book Club and rolling out steady and seamless changes within your real estate team.

With that in mind, let's move on to the first stage in effectuating change and growth at your real estate team.

the
High-
performing
**real estate
team**

PART 1

What's Your Viral Goal? Commission Earned, Volume Closed, or Units Sold?

CHAPTER 1

Viral Goals Propel Team Members to the Next Level

Understanding the Viral Goal

For your real estate team to grow, team leaders and team members must shift the focus away from the day-to-day and the 80% tasks that don't make much of an impact, and turn the attention to activities that will drive expansion, results, and greater success. But, to do that, you will need to create clarity around what success and growth mean to you. Whether you are the team leader or a real estate agent on the team, you must ask yourself: "What is it that I want for my real estate business? What is the *end goal*? What should my daily, weekly, and monthly efforts *really* help me achieve? In short: growth for your real estate team will require some serious contemplation and setting concrete goals.

Setting goals seems like a simple concept. You think about what you want to achieve and when you hope to achieve it by and determine some of the steps you'll need to take to get you there. Few people would argue against setting goals, or disagree with breaking goals into smaller, more manageable steps to increase your chances of successfully realizing your dreams. You will hear no argument from us on that point, and we'll explain just how to do that a little later in the chapter.

So why, then, do so many real estate teams fail to grow or achieve their goals, despite having a clear endpoint and a long list of things that will need to be done to get them there?

We'll give you a clue. In the first few paragraphs earlier, how many times does the word "you" or "your" appear?

You think.

You hope.

Your dreams.

Your daily, weekly, and monthly efforts.

The steps *you'll* need to take to get *you* there.

What does success mean to *you*?

What is it that *you* want?

Too often, either willfully or simply thoughtlessly, real estate leaders and team members fail to include their team as a whole in their vision for growth and in the goal-setting process. It's easy to mistake your personal dreams for the dreams of everyone on the team and assume that success and growth means the same thing to everybody. You may establish your goals in isolation and figure out what everyone else needs to do to make it happen.

When team leaders fail to recognize their team members' personal goals, without warning or adequate explanation, they present their people with a laundry list of changes to implement and targets to meet. These team leaders even speak excitedly about "our goal" and "our vision" to a group of people for whom *this* goal means very little and who often don't stand to benefit from it in any meaningful way.

Is it any wonder that real estate team members often feel disconnected from their leaders and apathetic to growth? When we talk about your real estate team's goals, and the end toward which your daily, weekly, and monthly efforts will be directed, team leaders need to rewrite the sentence, replacing "I" and "Me" with "We" and "Our."

In a similar fashion, real estate agents on a team may find themselves so laser-focused on their own personal goals that they fail to consider how they may benefit from plugging into the group's goal or vision. Team members must ask themselves, "Why did I join a team if the only goal I am focusing on is my own?" While it is important to feel motivated to hit your own personal goals, that personal goal must fit into the bigger goal of the team – and that is where you will find the greatest impact and opportunity for growth.

What are our collective hopes and dreams as a real estate team? We must consider each member of the team, from the sales side to the administrative side. This book is not just for team leaders. What does growth look like for the up-and-coming buyer's agent, Anne, or the administrative assistant, Toby, who volunteers his time once a week at the food bank down the street? What motivates and excites each individual person on the team? This conversation is as much about fixing the "I" and "Me" problem that leaders have as it is about making sure that each member of the team has a reason to feel motivated. In getting started, we must determine the personal motivations for every person on the team.

Understand that people are less likely to say "no" to their own goals. If leaders are going to have their real estate agents doing uncomfortable activities, like picking up the phone five times a day to add contacts to their sphere of influence (SOI), that can be very uncomfortable. But if that activity is directly tied to the agent's own financial goals, and they can clearly see how their financial goals are linked to the team's overall success, then the agent will want to complete that task or activity. The task may be uncomfortable, but if the agent can clearly see a direct path to personal reward as a result of completing the task, they will be more motivated to do it than if it was just something on a to-do list.

So, now we must define this viral goal. What are the steps that we'll need to take to get us to this place? What do we want as a team? What is the end toward which *our* daily, weekly, and monthly efforts will be directed?

The first component of team growth demands that you *make it about everyone* as you *devise a viral goal* in which the respective goals and ambitions of individuals on the team are intrinsically linked to the real estate team's overall growth goals.

When this occurs, all team members will feel personally connected to – and highly invested in realizing – the goal. Just like a video or meme that captures the attention and

Component 1: Devise a Viral Goal

FIGURE 1.1   Component 1: Devise a Viral Goal

imagination of millions across the internet overnight, a viral goal creates a social buzz around and within your team. Enthusiasm spreads from person to person, engaging and motivating every single member of the team.

FIGURE 1.2   Enthusiastic Spreads

Note that we used the word "demand" when explaining the first component of team growth. Devising a viral goal for your real estate team is not a suggestion nor is it a component that you can put off for another day. All of the subsequent components for growth build on this first important principle, so it's essential that team leaders and team members alike make significant efforts to include the whole team in the goal-setting process and never forget the intrinsic part that each team member will play in achieving the team's collective goals.

If the viral goal you devise does not capture the imagination and motivation of every real estate team member, then the entire team will fail to grow. It's as simple as that. While you might experience short-term results and periodic successes, exponential and sustainable growth cannot occur in the absence of a viral goal.

Before we outline the specific steps for devising a viral goal, allow us to explain the reason we came up with that term and what, exactly, we mean when a real estate team's goal goes viral.

Resource Library of Job Descriptions

> In the online resource appendix of this book, you will find job descriptions for everything from Sales Manager to Showing Assistant. Why are we giving these to you? Because good job descriptions are the key to hiring the right people for your brokerage or team. Good job descriptions also help employees redefine what their job duties, expectations, and training should include. You don't have to reinvent the wheel. The Icenhower Coaching and Consulting (ICC) job descriptions provided in this book include the key activities and duties, job specific skills, performance benchmarks, training opportunities, compensation, and more for each real estate team member's job.
>
> *All resources can be downloaded from this book's online appendix at therealestatetrainer.com/teambook.*

What Is a Viral Goal?

At ICC, we coach many of the top-producing teams across North America. A common complaint we hear from real estate team leaders and brokerage owners is that their people lack enthusiasm and urgency, that they are engrossed in gossip and social media when they should be engaged in productive activities and getting things done. Conversely, we often hear from many team members, too, who say they feel disconnected from the team. Or, they feel that they lack any concrete training or push to get them to the next level. These team members don't feel invested, and many who feel this way end up leaving the team on their own to go solo, or they find a new team that excites them. Lack of engagement works both ways and is equally detrimental to a real estate team.

Regardless of company policy, the average employee spends about 1.5 hours on social media every single day, not to mention taking personal calls and chatting excitedly with other team members about the latest binge-worthy TV show. Numbers vary, but every year organizations experience billions, if not trillions, of dollars in lost man-hours and productivity. It's understandable that real estate teams are adversely affected by this misspent time and the many wasted opportunities that result.

However, if you conflate an overuse of social media with a lack of enthusiasm and urgency, we fear that you are missing a crucial point. Your fellow team members are not inherently *lacking* in excitement and energy. Exuberance, curiosity, and an eagerness to respond to something swiftly and with a sense of importance are not finite resources that are simply present or absent within us. Set aside the question of whether a video of a cat playing a keyboard is a dumb waste of valuable time. The fact that an individual will watch a video of a cat playing a keyboard and then *immediately* share it with a dozen other people, who go on to share it with a dozen more, tells us that something else is at play here. The problem is not a lack of enthusiasm and urgency, but where that energy is being directed.

When something captures our imagination, we not only respond to it with *personal enthusiasm*, we also respond to it with an enthusiasm that compels us to *share it with others at lightning speed*!

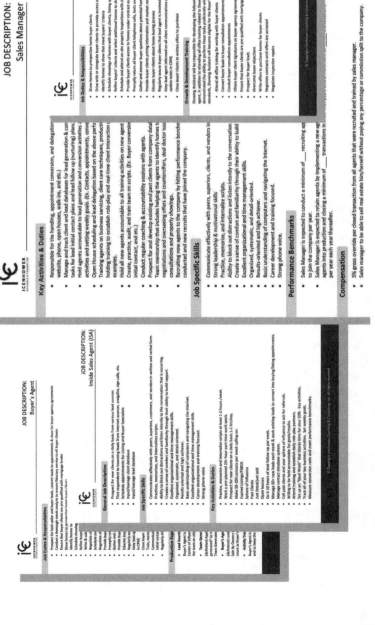

FIGURE 1.3 Library of Job Descriptions

But what if the tasks or responsibilities were "share-worthy" or a compelling topic of conversation for team members? What can be done to make the real estate team – and an employee's place and purpose within it – capture each team member's imagination, absorb their attention, excite them, influence them, rouse them into action, or inspire them to share their passion with the people around them?

Certain that devising a viral goal is the most critical component for achieving true team growth, we hunted out some of our old schoolbooks and taught ourselves a little bit more about the attributes that make a virus so productive and successful.

What Viruses Have Taught Us About Devising Viral Goals

We get it. You didn't sign up for a course in Biology 101, but we promise that these simple little microbes have a lot to teach us about the importance of devising and spreading a viral goal within a real estate team.

We also recognize that some of you might be a little unnerved right now. In light of the COVID-19 pandemic, the idea of a super contagious and harmful virus gives everyone pause. In the natural world, there aren't many good things about viruses, so we understand that speaking positively about viruses might strike you as somewhat odd.

But bear with us! The underlying attributes that make viruses so successful in the natural world are exactly the attributes that can be harnessed to create rapid, widespread, and lasting positive change and growth within your real estate team.

Viruses are simple microbes – they can't do much by themselves and need another living organism to give them everything they need to work and be effective. Likewise, no matter how worthy or inspiring the objective, a goal that's just written down on a piece of paper, or only known by a small handful of people, won't get very far by itself either. In and of itself, a goal is an inert and ineffectual thing, an idea or a collection of words rather than a reality. In the real world, goals are achieved by the efforts and energies of living, breathing people. Goals need a "host." Of course, that's the case for any goal whether it comes as a dictatorial command from on high or whether it's a goal that captures the imagination and enthusiasm of your people. All goals need a host, but there's a big difference between a person who carries out a goal due to nagging, pressure, criticism, or a fear of losing their job, and a person who strives to achieve a goal because it connects personally with their values and motivations, and because a sense of purpose is deeply embedded within their entire being.

> *Goals need a "host." Goals are achieved by the efforts and energies of living, breathing people.*

What's more, your goal is not going to survive or take off if it is not in constant contact with the members of the team, and if team members are not spreading the good word about the advantages and benefits of growth. As you know, most viruses spread through physical contact with another person. We're big believers in good manners and polite personal hygiene, but when it comes to spreading a real estate team's growth goals, you should not keep your mouth closed.

When devising a viral goal, team leaders need to apply strategies that not only inspire individuals on a personal level but inspire them to pass on a growth message to others, creating the potential for rapid and exponential growth in the message's exposure or influence. And, to allow the viral goal to spread across the team, team members need to be active participants on the team. As we explore in just a moment, the best way to inspire team members about growth on a personal level is to *make it about everyone*. Determining the personal motivations, wants, and needs of every team member is the first step in devising an exciting and meaningful viral goal for the team.

The best way to inspire team members about growth on a personal level is to make it about *everyone*.

FIGURE 1.4 Everyone

Some leaders employ a personal interview technique to figure out what motivates each team member. However, in our experience, the Team Book Club is the best strategy for uncovering motivations *and* creating rapid and exponential exposure to a message of growth. You learn more about your first book club meeting at the end of Part One.

What makes a virus so successful and effective is its ability to replicate and multiply itself. A biological or computer virus turns individuals or laptops into *passive carriers*, but when your people are inspired and enthused by your vision of growth, they become enthusiastically *active participants* in spreading the message.

Every single person on a real estate team can be a powerful and active participant in making the team's growth goals go viral. At the same time, every team has certain people that others especially admire, respect, and listen to. When a small handful of "social influencers" are excited about growth and expansion, it's incredible how quickly the rest of a team will buy into the need for change, so these are some of the first people that a team leader should target with a positive message of growth. However, in real estate teams that have reached a point of chronic apathy, you may find that these same social influencers have been the biggest contributors to the overall spread of negativity and cynicism, and are extremely resistant to hearing about the benefits and advantages of growth.

Viruses can spread rapidly and self-replicate systematically. They adapt through mutation to resist destruction. Likewise, it is important to pay attention to weak links or resistance within the team and be ready to respond and adapt accordingly. When team members begin to believe that they are unable to grow or reach their goals, they may blame other team members or the team as a whole. To justify the validity of this blame, they will often complain to one or more other team members to obtain their agreement in blaming the team as well. This is a common coping mechanism; it's much easier to blame someone than to accept that I may be falling short. To the detriment of everyone on the team, this is how poisonous negativity can spread like a virus and eventually erode the team's culture.

No one wins when this type of distraction occurs, especially the team members who are promoting the negative thinking. They will be much more focused on this drama than on generating commission income. This is why it's essential for team leaders to be aware of these types of negative undercurrents within the team and address them before they simmer to an eventual boil. Considering the tested leadership paradigm to "praise in public, criticize in private," both the team leader and the agent(s) involved should privately meet to air out their issues and come to a mutually agreeable solution as quickly as possible.

More on Viruses and Teams

In the natural world, when antibodies build up a resistance to a virus, the virus responds by *gradually mutating* so that the antibodies no longer recognize it as a threat. Similarly, team leaders must respond to extreme resistance by adapting their strategy for delivering their message and implementing the goal in a way that is less threatening to the most fearful and change-resistant among you.

Growth is often a gradual process, and there is no one-size-fits-all strategy for getting people on board. It may take some time for the most change-resistant people on the team to buy into a message of growth. They may not want to listen to other people, and they may even attempt to undermine efforts with negative speech, so it's important to not rely *exclusively* on team members to spread the word about growth. Instead, leaders must be persistent in proving how growth and change will help team members reach their goals.

Viruses hang out anywhere and (almost) everywhere, so always carry hand sanitizer!

Seriously though: communicate, display, and share a positive message of growth in unexpected places, or the everyday things that people interact with on your real estate team. Team leaders and members alike must find a variety of ways and places for the message that "growth is good for everybody" to come into contact with everyone. Successful teams will openly celebrate this growth culture in a variety of ways. For example, one top ICC-coached team has "Are You Coachable Today?" painted on the wall of their team's weekly meeting room. Another team includes "Being Learning-Based" as one of its team's core values. Many top real estate teams regularly meet with their agents to discuss each agent's personal and business goals to consistently motivate everyone to better themselves.

Some viruses are very clever. They don't die off if they don't have a host; they simply hibernate or become dormant until the right conditions come along. Oftentimes, team members are resistant to growth because they're currently content with their situation. A single person with a decent income and a busy social life is perhaps not quite as open to the idea of working harder or making a lot more money. However, as you well know, life can change on a dime. People get married and have babies, while others get divorced and need more money to support their change in circumstance. While we certainly hope that every team member's life is always changing for the better, our point is that sometimes a growth goal won't strongly resonate with someone until the right conditions come along. You must be patient and trust that everyone on the team will eventually become excited and invested in growth.

> *Sometimes a growth goal won't strongly resonate with someone until the right conditions come along.*

We recognize that the inner workings of invisible microbes were the last thing most of you expected to find in a book about real estate team growth! However, like us, we hope that you can see how the underlying attributes that make viruses so effective in the natural world are precisely the characteristics you want present on your real estate team in order to see growth happen.

As you know, certain factors make us more susceptible to viruses; we're more likely to catch a cold if we're stressed out and run down, for example. Similarly, certain factors or motivators make people more susceptible or likely to respond positively to the idea of growth and its accompanying goals. If a beneficial motivator reaches a "susceptible" individual, then that individual is more likely to respond positively to growth and internalize the goal. And, once the goal is in their mind, they will then go on to share a positive message of growth with other susceptible individuals.

Up Next: Make It About Everyone

As we explore in the next chapter, team growth is necessary before certain areas of personal growth can be achieved. Almost everyone is motivated by financial gains, professional growth, and a sense of purpose. As we learn how to *make it about everyone* on the team, we take a closer look at how to harness the personal goals and desires of each team member and link them with the team's overall goal in order to achieve the growth that every team member is looking for when they join a real estate team in the first place.

CHAPTER 2

Make It SMART: Specific, Measurable, Achievable, Relevant, and Time-Bound

Get SMART

At the beginning of Chapter 1, we asked why so many real estate teams fail to grow or achieve their goals, despite understanding the common knowledge that goals need to be specific, time-bound, and broken down into smaller, more manageable steps, and so forth.

Now that we have explained what a viral goal looks like, and how to include everyone in the process, you are ready to step back into more established territory and connect your newfound understanding about goals to more standard goal-setting practices and commonly understood best practices.

For years, industry and thought leaders have utilized what is widely considered the most effective method for goal setting. Although the SMART goal-setting process was originally popularized by George T. Doran in 1981, it is still widely accepted and utilized by some of the most successful people and organizations in the world today. So how does it work? To make sure your goals are clear and realizable, they must be SMART:

- **S**pecific
- **M**easurable
- **A**chievable
- **R**elevant
- **T**ime-bound

Specific

Measurable

Achievable

Relevant

Time-bound

FIGURE 2.1   SMART Goals Infographic

Specific

All goals should be clear and specific. If a goal is too general or vague, you will struggle to find concrete efforts to focus on or motivate yourself to take action.

For example, we often work with real estate teams whose goal is to create "a happier workplace." While we appreciate the good intentions behind that goal, if there were ever an award given for "Vaguest Organizational Goal," this one would take first place. Similar examples we've heard from the real estate team leaders we've worked with include imprecise and indefinable goals like "a more open workplace," or "a more relaxed workplace."

With each of these goals, the one thing they all have in common is generality. There's simply no way to quantify the desired outcome. How, for example, do you quantify the goal of a "happier workplace"? Do you count the number of smiles or high-fives exchanged between team members?

When formulating goals, the following five "W" questions can help you hone a more precise and detailed goal:

- **What** specifically do you want to accomplish?
- **Who** is involved?
- **Where** is the goal located?
- **Why** is this goal important to you?
- **Which** opportunities or obstacles are involved?

You can also ask yourself **How** you will achieve your goal, as long as your answer is *specific*. Again, when asking these questions, keep in mind that there must always be a rational relationship between what the team leader wants to accomplish and what every team member wants and needs.

All goals should be clear and specific. If a goal is too general or vague, you will struggle to find concrete efforts to focus on, or motivate yourself to take action.

Measurable

When it comes to setting specific goals, however, we highly recommend setting *concrete, numeric growth goals*. For a goal to be effective, it must be measurable. This will help you stay on track, and the most efficient and straightforward way to measure something is in numeric units. Your individual and overall growth goals should be specific, measurable, and made clear to the entire team.

Concrete, numeric goals also allow you to easily break the goal down even further. How many homes will need to be sold each quarter, month, or week to meet your team's annual growth goal? How many open houses will the team need to host each quarter, month, or week to meet your team's annual growth goal? How many sphere of influence (SOI) contacts will each team member need to make each quarter, month, week, or day to achieve your team's annual growth goal? How much should each team member be growing their SOI database each quarter, month, or week? These are just a few examples of how the actionable items can be broken down into daily activities to meet the overarching goal.

As we explore in Part Four of this book, a team dashboard drives growth and helps you determine if you're on course to achieving your overall growth goal. If you don't apply metrics to your goal, you won't know when you're following through or falling short.

Achievable

Of course, your goal should also be achievable and reasonable. Is selling 100 homes in a year achievable? Of course it is, depending on the size of your team. And, again depending on the size of your team, 200 or 400 might be completely achievable, too. If you're a small real estate team like Bob and Mary and Phil and Anne, then selling 400 homes is probably not achievable.

How many sales are ambitiously, but reasonably, achievable for your real estate team this year?

At Icenhower Coaching and Consulting (ICC), we often think of achievability in terms of "stretching." By this we mean the extent to which a viral goal makes a real estate team stretch. Your real estate team's viral goal should cause everyone in it to stretch, but at the same time a viral goal must not make unrealistic demands. If the goal is too far out of reach, motivation will decline. There needs to be balance and moderation.

Like a relentlessly determined marathon runner who can stretch a muscle to the point of rupture and irreparable damage, ambitious and determined real estate teams often put themselves and their people under undue strain. At ICC, we see this happen when teams create a single, gargantuan goal that is hopelessly impractical or ridiculously ambitious. We are going to talk about this more later in this chapter. Real estate teams also overstretch themselves when they create too many distinct and separate viral goals.

In the course of determining real estate team members' motivations and transforming those motivations into concrete subgoals that tie into the organization's overall growth goal, you may find yourself coming up with several different goals that are very exciting and worth pursuing. However, we highly recommend adhering to the conventional wisdom of selecting a single goal that will have the greatest impact on your team and is most likely to achieve everyone's big *Why*. Devising more than three big goals at any given time fragments your focus, dilutes the power and nature of a viral goal, and will push your real estate team to its tipping point.

Real estate teams overstretch themselves when they create too many distinct and separate viral goals. Devising more than three big goals at any given time fragments your focus, dilutes the power and nature of a viral goal, and will push your real estate team to its tipping point.

When a real estate team overstretches, it doesn't just fail to achieve the goal. Over-stretching also injures the team in a more critically damaging way. Disappointment, disillusionment, and depression can cripple the members of a team that fail to meet a viral goal that was too much of a stretch in the first place.

GOALS THAT STRETCH

- achievable
- use balance and moderation
- must push, but not too hard
- motivate team members to work harder

GOALS THAT OVERSTRETCH

- not achievable
- unbalanced, too hasty, unrealistic
- push too hard
- motivate in the beginning but will discourage in the end

FIGURE 2.2   Stretch versus Overstretch

Recognizing the perils of overstretching, a team might be tempted to set an ultra-conservative viral goal. This can be equally as dangerous, however, if it leads the team to avoid stretching entirely. A cautious, wary, and unambitious goal is uninspiring and will fail to capture the imagination and enthusiasm of team members. A viral goal needs to be challenging and robust if it is to motivate people and maintain momentum over the course of a year. If an annual goal can be achieved in a two-month dash to the finish line, without team members breaking a sweat, then clearly that's not much of a stretch.

Your goal-setting stretch must be balanced, so it results in a little bit of pain, a little (or a lot) of gain, and absolutely no harmful strain. Setting your course for an impossible goal is a sure-fire way to doom your real estate team to failure. If, however, you consider all the factors and it seems doable, then run with it. Be confident and optimistic about what is and isn't achievable. Be realistic, but don't allow a negative mind-set to creep in and convince you that you can't do something big or life changing on your team.

As well as Achievable, "A" can also stand for Actionable. There may be times when your targets seem unachievable, but there is always something *actionable* you can do to stay on track and achieve things you never thought possible. We discuss that in more detail in Part Two of this book, when we explain the importance of the second component of team growth: *focusing on activities first.*

As with the growth goal itself, growth activities can be broken down into smaller, more manageable components. Setting goals around each growth-building activity means you have multiple goals to hit not only every week or month but every single day. Rather than focusing on the end of the year or even the end of the week, focus on the activities themselves and how many growth-building activities team members have done *today*. This will make the real estate team growth goal both actionable and eminently achievable.

Relevant

Is the goal worthwhile and will it meet your needs? Is your goal actually relevant to you? For a goal to be relevant it must make sense and align with other goals you've set for yourself.

You might be surprised how frequently issues with goal-setting relevancy occur in real estate. For example, a team leader might become consumed by selling more homes than any other agent/team in her city. To help reach this new goal, the team decides to reduce commission in an attempt to attract more clients. As a result, the team *did* succeed in selling the most homes in the city, but they made very little income due to the reduction in commissions. In this case, the team leader's goal of being the number-one team in town through reduced commissions did not align with her need to make a living by earning income. The team just ended up sacrificing one goal to further another.

Remember that for a goal to be relevant it needs to matter. It needs to have significance or, otherwise, it can be easily ignored. Suppose an agent on a high-performing team sets an uncomfortably high sales goal of selling 50 homes in the year right after having a newborn baby. Because there are so many top-producing agents on the team, this new mother felt compelled to set a high sales goal for herself to try and keep up with the goals of the other team members. However, her real and most pressing concern for the upcoming year was to effectively balance her life between being a new mother and earning income for her family. Consequently, her goal to sell so many homes next year was not in alignment with her true goal of balancing her business and personal life. In this case, her goal was not even her own goal. Instead, it was actually the other team members' goal that she chose just to fit in with the rest of the team. For a goal to be relevant, it must be your own goal. Not someone else's.

The fact that you're reading this book is obviously a great indicator that you are ready to dial in on growth, expand your real estate team, and take a lot of market share. However, it's always worth taking the time to do some soul searching and take your broader life and objectives into account when creating any challenging and life-changing goal.

Time-Bound

Time creates a *When* to balance against the *What* of your viral goal.

Every goal needs a target date so that you have a concrete deadline to focus on, and something to work toward on a quarterly, monthly, weekly, and daily basis. Time gives you a means for plotting your progress and determining if you are ahead, behind, or on the predicted track to achieving your goals.

Your target dates should be realistic. Anyone can set goals, but if you're not realistic about timing, your likelihood of success is slim.

When formulating your goals, think about the end date and all the dates in between.

For example, the question, "When do we want to achieve our goal by?" might become your real estate team's annual goal (we explore this process in more detail in Part Five when we discuss how to create a "1-3-5" Annual Business Plan).

Then, once you've established your annual goal, you will need to ask yourself where, exactly, you need to be at various stages in the process if you are to stay on track with meeting that year-end goal.

The question, "Where, exactly, do we need to be in Q1, Q2, Q3, and Q4?" becomes your real estate team's quarterly goals.

The question, "Where, exactly, do we need to be in January, February, and March to meet our Q1 goals?" becomes a manageable subgoal for every month in that quarter, and you will repeat the same process for April through June, July through September, and October through November.

The question, "Where, exactly, do we need to be this week to meet our January goal?" becomes a series of weekly goals for that month. And, "Where, exactly, do we need to be today to meet this week's goal" provides a daily and hourly sense of purpose.

This process applies to any real estate team, whether you're a small group of five people or a massive brokerage with multiple branches and locations. No matter your size, purpose, or structure, every person, team, or department should have individual goals and expectations, as well as yearly/quarterly/monthly/weekly/daily activities that tie into the team's overall growth goal. This frequently pertains to individual agent annual sales production goals helping contribute to the team's annual sales goal. However, it can also apply to administrative staff members having goals like setting up specific systems or workflows, or even goals to hire and train new personnel by the year's end.

From "When do we want to achieve our goal by?" to "What can we do *right now*, this very minute?," breaking your goal into super-specific, time-bound goals and activities is what will cause a vision of growth to go viral. Establishing mile markers provides an infectious and irresistible sense of urgency that ensures the moment-by-moment spread of enthusiasm and motivation around the real estate team's goal.

Conventional goal-setting practices are powerful elements in devising the nontraditional reimagining that is a viral goal.

Just like a virus needs to be in constant contact with people to multiply and spread rapidly, the members of a real estate team need to be in constant contact with the goals that will help them to achieve their personal dreams and aspirations. Though they are conventional

FIGURE 2.3 Team Growth Goal Flow Chart

and long-established concepts, specific, measurable, achievable, relevant, and time-bound goal-setting practices are nonetheless powerful elements in devising the nontraditional reimagining that is a viral goal.

What Happens When the Goal Is Too Big?

At ICC, we often advise our clients to pick a bigger goal and we tell them to stretch themselves. We talked about this a bit earlier in this chapter, but I want to dive a little deeper with you. Having a goal that stretches you is all well and good; however, here is a cautionary tale about picking a goal that is too big.

This issue is common, especially with teams that have an energetic, super-positive culture, with exuberant agents that possess "I can do anything I put my mind to" attitudes. Now, this is a wonderful thing. It's important to have a positive outlook and motivated agents who feel very positive about their work. The problem lies in the resulting unachievable goals that may be set. With a "pie in the sky," goal-setting team, we find that missing those goals makes failure even more difficult to stomach.

For example, if a team goal is so far out of reach that after the first three or four months of that year, team members see that they are so far behind, that goal may become irrelevant. Team members won't pay attention to it anymore because there's no chance in this universe that they'll reach the goal. Or, team members may get very depressed by this harsh reality. They are constantly reminded at each weekly team huddle that the goal on the dashboard is getting further and further out of reach. It's a depressing weekly reminder of how far behind they are from reaching their goals. That can wear a team down that is otherwise doing very well. Suddenly, the goal becomes a negative topic. It's a dark shadow that hangs over the team meetings, so they tend to push the goal away, and may even miss team meetings. It creates a negative culture within the team, especially when the culture was so super positive before.

You'll find that many of the agents and teams that set unrealistic goals rely heavily on positive, sometimes cliché, mantras. "I can do anything!" "It's up to me!" "If we put our minds to it, we can achieve it!" "If we shoot for the moon and miss, at least we'll land among the stars!" While these positive mantras represent a great mind-set for team members to have, it opens up the door for your team members to get crushed if they find their goal is actually not attainable. I don't want to downplay the power of a good motivational quote, but there's also a dangerous side to them.

You must be cautious. Don't be too aggressive with goal setting because, as we have seen with many of our clients here at ICC, it can be damaging. Trying to double, triple, or quadruple your numbers from last year without some kind of tangible way to rationally explain such a significant, dramatic increase, can be detrimental and dangerous to the team's production.

I've seen many agents and many teams get too aggressive with their goals, and they pay for it. In one case, the team leader I worked with had a goal to increase the number of units they sold last year, which was 100, to 200 this year. They reached 150 instead, which is phenomenal! Instead of feeling accomplished by incredible growth, the whole team got discouraged. Everybody was behind their goals because the goal setting was too aggressive. It's very delicate. Even though this 50% year-over-year increase would normally be celebrated, because they set their goal at a 100% increase over last year's numbers, they felt let down.

The New Agent with Unrealistic Goals

I've seen this happen many times. It all starts when the team leader holds the annual business-planning retreat with the team to set goals and build the annual business plan (which we discuss later, in Part Five of this book). The whole team gets together to build this plan, and the team leader will talk to all the members of the team to learn their individual goals.

For the sake of this example, say there are four agents on a team. On this particular team, three buyer's agents want to sell 25 homes next year, and one wants to sell 50 homes next year. Let's say the agent that wants to sell 50 is not licensed yet, and he's set to take the test in February of next year. He just moved to the area and doesn't know anyone yet. He's a really positive, exuberant, excitable fellow, which is often the case with people who set goals that are too aggressive.

This is a hard situation for the leader because the leader doesn't want to squash his spirit, but it's also important for goals to be realistic and achievable. Even if the team is meeting the overall team goals, this one agent who is failing to reach his own personal goal is getting very depressed. He may be doing very good for a brand-new agent, but he is so far behind the goals he set that it's discouraging to him, and he is questioning whether he is good at this job. He loses confidence in himself, which is very dangerous in real estate sales. Ultimately, it damages his own self-confidence, and it can also bring down the other team members. The team as a whole could suffer simply because this new agent did not set an achievable goal for himself. As members of a team, it is vital that we all help each other to set realistic goals. At least for goal-setting purposes, we must temper the exuberant, excitable, and ambitious members of the team because a failure to do so could throw the entire team off its goals.

As leaders, it is vital that
we help our team members
set _realistic_ goals.

FIGURE 2.4   Set Realistic Goals

The Sum of All Parts Does Not Always Equal the Whole

We never want to be too obsessive about adding up each agent's goals to make the over-arching team's goal. This can derail your team easily. For example, using the same numbers from the story of the unrealistic new agent, if the three agents with a realistic goal of 25 units add their goals together with the unrealistic new agent's goal of 50, the team as a whole is set on selling a total of 125 units as a team this year. The problem with that is, what if the new agent quits after a few months of struggle? Or, what if the team brings on three more agents to the team? Then, that goal of 125 units might not be accurate anymore.

The Common Sense Test

Always use the Common Sense Test. It's simple. During your business-planning retreat with your team, take a look at last year's production. What do you think you can realistically increase to next year? What is reasonable? Based on the personalities and the people on the team, along with the leader's vision for how many new agents to bring onto the team next year, you will come up with a SMART goal.

Case Study

The Eric Craig Real Estate Team in Smithville, Missouri

I have been working with the Eric Craig Real Estate Team for more than seven years. This team guards against aggressive goal setting better than any team I've seen. We started working with the Eric Craig Real Estate Team when it was only Eric Craig plus one administrative assistant, and back then, they sold less than 100 homes a year. Now, they are selling over 500 homes a year. They didn't get there overnight, however.

Every year, they are very conservative with their goal setting. They've stayed true to this style of goal setting since day one. His team has grown steadily, year over year, for seven straight years. Usually, his team sets a goal of about a 15% increase year over year.

Now, here's the deal. If they only met their goal each year, that would mean 15% the first year, 15% the second year, and so on, the growth would indeed be slow. For example, if you set a goal at a 15% increase and you sold 100 homes last year, then to meet the goal this year you would need to sell 115 homes. Over the course of seven years at that speed would not get you to over 500 homes, like Eric Craig. So . . . how is his team doing so well, and now hitting over 500 homes per year after only seven years?

What's the secret? His team always far outperforms their goal. You may think that they need to set higher goals for themselves since they are always outperforming. That is not so, and here's why. There is a huge benefit to exceeding your goals – and it's more than just monetary!

At the start of every year, this team has their goal. They are often very competitive about it and work hard to get ahead of it right from the start. The team usually hits their goal, or even passes it, by late summer or early fall. The Eric Craig Real Estate Team is pumped! They get so excited about hitting this goal, and the timing is good because typically these late summer, early fall months are usually the months where agents and teams start to burn out.

August through October is usually the end of the "harvest season" in real estate. Most commissions are earned and most homes are sold during the harvest season, so when it's over, people are feeling drained and unmotivated, and also worried about business slowing down. The Eric Craig team, at this same time, is pushing hard to meet that goal that they are very close to hitting. Each member is watching the dashboard (we cover this later in Part Five of this book) closely during the team huddles and celebrating this positivity.

When the team passes the goal, they feel so strong and positive that they've already accomplished their goal before the end of the year. They move into the holiday season with one of the highest senses of positivity that I've ever seen in a real estate team. Believe it or not, of all the teams I've coached, this team has the highest retention rate. They very rarely lose any agents. The holiday season is a popular time for agents to move around. Business is slower, and agents have less income, and they worry if they'll get another check for a while. They start to make New Year's resolutions – they think making a change will fix everything for them, and they have a "grass is greener on another team" mind-set. It is super important as the holidays approach that teams have a sense of community, positivity, and a reason to celebrate. This helps keep team members engaged and happy so they don't start making bad decisions and quit.

Teams that create achievable and realistic goals for their team members help preserve the positive mind-set and exciting culture that is attractive in a real estate team, even during "moving season." Moving season is the opposite of harvest season – this is when agents "move" around because they don't want to stay on their current team.

In those last couple of months of the year, teams should be sitting down to craft a business plan (as we explain in Part Five of this book) for the next year. This gets the team members excited for what is to come next year. Remember, the culture that is created by having a goal that is achievable as opposed to aggressive keeps us in the game.

As a worst-case scenario, what happens if a team races far ahead of the annual goal – so far, that the team hits that goal early in the year? What if the goal is met in spring? You may worry that it makes that goal meaningless. In this case, the team should plan a mid-year planning retreat in the summer and reset the goal and raise it higher. That will do no harm, and it will actually excite the team because they crushed their goal so hard that they need to raise it now or choose a new goal.

If you look at the converse scenario and a team picks a goal that is too aggressive or too high, it's not pleasant to have a mid-year business planning retreat to lower the goal down to a reasonable level. That's deflating and will hurt the team culture and morale. This action admits defeat right in the middle of the harvest season.

Remember – it's better to move your team's goal up than to move the goal down. This is what the Eric Craig Real Estate Team has done so well year after year after year. They surpass their goal early on, have the highest rate of retention, steady growth, and motivated team members. They use SMART goals to get where they want to be.

Up Next: Motivate Everyone

Now that we have a handle on how to make our viral goal SMART, in the next chapter we dive in and explore how to make this goal motivate everyone on the team.

CHAPTER 3

Make the Viral Goal Motivate Every Team Member, Regardless of Their Role or Season of Life

Determine Their Motivations

The best way to inspire your real estate team members about team growth on a personal level is to *make it about everyone*. Determining the personal motivations, wants, and needs of your team members is the first step in devising an exciting and meaningful viral goal.

Every real estate team is unique. Your particular real estate team will differ in purpose, values, structure, and size to others. Therefore, the exact process of determining the motivations of each of the people on your team will differ from team to team and leader to leader.

A notable exception, of course, is the process of implementing a book club. At every real estate team, no matter the structure or size, your book club provides a space and opportunity to uncover and listen to the wants and needs of all team members. What's more, a book club is the best strategy for uncovering motivations *and* creating rapid and exponential exposure to a message of growth at the same time. We discuss your first book club session in more detail immediately following Chapter 5.

It's All About Mind-Set

At Icenhower Coaching and Consulting (ICC), our coaches work with leaders and team members from the top teams and brokerages across North America. One of the biggest issues that our clients face is the disconnect between the team leader and the team member. Often, the team leader feels frustrated. They sometimes come to us and say their main issue is their inability to get the agents on their team to sell more real estate. These team leaders are frustrated that their agents "just aren't selling." "They won't do what I tell them," "They don't try that hard." "They aren't doing the activities, so they aren't getting the results."

We also talk to many team members who feel equally frustrated. They may feel that the team is of no benefit to them. "My team leader expects too much of me." "My team leader provides me no training and expects me to double my business this year." "I don't understand what I need to be doing to grow my business, and my leader is putting a lot of pressure on me." They may even be shopping around for a new team because their current leader is not providing them with the support, motivation, and training they feel they need to succeed.

Our clients come to us and say, "What can we do? Tell us what to do to get our team producing more." Oftentimes, the problem isn't the low-performing team member – it's the leadership.

When a real estate team leader tries to motivate a member of the team, it must resonate. As we talk in this chapter about how to create a viral goal, and how to fuse our own personal goals to everyone's goals on the team, we focus on *making it about everyone* by way of motivation. And yet, a lot of leaders out there don't make it about everyone.

Many team leaders don't attempt to address concerns that they're having with production by sitting down with each team member and asking them pointed questions about their motivation. Respect and trust is essential in any relationship and is a requirement when engaging in discussions about the things that are most important *to everyone*. When real estate team leaders ask questions and listen attentively to the answers, it is a simple but powerful way to demonstrate respect and assure everyone that their wants and needs are important. This helps everyone on the team to trust that their best interests are being considered.

The questions a good real estate leader should be asking sound like this: "Well, what about the income goal that you have?" "I thought you wanted to reach this goal so you could move into a better neighborhood." "Didn't you want to reach this level of commissions so that your son could get into that nice private school?"

All the different goals of each team member must be known and understood by the team leader. Team members must be reminded that they can achieve their goals as a result of selling more real estate. Increased commissions come from increased sales. Selling more comes from doing more. Most real estate agents easily lose sight of their own goals, so leaders must act like coaches. Fact: to be a good leader, you must also be a good coach. Good leaders must motivate and refocus their agents. This is how you *make it about everyone* on the real estate team.

To be a good leader, you must also be a good

coach .

FIGURE 3.1 Leader and Coach

There are a lot of examples of poor leadership in the real estate industry. In these cases, the leader does not make it about their agents. Instead, they make it all about themselves. These leaders say things like, "Well, I don't have any spare time to train you, and that's why I brought you on." "I need more help, I'm too busy, and I have no time to hold your hand and walk you through this." "You're supposed to save me time, not cost me more time." That is the mind-set of a leader who doesn't want to invest in their people. "I'm paying for all of these leads, and you're not converting them. I'm wasting money on you." No team member wants to hear this.

In this scenario, the leader is focused on her own needs and concerns, not those of her team members.

A mind-set centered on what is best for the leader will not motivate the team members. If anything, they'll get defensive. This kind of conversation coming from a team leader would make any team member feel attacked. The last thing that they are going to do is listen to the leader and get motivated to work harder. If the leader instead reminds each team member of their personal goals and why they need to be doing what they are asked to do, they will feel motivated to move forward and do the activities, as uncomfortable as they may be, to get the results that they want.

Instead, so many examples of poor leadership persist. Leaders try explaining to their team members why they are failing the team, and almost *guilt* them into action – which will not work in the long run. If anything, team members will just nod and agree, trying to get out of this uncomfortable conversation. The message is not hitting home. The leader is failing to motivate the team members in any way, shape, or form. Of course, later down the road when they leave the team, the leader may scratch their head and wonder why.

Leaders that do this tend to adopt the mind-set of, "Good riddance! He/she didn't do anything for the team anyway." Emotions can run high when an agent leaves the team. Instead, leaders must shift their mind-set here. When any agent joins a team or brokerage, they are looking for leadership. They want and need a leader. If the agent doesn't perform, it is the leader's job to guide them and refocus them.

Team members must adopt a positive mind-set, too. As each team member holds up their end of the deal and works with the team leader as well as fellow team members, they must be coachable. At the end of the day, the best leader will not be able to change a team member who is unwilling to be coached or motivated. If a team member has the mind-set going into the team that it's all about their own personal goals, perhaps they need to reevaluate why they joined a team in the first place.

Every real estate agent needs the leader to help them, motivate them, and refocus their energy. Leaders are responsible for holding each team member accountable and holding their feet to the fire. When a team member has difficulty focusing on their daily activities, and as a result, is struggling to convert leads, this evidences the value of being a part of a team. The last thing a leader should do is go on passive-aggressive monologue about why these low-performing agents are costing too much money, or asking the agents why they aren't doing the work . . . or just complaining in general.

Leaders must *make it about everyone* because if they don't, they fail to realize that they are complaining about the very reason agents join a team in the first place. Team members need their leaders to step up. If agents didn't have issues and need support, they wouldn't need to join a team. Instead, they would go off on their own, become a competitor, and start their own team.

So, team leaders must understand that all the issues agents have with production are actually opportunities to lead and demonstrate the value of being on the team. *This is the leadership mind-set that leaders must adopt!* If coaching and leadership conversations are focused on *making it about everyone*, the team leader will achieve the proper mind-set around effective leadership.

And as for team members, ask yourself, "Am I willing to be coached?" "If my team leader is *making it about everyone* on the team, what is my responsibility in that?" "What do I need from my team leader?"

The Power of a Personal Conversation

In addition to the book club, for smaller real estate teams it is easy and natural to sit down and speak privately and personally about motivation.

It's crucial to avoid a "tell-and-sell" type of conversation. Leaders, we're talking to you, here. Endlessly listing all of the things *you* want to do, or trying to sell people on *your* goals and vision for the team, just plain isn't going to fly. For team members to truly hear and believe that change is desirable, and that team growth is a good thing, they must first be engaged. To be engaged as a team member, you must participate, and to participate, your leader must involve you by coming from curiosity and asking questions. As we mentioned earlier in Part One, people can't say no to their own goals, so it is essential to help each team member realize what their dreams and goals actually are.

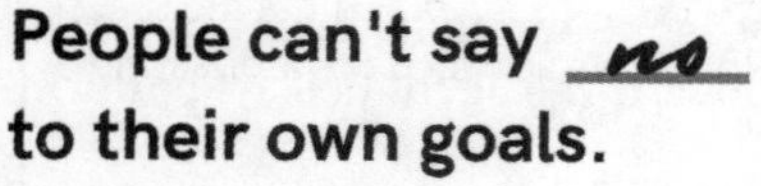

People can't say _no_
to their own goals.

FIGURE 3.2 Can't Say No

Back to the Future

At ICC, we employ a multistep process of "self-discovery" in which we guide our clients through an exhaustive past-present-future line of questioning that helps them to identify their deepest desires and motivations.

Essentially, the self-discovery method involves asking probing questions that pinpoint specific motivations, prompt an individual to reflect and think, and engages them to author their own goals (that will later be tied to the team's overall growth goal). We find that it is helpful when people are encouraged to *compare their current situation to where they want to be in the future.*

Though obviously this process is built for team leaders to use with their team members, as we mentioned in the last chapter, there may be multiple leadership positions on your team. And everyone on your team should be learning leadership skills so they can continually learn and have the opportunity to grow their role. Whether your goal is to become a Lead Buyer's Agent or an Administrative Manager, learning how to lead, motivate, and coach others is essential. For this reason, everyone on the team should fundamentally understand the self-discovery process, and know its value.

Self-Discovery Process

Here's how team leaders can use the process of self-discovery with team members:

1. Ask each team member the following questions
2. The questions get each team member thinking and providing extended answers.
3. As the team member gives their answers, leaders should guide them onward, letting the team member's own answers knock down whatever roadblocks they've been facing.

 ## Self-Discovery: Questions to Ask

1. The Catalyst Question – "What's the most important thing for us to talk about today?" This clarifies where to start in helping your team member as their leader.
2. The Probe Question – "What else about that . . . ?" This question helps you fully grasp the "icebergs," those major issues impacting your team member, which are often hidden below the surface.
3. The Pinpoint Question – "What's the MAIN Issue here for YOU?" This pinpoints the root causes of your team member's problems, so you can help clients advance toward lasting solutions rather than a quick fix, Band-Aid over the issue.
4. The Finish Line Question – "What's your ideal end goal here?" This question focuses your team member on the ideal end goal (the "finish line"), so they'll be willing to go through whatever discomfort is needed to achieve that goal.
5. The Support Question – "What's the Best Way I Can Help You?" This gets your team member to think about how they can solve their problems individually, and then, with your support on specific items.
6. The Execution Question – "What do you need to do . . . by when?" Finally, this helps your team member get clear on their next steps.

Does this method actually work? If you are still unsure about the concept of self-discovery, here are seven additional reasons why it is worthwhile.

1. **Each team member's strengths are incorporated into the goal setting.** By incorporating these unique attributes into the team's overall goals for growth, the team member should feel like an integral part of the real estate team's structure and vision for the future.

2. **Leaders are able to see whether each team member is really engaging** with the team, and with the leader.

3. **Are they figuratively "asleep" on the team?** Are they taking in what is being told but NOT thinking about it? The self-discovery questions build continual agreement with each team member – confirming that they are, in fact, buying into what the leader says. With team member "buy-in," leaders can solve the whole "why don't they take action?" problem.

4. **Similarly to #3, from the team member's perspective, they have the sense of having authored the change and therefore owning it** ("If they author it, they own it"). As a team member, you must author the change. Your leader can't be the one telling you how to make a change. You need to see the change as one you have mapped out ("authored") for yourself. As the author, you will feel that you are the rightful "owner" of the change/solution and therefore entitled to keeping it.

5. **Puts the team member's self-confidence in turbo mode.** This self-discovery approach allows each team member to be the one creating their own solutions. As they create solutions, each team member gains the confidence to dig deep within themselves and try to find a solution – even without the leader's help.

6. **Brings out each team members' leadership abilities.** As a team member, you will find that you reach the point where you're the one who owns up to your challenges and then leads the charge toward solutions. In this position, team members can thus see themselves as leaders when facing their challenges.

7. **Creates a bond between the leader and each member of the team.** By asking questions, leaders can achieve a true understanding of each team member. If leaders can understand their team members at such a high level, both the leader and the team member will care more. This leads to more trust on a team. It'll also lead to a team structure that works because team members will feel as though "my leader gets where I am coming from."

Quick Tip for Leaders

As you go through the self-discovery process with each team member, make sure you have a pen and paper to take notes because their motivations will soon spill out one after the other. Every time they give you an answer, reply, "Great. That makes sense," or similar words of support and encouragement. Thank them for their feedback and prod them to expand upon their answers: "What exactly would that look like?" "How would that change your life?" And so on. Continue probing and prompting until you get to the heart of what motivates and excites your people.

There is power in a personal conversation. Meeting face-to-face, in person or through a video conference, may also be a viable process for medium-sized and larger real estate teams. As we mentioned in the previous chapter, at larger teams it's highly advisable for the leadership team to read this book in advance and conduct their own book club. It's perfectly possible for larger teams to conduct a personalized approach to discovering their team members' motivations.

Don't allow the real estate team's size or set-up to deter you from uncovering what each team member personally wants and needs. Whether it's achieved through personal conversations, or as a component of the book club process, the best way to inspire everyone on the team about team growth is to *make it about everyone*, so it's imperative to not skip this self-discovery crucial step.

Visualizing Goals

Visualize the actual impact that a promotion or an increase in income would make to your life. Dig deep into the emotional motivations. If you want to buy a vacation home at the beach to be closer to your grandchildren in Florida, the goal is for you to feel the sand beneath your feet and the sound of your grandchildren's laughter. If you want to send your child to a good college or begin to save for retirement, the goal is for you to visualize and feel the peace and reassurance of having savings in the bank. The more you visualize your own personal, desired results, and picture yourself in a pleasurable future, the more likely you are to take uncomfortable but necessary actions now.

An Educated Guess

No doubt, your discovery process will reveal some unexpected and interesting insights. As we've repeatedly stressed, it is crucial that leaders make this process about everyone and adopt as personalized an approach as possible.

Having said that, knowledge and experience allows us to make an "educated guess" about the most frequently cited motivators for members of a real estate team. Broadly speaking, real estate agents on a team tend to be motivated by (a) more money, and (b) more opportunities for professional growth and advancement.

MOTIVATORS FOR TEAM MEMBERS

1 **More money**
2 **More opportunities for professional growth and advancement**

FIGURE 3.3 Motivators

Money as a Motivator

If you are troubled by the thought of cold hard cash being the main motivator for your team, or if you think that everyone must have a more "virtuous" viral goal or be driven purely by their passion in the real estate industry, this may be a wake-up call for you. An intrinsic desire to do good work or a call to contribute to a higher purpose is, of course, amazing; and if that's what genuinely motivates someone, that's wonderful. However, there is absolutely nothing wrong with team members who are excited and motivated by the prospect of making more money.

Often, those who say it's wrong to be motivated by money are those for whom money is no object. Those who are struggling to pay their bills, send their kids to college, and have any hope of saving for retirement would very much beg to differ! When you assume that people are motivated primarily by pride in their work on a real estate team, it can lead to a sense of exploitation on the part of the team, and resentment and apathy on the part of the team member. Dismissing money as a motivator leads to low morale and high turnover on a real estate team, as people will leave to seek out better opportunities to get what they need.

Bottom line, there is absolutely nothing inherently wrong with money as a motivator. There's nothing "evil" about running a real estate team in order to make more money. Frankly, isn't that the whole point of creating a real estate team in the first place? If you think about it, the team leader got here as a successful real estate agent. The leader realized that in order to fulfill their own personal desire for continued growth and success, they needed to create a team. It's perfectly legitimate for a real estate team to be extremely profitable and grow to whatever size its leader desires. No justification required.

Sure, it can feel uncomfortable to talk about money with the team. That said, observing the taboo of talking about money prevents team members from achieving their financial goals and attaining the life that they want. For that reason, you must get rid of any misgivings about money as a motivator, and create a space in which leaders and team members alike feel free to articulate a desire for increased income and financial opportunity.

Growth Opportunities

There are few things as exciting and rewarding as working on a rapidly growing real estate team that is going from strength to strength and success to success. The days may be long, challenging, and sometimes chaotic, but they are also full of energy, opportunity, and incomparable experiences that you'll remember for the rest of your life. The thrill that comes with knowing you are part of something bigger, and that you're doing something different that nobody else is doing is, quite simply, phenomenal.

Along with financial stability and increased income, the most talented and driven people on any real estate team crave opportunities for growth, and the responsibility and excitement that those opportunities bring. Too often, however, only a few key players have the privilege of actively participating in a team's growth and experiencing that excitement and sense of purpose for themselves. They sit on the sidelines or watch a select group of people advance while they stay in the same place year after year or leave for something better and more challenging.

According to LinkedIn's most recent *Workforce Learning Report*, a staggering 94% of employees would stay at a company longer if it invested in their career development. A real estate team is like any other organization in this way. Growth opportunities and professional development are essential for retention, not to mention building respect and rapport on a real estate team.

94% of employees
would stay at a company
longer if it invested in their
career development

FIGURE 3.4   LinkedIn Workforce Learning Report

As *Forbes* business magazine put it: "Development is no longer an optional perk or reserved for only certain positions; it's *expected* by today's talent. It signals that the employer values their people and are actively interested in their success – not just on the job, but over the long haul." We couldn't agree more.

Growth Opportunities in Practice

"Growth opportunities" are exactly what they sound like. They're opportunities for real estate team members to advance, develop, improve, and grow. Growth opportunities come in the form of promotions with increased responsibility, autonomy, coveted titles or designations, and challenging, stimulating tasks and projects. Providing people with educational and training experiences or the opportunity to attend exciting conferences or classes also creates a culture of growth.

Increasingly, real estate team leaders are placing more emphasis on the development of "soft" interpersonal skills than easily quantifiable "hard" skills. See below for a few examples of these skills. The very best real estate teams create multiple and endless opportunities for development and growth, and strike a healthy balance between concrete, technical skills, and skills that help individuals to grow personally as well as professionally.

The same *Workforce Learning Report* also showed that talent developers must meet employees where they are with experiences they want. So, as far as is practical and possible, when it comes to creating opportunities for development, team leaders should look to their people for the type of growth experiences that motivate them most. Again, leaders can solicit feedback through personal conversations, or as part of the book club process. While it's safe to make an educated guess that most team members will be motivated by growth

SOFT SKILLS

- Leadership
- Mentorship
- Communication
- Collaboration
- Problem-Solving
- Patience
- Time Management

HARD SKILLS

- Typing
- Accounting
- Copywriting
- Web Design
- Marketing
- Social Media
- Graphic Design

FIGURE 3.5   Soft Skills versus Hard Skills

opportunities in general, it's important to make this process as specific to them as possible if you want to create a viral goal that motivates people on a deep and personal level.

A Visible Path to Growth

For growth opportunities to work as an effective motivator, they must be readily apparent. Growth opportunities must be out in the open, where everyone can see them and have a clear understanding of the career path or opportunities and experiences available to them. Growth opportunities keep talented people from feeling as though they've hit a "ceiling" in a real estate team, and leaving as a result; so it's important that your team is transparent and publicly messages the varied and endless opportunities for growth that exist.

A single growth opportunity can become a powerful motivator, driving multiple people. When a buyer's agent on a real estate team is given the chance to recruit, train, lead, and manage a team of buyer's agents, they will naturally be excited by the opportunity to grow into a lead buyer's agent. Yet the excitement doesn't stop there. Others at the business will see the growth opportunity given to the employee and feel excited, too. Their excitement will come from an understanding that similar growth opportunities may await them in the future. Another example of a growth opportunity would be for an administrative assistant. As the team grows, more administrative staff will be necessary, and the existing administrative assistant may have the opportunity to become the administrative manager of a team of administrative staff.

As more units are sold by the team, there becomes a demand for more people to service the needs of the team. A single growth opportunity can paint a vivid picture of productive career growth where every individual has the potential to progress to positions of leadership and climb the organizational ladder simply by virtue of the many more rungs being added beneath them! When more units are sold by the team, there becomes a demand for more people to service the needs of the team.

In the book *Contagious: Why Things Catch On,* Jonah Berger provides evidence that *visibility* is a key factor in whether a product catches on, or an idea "goes viral." Seeing others do something makes people more likely to do it or want it for themselves. Making something more public or observable makes it easier to imitate and replicate. Remember that when devising a viral goal, team leaders not only need to inspire individuals on a personal level but inspire them to pass on – explicitly or implicitly – a growth message to everyone on the team, creating the potential for rapid and exponential growth in the message's exposure or influence. Team members don't necessarily need to talk about growth to spread a message of growth: sometimes, "seeing is believing."

Up Next: You've Got Your Viral Goal – Now What?

So far in the first three chapters of this book, we've covered several tactics that will help you in creating the viral growth goal for your real estate team. We talked about the reason why a viral goal is essential for driving growth and taking your team members to the next level. We also talked about making the viral goal about everyone on your team. And, of course, in this chapter, we talked about making sure your viral goal is SMART. In the next two chapters of Part One, we will pivot to tackling two topics on your mind whether you're a team leader or a team member: org charts and compensation structures. Time to dig in!

CHAPTER 4

The Org Chart: How to Structure a Real Estate Team for Maximal Growth

Growth Opportunities and Team Growth

Generous bonuses can't happen unless the real estate team is growing. Promotions can't happen unless the real estate team is growing in ways that support expansion. Increased agent income can't happen without increased team production. If team members desire permanent workplace flexibility, the team will need to raise a specific amount of extra revenue to invest in the technology that remote agents need to get their work done. If team members are motivated by health and wellness, the team will need to raise a specific amount of extra revenue to invest in a weekly meditation program, healthy snacks in the kitchen, or an on-site gym.

As we said before: money is a medium of exchange – a way for us to trade one thing for another. As much as team leaders want to provide more commissions and raise team member salaries, send their agents to out-of-state training conferences, or lead an altruistic campaign, they simply cannot do so if the real estate team cannot reasonably and sustainably support those ideals and goals. Revenue both justifies and enables expenses.

Of course, if it's realistic for a team member to immediately provide some of the smaller perks that will boost morale on the team and give everyone a taste for more, that's a fantastic way to catalyze the drive for growth. To some extent, however, overall team growth must first occur before team leaders can deliver on the promises of individual goals. Leaders who skirt around this dilemma, or attempt to provide the *rewards* of growth without the *causal activities* of growth, create unrealistic expectations and run the risk of disappointing and losing their team's trust.

A *rational relationship* must exist between everyone's individual reasons for wanting growth and the overall growth goals of the real estate team. This is where the viral goal comes into play. Once the team leader has determined the motivations of the people on the team, the second step is to create a viral goal that links each team member's desired outcomes and aspirations to the organization's overall growth goal.

Remember, *your* goal for your team may not go viral, but a goal that is attractive to *all* team members will.

The Importance of an Org Chart

It is essential to have a team culture that embraces growth. To embrace a culture of growth, it is very important that everybody embraces a team structure that will lead to increased profits. If everyone on the team wants to make more money, the team must grow.

Team growth is the only way administrative staff members will get raises. If administrative staff seek promotion opportunities or want to lead other people on the team, the only way these opportunities will present themselves is if all team members embrace growth. On the sales side, as the team grows, you will need more agents. This will create opportunities for leadership roles on the sales team.

This culture of growth must be based on an org chart. With an org chart, everyone on the team can visualize this goal of growth. Here at Icenhower Coaching and Consulting (ICC), we coach many of the top real estate teams in North America, and they take on many different shapes and sizes. The larger a team gets, the more unique the org chart. Later in this chapter, we provide you with several general examples of what an org chart can look like for a real estate team.

It is essential to see where you are going. Even if you are on a smaller real estate team with only three sales agents, looking at an org chart that shows what a team of 25 agents would look like can be very beneficial. Team members will see all the leadership opportunities that would come from that kind of growth. Visualization cements the idea in everyone's brain and makes the goal tangible. Suddenly, it's not just an abstract idea – it becomes achievable.

Once you create an org chart, you can start creating benchmarks. For example, if you are a Buyer's Agent and you sell a certain number of houses, or if you are able to generate a certain amount of business from your own sphere of influence (SOI), you might graduate to the position of Lead Buyer's Agent. Or if you are a Transaction Coordinator, once you are able to comfortably manage 40 pending transactions, you might be able to get a Transaction Coordinating Assistant or possibly graduate to Administrative Manager. Those are just a few examples.

The entire team must see team growth opportunities visually, and an org chart accomplishes this. The org chart allows team leaders to be transparent with their plans for the team. When talking about team performance and creating goals, all team members must be able to see what the team is working toward. If team members can visualize the team's goal, it becomes real. It becomes something that every team member will think about, and it keeps everyone focused on the hard work that must be done to reach those goals.

The quickest way to lose motivation is to lose sight of your goal or think it's unachievable. The more you can keep the goal front and center visually, the more the entire team will embrace growth.

Another reason to use an org chart: goal fusion. The org chart demonstrates goal fusion visually. It helps create a positive team atmosphere. If everyone on the team has a similarly aligned goal (i.e. team must sell 250 homes in a year), everyone has their part to play in reaching that goal, and everyone will know that all team members are on the same page, it creates a positive, team-oriented culture. Team members will think in "we" not "I" statements. This team-oriented culture will encourage team members to help each other and desire success for everyone on the team. This is a true team. We talk in more detail about goal fusion later in this chapter.

Remember that none of these org charts become possible without a high-performing team that is focused on increasing production. Teams must generate increased income before increasing all the expenses associated with growing the team in agent count and administrative staff count.

By using the principles in this book – all five components of team growth – your team will be focused on increased production. And if everybody on the team focuses on increased production, the org chart will reflect that growth. Because your team will experience increased production, increased income, increased staff, and increased marketing, everybody achieves more. Everybody gets more opportunities. Everybody gets increased pay and increased leadership role opportunities. This is why you must not ignore the importance of the org chart!

United We Stand

We cannot stress enough that a real estate team's growth is a collaborative, cooperative, and coordinated group effort. A viral goal unites an abundance of personal motivators under the umbrella of a common objective and purpose, and it is essential that everyone join forces to realize a mutually beneficial vision of growth.

Determining each team member's personal motivations taps into everyone's big *Why* – the main thing that will motivate them to embrace change and perform the sometimes uncomfortable and challenging growth activities necessary to achieve the overall goal. This first step is an exciting and energizing process that creates a rejuvenating and invigorating social buzz within a real estate team. That's phenomenal. That's what's going to make a vision of growth catch on and go viral. That's exactly what we want.

 Resource   **Organizational Structure Charts**

In the online resource appendix of this book, you will find several organizational charts for leaders to use for their team. We have provided four different organizational structure charts, and the one you use will depend on the size and structure of your team. Remember that every team looks different, and these are only a few samples of how your team may look! These charts are fillable PDFs – making them super easy for you to use and customize for your team.

All resources can be downloaded from this book's online appendix at therealestatetrainer.com/ teambook.

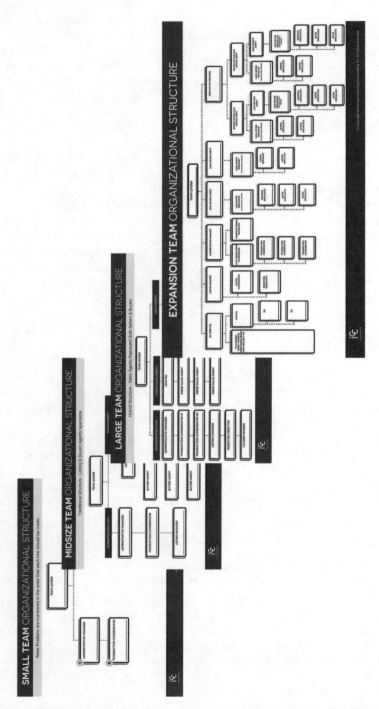

FIGURE 4.1 Organizational Structure Charts

However, it can sometimes look a little like the following illustration.

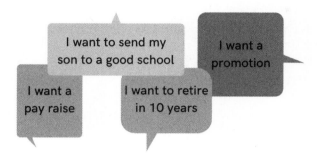

FIGURE 4.2   A Myriad of Motivations

When a team leader first sits down and wades through each team member's motivations and aspirations, the results may seem a little scattered and disconnected. At this point, the leader has spent so much time *making it about everyone*, but now they must *make it about their goal for the real estate team as a whole.*

What's more, from a practical perspective, these personal, emotionally charged hopes and dreams must be translated into concrete growth goals that can be quantified, measured, and tracked. "Sending my kid to a good college" is a great motivator for any parent, but it is not a great goal from a practical, implementable perspective. "Doubling my income" is a little more specific and quantifiable but, again, a real estate team can't increase salaries or distribute generous bonuses unless the team itself is growing, so this statement is also more of a motivator than a concrete goal.

In short: team members' personal motivations must translate into individual concrete growth goals that, *fused together*, create a single real estate team growth goal.

Goal Fusion

In its simplest terms, fusing individual team member goals together results in a single real estate team goal. When you do this correctly, the overall goal won't unravel into individual and potentially divisive goals. Rather, the overall team goal will remain intact, synthesized as a unified and coherent source of guidance.

Let's provide a very straightforward example for the team leaders reading this. Suppose you are running a small real estate team in Central California. On the sales team, you have four agents: Bob, Mary, Phil, and Anne. In terms of *motivation*, Bob would like to start saving up for a boat and retire early, while Mary would like to send her children to a private college when they graduate from high school in three years. Phil would like to take six weeks off and travel to Europe with his wife next summer; and Anne dreams of buying an investment property in wine country.

Four different people with four different motivations but one thing in common: they're all part of the same real estate sales team. In order to realize their personal dreams, they're going to need to increase their income, which means they're going to have to increase the number of homes they sell. In short: if they are to make more money, their personal motivations must translate into concrete growth goals.

Again, in very simple terms, among these four people each now has the following sales goal:

- Bob: 20 homes
- Mary: 25 homes
- Phil: 25 homes
- Anne: 30 homes

But remember: personal motivations transform into individual concrete growth goals that, *fused together*, create a single organizational growth goal.

Faced with these individual's growth goals, the team leader would add the goals together to create a single, team growth goal. In this case, adding the individual goals together literally means adding them together: $20 + 25 + 25 + 30 = 100$ total homes. That's the total number of homes for the agents on the sales team, when everyone meets their individual sales goal.

Logically then, the sales team's single, overall growth goal would be "100 Homes Sold." That total works because it supports what each person individually wants. There is a *rational relationship* between the organization selling 100 homes (its goal) and each person on the team achieving their goal (i.e. the number of sales that contribute to 100 homes sold). Everyone's personal motivations have been transformed into individual, concrete goals that fuse together to create a single organizational growth goal for the entire sales team.

When the team hits their target (100 homes sold), its members will then be rewarded in some way. They may earn increased commissions, bonuses, a promotion, a paid vacation, etc. While their ultimate motivation to send their kid to college or buy a boat and retire early may not yet occur, they are well on their way to realizing those dreams and have tangible proof that growth is benefiting them personally.

Easy, right? In the example above, a straightforward numeric value creates the rational relationship, and everyone participates in achieving the benefits and rewards of growth. In reality, it's not always so straightforward. It would be wonderful if we could simply make a quick back-of-the-envelope calculation and arrive at our real estate team's overall growth goal, but for many teams the fusion process will be a little more complex.

$1 + 1 + 1 + x =$ Not So Simple

Let's say that the aforementioned real estate sales team relies on an administrative assistant/office manager named Toby. Like his coworkers, he is also motivated by making more money, and would like to go back to school in the evening to get a degree in marketing. However, as his role is administrative in nature, it's not as easy to transform his personal

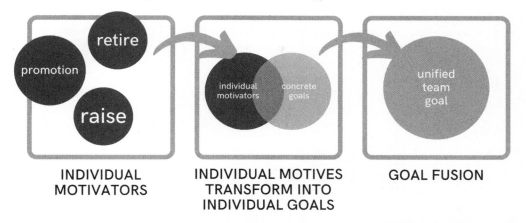

FIGURE 4.3   Individual Motivators to Goal

motivations into a concrete goal that has a rational relationship to the real estate team's overall growth goal.

If we can't measure this person's individual sales, it seems we can't tie their goal into the larger goal of increased sales and profitability, but there is always a way for team members to support the greater team growth goal. For example, as part of Toby's weekly activities, he may be tasked with reaching out to past clients and obtaining a certain number of favorable online reviews. Or, perhaps Toby can start using his interest in marketing to create dynamic mailers and other marketing materials to promote client events. These are both areas that an administrative assistant can have control over.

When the team receives a certain number of five-star online reviews, or sees an increase in interest in client events due to Toby's marketing efforts, Toby's goals (and related activities) indeed tie into the overall real estate team goal. These decidedly "un-salesy" areas help the entire team to "move the needle" on sales and achieve the team's growth goals.

Like his colleagues in sales, Toby is also a crucial player in the "If, then" sequence of the process. If the team hits their *overall* target, its members will then be rewarded in some way. Toby may also receive a bonus or a pay raise, or the flexibility and support he needs to work and take college classes at the same time. As he studies marketing, his newfound knowledge and ability to effectively market to a wider audience will have a positive impact on the real estate team and deepen his connection to the company's culture of growth. As the team grows, he may find himself a shoo-in to be promoted to marketing director.

When devising a viral goal, it can't be about some of them: You must make it about everyone.

Again, this is a relatively straightforward example, but the message is clear. No matter the size of the real estate team – and no matter each person's individual role or position within the team – with some creativity and considered planning, you can transform each team member's personal motivators into concrete and actionable goals that, when fused together, will result in a single, unified real estate team growth goal.

At larger real estate teams with different divisions, departments, teams, or branches, the breakdown will look something like this:

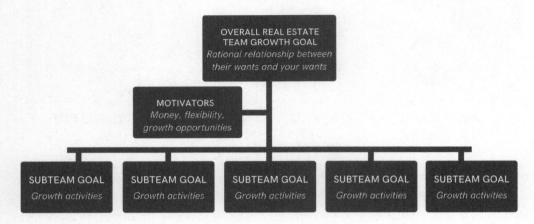

FIGURE 4.4   Team Goal Chart

Each subteam may be made up of several people with distinct roles and abilities but, again, note that every subteam goal is linked to the overall real estate team growth goal. Not only will the team goal inform and drive the creation of any ensuing subteam goals, but the related activities, not to mention the successes and outcomes, of those goals will be measured against whether they contribute to the success of the overall growth goal. People's motivators remain an ever-present factor and visible reminder about what everyone is personally working toward; but, in a sense, they sit somewhat to the side, having been transformed into more concrete, quantifiable, and actionable team goals.

Remember: every single person on a real estate team can be an active and powerful participant in making growth go viral. Goals need a "host," and a viral goal is one in which everyone is driven by infectious enthusiasm and an irresistible desire to bring the goal to fruition. Goals are achieved by the efforts and energies of living, breathing people, and the success of a viral goal depends on its inclusivity and ability to impact everybody. When devising a viral goal, you can't just make it about *some* of the team members: you must *make it about everyone.*

Up Next: Compensation

Now that we've discussed the importance of creating an org chart, we will dive into the typical compensation structures for each member on a real estate team.

CHAPTER 5

How to Pay Real Estate Team Members: Typical Compensation Structures for Each Role

First a Quick Recap

In the first four chapters of this book, we talked about devising a viral goal that will propel team members to the next level. We also talked about ensuring that the viral goal motivates everyone on the team. We discussed how to make the viral goal SMART, and we talked about how an org chart will help create a culture of growth.

This chapter is devoted to the topic that inspired many readers to pick up this book in the first place: commissions and compensation.

If you are the team leader, how much are you paying your people? And if you are the team member, how much should you expect to be paid? Compensation structure is a hot topic for many of our clients. We talk about all the ways that we can motivate people through a goal, but let's be honest. Compensation is a big part of your desire to increase your responsibility. When you move into a leadership position, you expect to be compensated appropriately. In this chapter, we outline the various positions on a real estate team, which will provide you a motivating path for growth within the real estate team.

This is what the top teams do. They do not have a structure with one team leader at the top of the organizational chart, and then one long line of people, all of whom answer to the leader directly. That model is not sustainable.

Our org charts show multiple levels of leadership and that enables the team leader to motivate agents and staff members on the team by providing them with different paths for growth within the team.

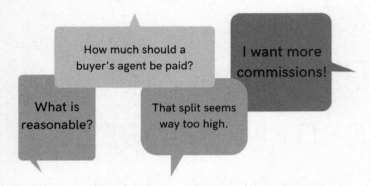

FIGURE 5.1 Questions on Compensation

FIGURE 5.2 Single-Level Org Chart

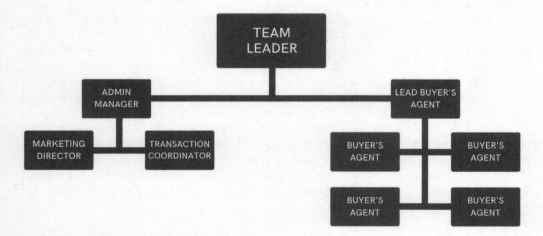

FIGURE 5.3 Multilevel Org Chart

Team members can continuously move up, and that will keep them motivated and prevent the feeling that they've hit the ceiling on the team. It will also help to prevent that awful feeling of burnout. Nobody wants to feel stuck in their current position. Nobody wants to feel that they can't ever make more money or get more responsibility or learn to do a new job. If there's nowhere for them to move up, no path for growth, no steps to ascend, no ladder rungs to climb, why care? If there is no room for growth, then the team member will not be motivated.

In Chapter 1, we gave you our library of job descriptions. Now, we break down each position on a real estate team in more detail and discuss how much each team member is typically compensated. We also talk about what each position's duties include.

Resource   Typical Compensation Structures for Each Role on a Real Estate Team

In the online resource appendix of this book, leaders will find this helpful resource on how to structure commission on a real estate team. At Icenhower Coaching and Consulting (ICC), we get questions on compensation all the time. As we learn about growth in this chapter, think about how much you are paying your team members. Of course, it varies depending on your market and location. This PDF packet includes the general commission structure that you can use to project compensation costs for each member of your team.

All resources can be downloaded from this book's online appendix at therealestatetrainer.com/teambook.

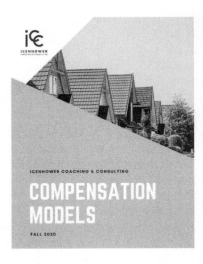

FIGURE 5.4   Team Compensation Models

Sales Roles

Inside Sales Associate (ISA)

Other names: Inbound Sales Associate

Compensation: Salary + Commission

Example: $24,000–$36,000 plus 5%–10% of gross commission income (GCI)

Duties:

1. Convert inbound leads
2. Make outbound prospecting calls

Also known as a telemarketer, this role is typically filled by a licensed real estate agent who works "inside" the office, as opposed to an outside sales agent who actually shows property and goes out and meets clients, lists property, and so forth. Oftentimes, the ISA role is where agents start out when they first get into the business. This helps them learn how to convert inbound leads and make outbound prospecting calls to generate new leads. Essentially, lead generation and conversion is an ISA's sole focus.

Starting out as an ISA on a real estate team is a huge benefit to new real estate agents, since the vast majority of solo real estate agents fail due to an inability to generate enough business and income to survive in the industry. ISAs on real estate teams develop amazing habits and learn the most crucial parts of the business, which will ensure that they will be more successful in their careers going forward. From their experience as an ISA, they will always be able to generate and convert business – earning commissions won't be a problem.

Typically most teams that utilize ISAs as a means of new agent onboarding and training will have a new licensee come onto the team and serve as an ISA for the first 6 to 12 months. During that time, they will be generating and converting leads for the other sales agents on the team.

Compensation Explained   ISAs convert leads and set listing or buyer consultation appointments from the leads they are working. They are paid a relatively nominal base salary, usually in the range of $24,000–$36,000, plus a commission of somewhere between 5% and 10% of the GCI. This commission comes when one of the leads that they convert actually closes and produces commission income. Of course, if one of the leads they convert does not successfully close on the purchase or sale of a new home, no additional commission is earned by the ISA on that transaction. Once the ISA has shown a proficiency and developed the skill set and ability to successfully generate and convert leads into appointments, the agent then graduates to become a sales agent for the team where they then can start conducting appointments, showing property, etc.

Showing Assistant

Other names: Showing Specialist or Showing Agent

Compensation: Commission

Example: 15%–20% of GCI

Duties:

1. Showing properties
2. Additional sales agent support

The position of Showing Assistant is another way to onboard and train new agents before allowing them to graduate to become a normal sales agent. As their name implies, Sales Assistants show properties. They are like a door opener. They exist on the team to assist the sales agents. So imagine a Buyer's Agent who generates leads, sets their own buyer consultation appointment, meets the client, explains everything to them, learns about what they're looking for, and then sets up a lot of showings of different properties. Then, the Showing Assistant would actually be the person driving the client around, opening doors, and showing them property. Once the buyer finds the house they wish to buy, the Showing Assistant takes the buyers back to the Buyer's Agent to write the offer for them, negotiate the contract, and so forth.

The Showing Assistant only steps in to open doors. Sometimes they will hold open houses, too, if the other sales agents are unavailable (too many listings, out of town, etc.) Showing Assistants will sometimes step in to help with open houses in these cases.

Quick Tip   Understand the Split

The Showing Assistant is typically paid by commission, 15%–20% of GCI on the buyers they represent. They provide a great service to Buyer's Agents on teams. Despite their value, most real estate agents are overly commission split-sensitive and may not see why they should give up part of their commission split to have a Showing Assistant. Most sales agents don't really understand business, economics, and financials, and because of that, they cling to their commission dollars. They don't want to give up any of their commission. All they want is a higher commission.

This is one of the big reasons why there are so few high-producing agents. The high-producing agents know they need to invest in their business. They do need to incur costs in order to increase their net income. You will see in most Multiple Listing Services (MLS) that the top agents are either team leaders or members of teams. Solo agents typically sell a lot less real estate and have a lot less income – all to protect their higher commission percentage.

Buyer's Agents should embrace the idea of utilizing Showing Assistants, and thereby give up 15%–20% of their commissions to compensate them. This is what many top Buyer's Agents do, because they know it works. A Buyer's Agent can usually only handle 40, maybe 50, transactions per year without burning themselves out. Showing property takes up about 80% of a Buyer's Agent's time. Writing offers doesn't take much time. Buyer consultations don't take

(continued)

Quick Tip *(continued)*

much time. Inspections and negotiations – not much time either. Buyer's agents spend the vast majority of their time showing property.

As a Buyer's Agent, if you could start getting paid 30%–40% on some of your transactions without having to show property, you might be able to start closing 70–80 transactions per year and make a ton more income. Not to mention, having a Showing Assistant on the team will also enable Buyer's Agents to take vacations or spend more time with their family. Buyer's Agents will achieve a better work/life balance as a result, since they won't have to work nights and weekends to show property.

It's important that Buyer's Agents begin to embrace the idea of hiring Showing Assistants in order to truly expand and grow in the role. As an added bonus, it gives new agents a way to train. Showing Assistants learn how to work with buyers. They can shadow the Buyer's Agent on the buyer consultation, or through the inspection process. They can start learning through other members on the team. It is almost like a built-in mentorship program where the Buyer's Agents mentor the Showing Assistant. And in return, the Buyer's Agent is provided with some extra coverage and help. It helps grow the team's culture through team member bonding, as an added bonus, because team members are working together and getting to know each other.

It really does benefit agents to leverage themselves. It's the same reason the team leader leveraged themselves initially by bringing on agents and staff, too. They hired administrative staff members, they gave buyer leads away to buyer's agents on the team, and as a result, the team leader ends up earning less of a commission split, too. This is the mind-set that top agents must have.

Showing assistants often come on right after they get their license, and they are able to get a lockbox key from their local MLS. That's when they can start showing property legally. And that's when they can start to help out Buyer's Agents on the team.

Learn to be *Less*
split-sensitive to earn
more **income.**

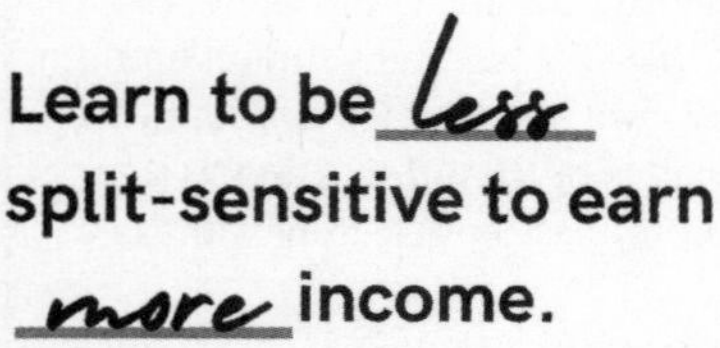

FIGURE 5.5 Learn to Be Less Split-Sensitive

ISA/Showing Assistant Hybrid

Combination of the ISA and Showing Assistant Roles
Compensation: Salary + Commission
Example: $24,000–$36,000 plus 10% of GCI

Duties:

1. Convert inbound leads
2. Make outbound prospecting calls
3. Show properties
4. Additional sales agent support

The role of ISA/Showing Assistant Hybrid is the best of both worlds. This is a great way to onboard new agents on your team, as it trains a very well-rounded agent with skills across the board. In the morning, the agent in this role acts like an ISA, converting and generating leads and working the phones. They learn how to prospect, convert leads, and develop great habits. And then, in the afternoon, the agent is out showing property as a Showing Assistant for the Buyer's Agents. They learn how to work with buyers and show property while shadowing the Buyer's Agents on all the different aspects of the Buyer's Agent's role. It's a great onboarding practice for the first 6 to 12 months of a new real estate agent's career on the team, until they demonstrate that they can perform all activities required on the team dashboard (more about that in Part Five).

The ISA/Showing Assistant Hybrid learns how to prospect, convert leads, and develop great habits.

Buyer's Agent/Specialist

Compensation: Commission

Example: 35%–50% of GCI

Duties:

1. Generating and converting leads
2. Following up and nurturing leads
3. Conducting buyer consultation appointments in person or via video conference
4. Showing property
5. Writing offers and negotiating contracts
6. Attending and negotiating inspection repairs

Traditionally, the industry-standard commission for Buyer's Agents is 50%. The vast majority of teams use a 50/50 split. Sometimes they are paid less and there are situations where they may be paid more, too. Starting with less is typically due to having ISAs on the team. The ISA needs to be paid, too, which brings down the cut that the Buyer's Agent will get.

Quick Tip Understand the Split

When you have an ISA on your team, it wipes out the first two duties of a Buyer's Agent (generating and converting leads, and following up and nurturing leads). These tasks are done by the ISA over the phone and the ISA gets the lead pretty darn close to the third task of a Buyer's Agent – conducting the appointment. As a result, a percentage of what the Buyer's Agent would normally get needs to be allocated to the ISA.

Usually, the part of the Buyer's Agent's job that an ISA does is the part of the job that the Buyer's Agent likes the least. Working the phones is not the part of the job that people tend to enjoy. So, a lot of Buyer's Agents are more than happy to take a reduced commission percentage if it means they won't need to work the phones all the time. Instead, they can get the lead handed to them in the form of an appointment set.

In a lot of cases, if the Buyer's Agents generate their own leads, they earn a 50% commission. If they get the lead from the ISA, they might earn a 35% commission. So, it can fluctuate depending on the source of the lead.

There are also situations when a Buyer's Agent will earn more income with a higher commission split. There are a few scenarios that require this. Sometimes, an agent generates and closes more business from their own sphere of influence (SOI) than they get from team-generated leads over the course of a year. Here, we are looking at the agent- versus team-generated closings ratio. Once an agent starts bringing more business to the team than the team is providing the agent over a sustained period of time, oftentimes, teams will seek to reward that success. This would be a valid reason for giving the Buyer's Agent an increased commission split on the leads that the Buyer's Agent is bringing to the team from their own SOI. So, for example, the Buyer's Agent might be graduated to a 75/25 split on leads the Buyer's Agent generates from his/her own SOI but still remain on a 50/50 split for those leads provided by the team to the Buyer's Agent (team-generated leads). This particular Buyer's Agent demonstrates an ability to outpace the team on the Matching Standard with the number of agent-generated closings exceeding the number of team-generated closings.

As an alternative, teams might implement graduated commission split increases once a Buyer's Agent demonstrates an ability to outpace the team with agent-generated closings. You might then graduate to a sliding scale where for the first 10 closings of the year, they are at a 50% commission split. Then, for the next 10 closings, they graduate to 60%. And then from closings 21–30 they would be at 70%, 31–40 at 80%, 41–50 at 90%, and then you could even say from 51 and beyond they would earn 100% of their commissions through the end of the year. Of course, these graduated splits reset at the beginning of each year, when all agents would then start over at their original 50/50 split. A sliding scale like this can also be used with sales volume. As an example, agent splits would start out at 50%, then after $5 million in closed sales volume the split would increase to 60%, then at $7 million 75%, and so forth. Either way, graduated commission splits can be great incentives for high-performing Buyer's Agents.

If you are a Buyer's Agent reading this, you may think that some of these splits are not favorable enough. Understand that it is natural to feel that way because by nature, agents tend to be overly split-sensitive. Just like all humans, we tend to shy away from costs because anything that costs us money is scary.

Understand that successful businesspeople tend to invest in their business and get ahead in their career and life a lot more quickly. Bill Gates is on one of the lowest "commission splits" of

(continued)

Quick Tip   *(continued)*

all time. For the sake of this example, let's say that Bill Gates, founder of Microsoft, would make $101 billion in annual revenue. With all the costs that Microsoft has, his costs add up to about $100 billion. So, his commission split is only at about 1%.

Would you accept a 1% commission split? Probably not. However, 1% of $101 billion means Bill Gates is still making approximately $1 billion. Bill Gates knows that in order to increase his business, he needs to increase his costs.

That's the way it works with real estate agents, too. The top agents are typically the ones that have the most costs. If you look at any community, you will see that most of the top agents are at brokerages where they pay a higher commission split and the lower-producing agents are at the discount brokerages. Success leaves clues, so be sure to pick them up!

If you look at the team leader of a real estate team, they have to pay administrative support, marketing costs, leads, and so on . . . by the time it's all said and done, it's not uncommon for a team leader to only keep 20%–40% of their GCI. However, typically the team leader makes more than agents on the team. Yet, they have the lowest split after all of these costs are factored in.

This is also true with Buyer's Agents. Many don't realize that Buyer's Agents on real estate teams receiving 35%–50% commission splits are in fact making hundreds of thousands of dollars in income. Much of this success is due to the value provided by the team. Leads, administrative support, mentoring, training, accountability, and so on, are all provided by the team. These Buyer's Agents can close a lot more transactions, sell a lot more real estate, and make a lot more net income because of the value a team provides. It's very important for Buyer's Agents to be less split-sensitive. They need to control that natural tendency and instead focus more on their net income. Even though they may feel like they are making less per transaction, the support of the team will propel them to earn more net income when everything is said and done.

Lead Buyer's Agents

Other names: Lead Buyer's Specialist

Compensation: Commission

Example: 5% override on the Buyer's Agents they manage + increased percentage on personal transactions (60% or 70%)

Duties:

1. Recruiting; identify potential candidates to join the team, meeting with them, overcoming their objections to joining the team, then assisting them in joining the team.

2. Onboarding and training new agents; ensuring they are going through an intense agent onboarding program, being there to answer all their questions, "deal doctor" issues when problems come up with their clients or transaction hiccups, they are there to help them.

3. Leading and managing; run weekly dashboard meetings, conducting coaching sessions.

Compensation Explained   This is a great path for growth for Buyer's Agents because they are attracted by the fact that they can get 5% override (5% commission) on all the sales of all the other Buyer's Agents on the team. This means that the Lead Buyer's Agent doesn't necessarily need to be doing all of their own sales to earn income. This is motivation for the Lead Buyer's Agent's number-one role: recruiting. The bigger and more successful they grow the size of the team, they can expect 5% out of every buyer side closing that the team generates. This becomes practically passive income. They have less income coming from their own sales so they don't have to be out showing property on nights and weekends. The role of Lead Buyer's Agent is almost like an additional team leader or the broker of an office, because they receive a percentage of the other agents in their care.

For Buyer's Agents to qualify to become Lead Buyer's Agents, the Matching Standard comes back into play. Just because an agent sells a lot doesn't mean they are necessarily going to be the best Lead Buyer's Agents. For a Lead Buyer's Agent, they also need to demonstrate that they can generate and convert a lot of transactions from their own SOI because we want that leader of the Buyer's Agents to lead by example. We want a team of agents that all know how to grow and cultivate their own business, and bring business to the team, not just become dependent on the team to bring business to them.

With the Lead Buyer's Agent, they need to have demonstrated that they did successfully establish an interdependent relationship with the team and brought a sufficient amount of business from their own SOI, and they weren't dependent on the team's leads to get their numbers each year. A Lead Buyer's Agent must also like to train and recruit, and it must be a person who really likes to see others succeed – often even more than themselves. That's a true leader. You don't want someone in this role who is just doing it for the compensation. This type of position is really best served by someone who wants to develop others. They don't want to be the rock star on the team – they would rather be the rock star maker.

We have had Lead Buyer Specialists who had earned $200,000 in GCI as a top Buyer's Agent, and when they are promoted to the Lead Buyer's Agent role, they actually scale back the amount of commission that they earn from their own business. As a result, their goal might be to earn $150,000 in GCI the next year but to earn $100,000 from their 5% overrides from the other Buyer's Agents on the teams ($250,000 total). They do actually make more money and sell less real estate themselves, which will start to give them better work/life balance, and they can enjoy more time with their family or their own hobbies. The next year, they may even go down to $100,000 in GCI but earn $200,000 from their 5% override ($300,000 total).

When to Hire   We have seen this successfully done by quite a few of our clients. It's a great role that works very well time and time again. Typically, we'll start thinking about bringing on a Lead Buyer's Agent once we've got somewhere around six or seven agents on the team. This is when the team starts to get harder for the team leader to manage. With six or seven Buyer's Agents, you're going to have a lot of issues and a lot of questions – all the things that go along with managing personnel. It makes it harder to recruit, and ultimately, harder to grow without extra managerial help. And in this case, the Lead Buyer's Agent will help recruit, train, lead, and manage all the Buyer's Agents. This takes a lot off the plate of the team leader.

Listing Agent

Other names: Listing Specialist

Compensation: Salary + Commission

Example: $40,000–$75,000 plus 5%–10% on the sellers they represent

Duties:

1. Lead generating for listings
2. Following up and converting listing leads
3. Preparing for listing appointments
4. Conducting listing consultation appointments
5. Providing listing marketing updates
6. When applicable, conducting price reduction appointments

Compensation Explained   With all the clients we have worked with here at ICC, we have found a lot more success making this person on the team salaried plus commission. Part of the reason for a base salary is because this position does not require as much urgency as that of a Buyer's Agent. A Listing Agent is usually more reserved, and doesn't need to be "Johnny on the spot" all the time. The following chart illustrates the differences between the two roles.

BUYER SIDE

- work nights and weekends
- hustle, "Johnny on the spot"
- show multiple properties to one client
- can be very time-consuming
- "salesman" position

LISTING SIDE

- usually work 9 to 5
- steady job with predictable hours
- lists one property for the client one time
- less time-consuming
- less of a "salesman"

FIGURE 5.6   Buyer Side versus Listing Side

Instead, successful Listing Agents possess more of a steady and stable demeanor. As a result, they prefer the security of being compensated with a salary and receiving a paycheck every couple of weeks. This calming characteristic of top Listing Agents helps give home sellers confidence in the agent that they've chosen to represent them.

Administrative Roles

When you first built your team, likely your first hire was an Administrative Assistant. When your team is relatively small or new, you may have only one administrative staff member to do all five of the following administrative roles. Though this is true and your Administrative Assistant may wear many hats, understand that this person will only be able to do bits and pieces of each of these roles. To expect one single person to do the job of five is unreasonable, and you must edit your expectations and modify the following five administrative roles to fit your situation.

Listing Manager

Other names: Listing Coordinator, Listing Assistant

Compensation: Hourly/salary

Example: Amounts vary greatly based on local standard and cost of living

Duties: Listing to contract

- Oversee all aspects of sellers' transactions from initial contact to executed purchase agreement.
- Prepare all listing materials: prelisting presentation, listing agreement, sellers' disclosures, comparative market analysis, pull online property profile, research old MLS listings, and so forth.
- Consult and coordinate with sellers all property photos, staging, repairs, cleaning, signage, lockbox, access requirements, and marketing activities.
- Obtain all necessary signatures on listing agreement, disclosures, and other necessary documentation.
- Coordinate showings and obtain feedback.
- Provide proactive weekly feedback to sellers regarding all showings and marketing activities.
- Coordinate all public open houses and broker open houses.
- Input all listing information into MLS and marketing websites and update as needed.
- Submit all necessary documentation to office broker for file compliance.
- Input all necessary information into client database and transaction management systems.

Transaction Coordinator

Other names: Client Care Representative, Contract to Close Manager

Compensation: Hourly/salary

Example: Amounts vary greatly based on local standard and cost of living

Duties: Contract to Close

- Oversee all aspects of buyer and seller transactions from executed purchase agreement to closing.
- Coordinate title/escrow, mortgage loan, and appraisal processes.
- Coordinate inspections, assist in negotiations regarding repairs, and coordinate completion of repairs.
- Regularly update and maintain communication with clients, agents, title officer, lender, and so forth.
- Submit all necessary documentation to office broker for file compliance.
- Coordinate moving/possession schedules.
- Schedule, coordinate, and attend closing process.
- Input all client information into client database system.
- Schedule 30-day, 90-day, and 120-day client customer service follow-up calls to assist with any home improvement provider recommendations and to ask for referrals.

Marketing Director

Other names: Marketing Manager

Compensation: Hourly/salary

Example: Amounts vary greatly based on local standard and cost of living

Duties:

- Manage client database management program and system.
- Create and regularly prepare all buyer and seller consultation packages.
- Coordinate the preparation of all listing and open house flyers, graphics, signage, and all other marketing materials.
- Manage and update agent website(s), blog(s), and online listings.
- Regularly assist agent to manage and enhance agent's social media presence.
- Track and coordinate all inbound leads from websites, social media, and other online sources.
- Coordinate all client and vendor appreciation events.
- Regularly obtain client testimonials for websites, social media, and other marketing materials.
- Coordinate and implement agent marketing videos and property videos on website(s), blog(s), social media, and client database email campaigns.

Administrative Manager

Other names: Operations Manager, Team Manager

Compensation: Hourly/salary; should also be a percentage of profits bonus or other production-based bonuses

Example: Amounts vary greatly based on local standard and cost of living

Duties:

- Oversee all aspects of the administration of the agent's business.
- Create and manage all systems for sellers, buyers, client database management, lead generation tracking, lead follow-up, and all office administration.
- Maintain all agent financial systems, profit-and-loss statement, bill payment, budget(s), bank accounts, and business credit card(s).
- Coordinate the purchasing of any office equipment, marketing materials, and any other business-related supplies and materials.
- Create and update a business operations manual and all job descriptions/employment contracts for any future hires.
- Manage the recruiting, hiring, training, and ongoing leadership of all future administrative hires.
- Hold agent(s) accountable for conducting all agreed-upon lead generation activities.
- Ensure that all agent activities are limited to listing property, showing property, negotiating contracts, and lead generation.

Runner

Compensation: Hourly/salary

Example: Amounts vary greatly based on local standard and cost of living

Duties:

- Putting out and picking up signs, flyer boxes, and lockboxes
- Delivering earnest money deposit checks and paperwork
- Picking up keys
- Fixing signs
- Taking photos
- Meeting people at the properties to provide access
- Miscellaneous tasks related to listing property management

It isn't until the team gets a little larger and is closing somewhere between 75 and 125 transactions a year that we would see the need to hire a second administrative person. At that point, you would divide the tasks. Maybe you would have the Listing Manager and the Marketing Director together as one role, and the Transaction Coordinator and the Administrative Manager as the other role, for example. Perhaps both administrators share the Runner duties. There are a lot of ways to hodge-podge it together.

Once your team reaches 300–350 closings, you might bring on your own independent Marketing Director. Understand that your team will grow depending on the need and depending on how many transactions you are closing each year. If your team is closing over 350 transactions per year, you are probably going to need a second Transaction Coordinator to handle all the duties from contract to close. Growth beyond that depends on many different factors. The structure of your team, how the team members lead generate, and what the lead flow looks like all come into play as you make new administrative hires. Not every team is the same, though most teams do start out the same and grow the same when they are smaller. Once a team grows, there are many differences in structure, and how each team handles their business creates different needs for various roles on the team. This is where an ICC coach can come in and provide that custom advise for your next hire.

Next Steps

In Part Two of the book, we turn our attention to the second component of real estate team growth, which asks you to set outcomes aside and focus on activities first. Again, this goes against conventional approaches and is a fundamental part of the nontraditional reimagining that is a viral goal.

If you're reading this book as the leader of your real estate team, we advise you to continue reading each part from start to finish. However, if you're reading this book as a member of a real estate team, then your next step is to get ready to attend the first of five book club sessions. The following section helps you prepare and gives you a sense of what to expect. When the first book club is over, you can then pick up where you left off and continue to Part Two.

The Team Book Club: Part One Discussion Guide

Before you hold your first book club (or simultaneous book clubs in the case of larger real estate teams), it's crucial that you understand that the purpose of the first five book club meetings is *not* to come to a particular conclusion or decide on what your real estate team's overall growth goal will be.

Remember that you and your real estate team members are simply having conversations, exploring ideas, and absorbing the material rather than immediately deciding on a specific viral growth goal, or setting to work on a particular course of action.

How Long Will Each Book Club Last?

Let's start with the most frequently asked question about holding or attending a book club – how long is this thing gonna last? The best book club sessions are those where everyone is talking and collaborating. At a *minimum*, you will need 30 minutes to create a productive and generative discussion.

However, we highly recommend allocating an entire hour on your calendar with some built-in leeway in case the conversation is particularly productive and worthy of extending.

The Role of the Facilitator

Most real estate teams have some form of regular group meeting but, even if your team members are used to being part of a group discussion and are good at listening to each other, you will still need somebody to lead or facilitate the book club – in part to make sure that everyone's voices are heard but also to come prepared with questions and thoughts about what needs to be discussed.

If you're the leader of a small real estate team, it's natural and best that you lead the book club yourself. Remember that the purpose of this first book club is, in part, to determine each team member's various motivations, so it's important that you facilitate conversation, encourage participation, and make it about them rather than you. In short: a good facilitator should only speak when the talking dies down, and devise ways to spark and stoke pertinent and relevant conversation.

At larger real estate teams and organizations, the leadership team will hold their own book club first and then break out into several, simultaneously held, departmental or team-based book clubs. Again, the role of the facilitator is to *make it about everyone* and encourage respectful and relevant conversation.

Take Note

In addition to a facilitator, you might also choose a team member to take notes. While it's unnecessary and impractical to document the entire discussion, it's worth taking note of the most salient points, or the most frequently cited motivators among your team members.

Distribute a Summary

A summary supports team members who read Part One early in the week and need to refresh their memory. It also supports those who may have not finished up Part One. The Part One summary you distribute will help get all team members up to speed so they can't opt out of participation.

Hold Each Other Accountable

We explore accountability in detail in Part Three, but it's never too early to cultivate a culture of accountability and personal responsibility. Facilitators should begin each book club session by asking the group who did and didn't read the assigned part. For those people who haven't read it, or didn't finish it, you can ask them the following four key accountability questions.

① How do you think you did?

② What got in the way?

③ What do you need to do
differently next time?

④ Is there any way we can help?

FIGURE BC.1   Key Accountability Questions

Not only will this encourage everyone to better prepare for the next book club session, it will also familiarize everyone else with questions they'll be hearing a lot in the coming weeks and months.

While it's important to hold each team member accountable for actually reading and thinking about the chapter, don't become overly distracted or derailed by those who haven't prepared in advance. Keep the accountability section to a minimum and keep your sight on the real purpose and subject of the book club meeting.

Part One Summary, Component 1   Devise a Viral Goal

The first component of team growth demands that you "make it about everyone" and devise a viral goal in which the respective goals and ambitions of individuals on a real estate team are intrinsically linked to the team's overall growth goals. When this occurs, the members of the team feel personally connected to – and highly invested in realizing – the goal. Just like a video or meme that captures the attention and imagination of millions overnight, a viral goal creates a social buzz around and within the team. Enthusiasm spreads from person to person, engaging and motivating every single team member.

Key Points

- Determine personal motivations. People can't say no to their own goals, so it is essential to help team members realize what their dreams and goals actually are.
- Get SMART. To make sure your goals are clear and realizable, they must be Specific, Measurable, Achievable, Relevant, and Time-Bound. All viral goals must have a finish line. Every goal must contain a clearly measurable goal, as well as the date by which that goal must be achieved.
- Main motivators are money and opportunity. Broadly speaking, people on real estate teams tend to be motivated by (a) more money, and (b) more opportunities for professional growth and advancement. When something has practical value, it's more likely to resonate with and inspire people.
- Growth comes first. Organizational growth must first occur before leaders can deliver on the promises of individual goals. Leaders can't provide more money or diversified growth opportunities unless the organization itself is growing.

(continued)

Part One Summary, Component 1   (*continued*)

- United you stand. People's personal motivations must translate into individual concrete growth goals that, fused together, create a single organizational growth goal.
- The importance of an org chart. It is essential to have a team culture that embraces growth. To embrace a culture of growth, it is very important that everybody embraces a team structure that will lead to increased profits. If everyone on the team wants to make more money, the team must grow.
- Compensation structure is important. It's good for everyone on the team to know not only their job duties in detail, but also how they should expect to be compensated. Commission splits are often a hot topic of discussion and it is important to not be overly split-sensitive. Everything should be seen through the lens of growth and opportunity for every team member.

Notes:

_____

_____

_____

_____

Questions to Spark and Stoke Conversation

Prewritten questions are a great way to spark conversation and ensure that everyone participates, even if they haven't had time to read the entire assigned part of the book.

For those of you reading this who are the leader or book club facilitator on your real estate team, the questions below are simply a starting point – you are, of course, free to create your own.

For those of you reading this that are members of your real estate team, these questions will give you an idea of what to expect at the first book club meeting. While it's unlikely that every single one of these questions will be asked at the meeting, thinking about each of them will help you to prepare for every possibility in advance. Even if a particular question doesn't come up, thinking about the chapter from all angles is still a useful exercise.

The best book club questions are those that are open-ended and can't be answered with a simple "Yes" or "No." However, it can be difficult to strike a balance between questions that are open-ended and inclusive, but not so broad that particular people can railroad the entire book club into a prolonged discussion about their personal life or motivations. This can be particularly tricky when discussing a chapter that repeatedly says to *make it about everyone*! Again, navigating balanced and relevant conversation and ensuring that *everyone's* voice is heard is the role and responsibility of a good facilitator.

Naturally, you can use the Part One summary provided earlier to guide the conversation in addition to, or instead of, the questions below. As you read through each bullet point in the summary, ask your people, "Did this point resonate with you?" "How?" "Why?" "Tell me more," and so forth.

Above all, any questions you ask should connect the concepts to how they relate specifically to your real estate team.

Book Club Conversations for Part One   Devise a Viral Goal

- What do you think the author's purpose was in writing this book?
- What ideas was he trying to get across in Part One?
- How do the ideas presented in Part One apply to us at _____ (insert the name of your real estate team)?
- How does a viral goal differ from traditional goal setting?
- How might we start applying some concepts around a viral goal at our team?
- How did the section about making it about everyone make you feel?
- How would growth personally affect or change your life?
- Do you agree that increased income and multiple growth opportunities are the two main motivations for most people?
- Apart from money and growth opportunities, what else motivates people in regard to growth?
- What did you already know about goal setting before you read this book?
- What new things did you learn?
- What questions do you still have?
- Are there any quotes, passages, or ideas you found particularly compelling?
- Do you have a new perspective as a result of reading Part One?
- Did you learn something you didn't know before?
- How has your attitude or behavior changed?
- How does this book relate to your life or experiences?
- Did you connect with the subject matter? Did it make you nervous or excited?
- What did you like best about Part One?
- What did you like least about Part One?
- Which topic(s) of Part One stood out to you?
- If you had the chance to ask the author one question, right now, what would it be?

No matter what questions you decide to ask your people, at the end of each book club session, you (or each book club's leader/facilitator) should ask yourself the following questions:

- Does everyone understand the material?
- Have we discussed ways that the material relates to us?
- Are my people excited and engaged? Is there buy-in?
- Did I make it about everyone?

If the answer to these questions is a resounding "Yes," then you are well on your way to devising a viral goal on your real estate team.

PART 2

The Sales Team Activities That Will Grow Your Pipeline

CHAPTER 6

Focus on the Right Metrics: ABIs versus RBIs

Deliberate, Purposeful, Systematic Activities

How do you know that you have the flu? You may experience the classic symptoms of the virus's activities within your body.

However, you may be infected and not feel sick for several days. Some people don't display any signs at all. Know it or not, the virus has been steadily and systematically performing its "work" all along. All viruses follow the same basic steps or activities in order to achieve its goal. Its deliberate, purposeful, repetitive activities produce the desired results.

Needless to say, in the case of the flu, the desired results are not at all pleasing for the virus's unhappy target, but once again we have found that the underlying attributes that make viruses so successful and effective in the natural world are exactly the attributes that can be harnessed to effect rapid, widespread, and lasting positive change and growth within your team.

Deliberate, purposeful, systematic activities produce the successful results you desire. While the symptoms confirm the impact, it's the activities of the virus – or in our case, the activities of real estate team members – that create that impact and give rise to specific effects. Real estate teams that focus less on results, and more on the activities that produce those results, are more likely to achieve their goals and less likely to be caught off guard by signs that tell you something serious is up. Focusing on activities enables teams to diagnose potential problems and apply their time and energy to those things that are most likely to drive growth and have the greatest impact on achieving the team's goals.

Icenhower Coaching and Consulting (ICC) is one of the largest real estate coaching companies in North America. We coach a large number of the highest-producing teams and brokerages. When new clients come to us, we often see that they are more focused on results than they are on activities.

We ask the leaders of these teams how many closings they've had year-to-date, and they'll know that number right off the top of their head. When we ask what their main problem is, they will say that they want more production, income, or profit. Every team leader or brokerage owner comes to us wanting to increase their results in some way. Then, we ask what activities they are doing on a daily and weekly basis to increase the likelihood

ACTIVITIES   DESIRED RESULTS

Deliberate ⎫

Purposeful ⎬ Success

Systematic ⎭

FIGURE 6.1 Deliberate, Purposeful, Systematic

of getting those results. This is when they give us a blank stare. Often, they have no idea what activities are being done on their team, and to what degree.

Most of the time, all the focus of the team leader is on the results and the desired outcome, and not on the activities that must be accomplished on a daily, weekly, and monthly basis in order to get those results. The same holds true for team members. It's true that most of the time, real estate agents have their eye on the prize but don't take into account the activities that must be accomplished with regularity in order to reach that prize.

You may think that the market or the industry is responsible for how much money you make. Give yourself and your team more credit! This may not be what you want to hear, but most of your business outcomes are within your own control. You control the results – regardless of the strength of the economy, or the strength of the real estate market. None of that matters. If you, as a real estate team leader or team member, focus on the activities, you can design your own outcome and get the results you want.

The vast majority of real estate agents allow the results to be delivered to them by default because they don't commit to activities and they just take what they get and what they are handed, and what the market "gives" them. This is troubling because with this mind-set, there is no control of the outcome, which leads to feeling stuck. This is a very common problem. It is one of the primary reasons team leaders come to us at ICC. We work hard to refocus team leaders on their activities by reminding them that they are an active participant in achieving the results they desire through the activities they do. You learn more about this important and vital component to growth throughout this chapter.

Are You Focused on the Right Things?

Real estate teams are under tremendous pressure to bring about growth and achieve the results they have forecast, often in tough and turbulent economic times. With the continued existence of their team on the line – not to mention the lives and livelihoods of other people, and indeed their own career and reputation – leaders can become so focused on results and outcomes that they fail to consider or identify the activities that drive growth to achieve the team's viral goal.

A failure to determine quantifiably impactful growth activities, and distinguish them from marginally impactful or insignificant activities, leads to ad hoc, arbitrary, and

Resource Production Ratio Planner

In the online resource appendix of this book, you will find our ICC Production Ratio Planner. This fillable form allows you to plan out the quantity of activities that must happen on a weekly and monthly basis to meet your production goals.

All resources can be downloaded from this book's online appendix at therealestatetrainer.com/ teambook.

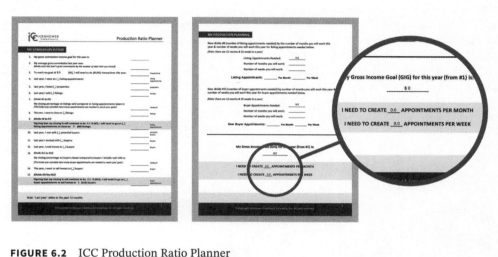

FIGURE 6.2 ICC Production Ratio Planner

reactionary decision-making, and the futile focus on the day to day. If team leaders fail to identify the important activities, how then can team members be expected to hit their own personal growth goals that contribute to the team's success?

From One Component to Another

Component 2 asks you to build upon lessons learned in component 1.

As you recall, component 1 of team growth transforms the personal motivations of team members into a unified and concrete "viral goal" that is then broken down into yearly, quarterly, monthly, weekly, and daily milestones with related activities that tie into the real estate team's overall growth goal. From, "When do we want to achieve our goal by?" to "What can we do *right now*, this very minute," breaking your goal into specific, time-bound goals and activities is what will cause a vision of growth to go viral at your real estate team.

While the overall growth goal is undeniably important, and every subgoal stems forward and backward from the overall team goal – and while it's absolutely crucial that you set your sights firmly on what you want to achieve – when you fix your focus on where you want to be in a year's time, you might forget about the actual process and activities that will get you there.

A football game, for instance, is measured by the final score and not by all the blocking, passing, and tackling prior to that moment. Those activities (blocks, passes, tackles) aren't on the scoreboard at the end of the game. No. The scoreboard shows the final score – the end result – and that's, arguably, all that matters to the fans or the team's financial investors.

However, the best coaches understand that it's the blocking, passing, and tackling – in other words, the component activities – that contribute to the final score in the first place. If you're only looking at the score, you're turning a blind eye to its cause. You're jumping over the things that affect a result and looking only at the result itself. When you focus on results rather than activities, you lose sight of the most critical things that occur along the way.

Building upon those principles, component 2 requires real estate teams to set end results and outcomes aside somewhat and *focus on activities first*, identifying and capitalizing on those activities that have the greatest impact and likelihood of helping you and your team members in achieving your goal.

Component 2: Focus on Activities First

FIGURE 6.3 Component 2

As with component 1 that breaks a large viral goal into smaller, periodic goals, with component 2 you will take a target end result and break it down into a series of activity-based targets to perform on a quarterly, monthly, weekly, and daily basis.

When your focus is fixed on results and outcomes, there may be times when your targets seem unachievable, but when your focus is centered on activities first you will develop a mind-set in which you see that there is always something *actionable* you can do to stay on track and achieve things you never thought possible.

Trust the Process

A word of emphasis before we move on: When we ask you to focus on activities first, we mean that you will not only focus on *performing* the most meaningful and impactful activities, but *identifying* and *quantifying* the most meaningful and impactful activities.

In short, a particular activity or course of action must be justified by facts, figures, or other supporting data that strongly *indicates* its effectiveness and value. The activities you focus on must be worthy of your time and efforts, so it is crucial that you invest time and energy assessing and considering individual activities before jumping in and doing them. Of course, there will be times when you will have to jump in and do something first to know if it works, but it's nonetheless essential that you can justify an activity's value with measurable and trackable supporting data. You can't just *do*. You have to do and *assess the effectiveness of what you do.*

The five components of growth apply to diverse and disparate real estate teams, which will experience unique factors and variables that will determine the precise course of action taken to achieve their goals.

We cannot provide a "one-size-fits-all" list of activities to implement in order to achieve your real estate team's goal. We cannot tell you which growth activities are extremely impactful, marginally impactful, or relatively insignificant at your team.

What we can do is to tell you that focusing on activities first *works*. And, we can provide you with examples of what we have seen work for other highly successful real estate teams.

It's very important that you do not assess whether something is comfortable or effective when you first start doing it. In order to become better at anything, we have to repeatedly practice it and do things that are initially uncomfortable, time and time again, until it ultimately becomes comfortable, natural, and effective. If we assess whether we like something up front when it's inevitably uncomfortable, we don't really know if we're going to like it once it eventually becomes ingrained and natural to us.

The ability and willingness to push through discomfort is what makes people great in their careers and in life. We just have to have the faith that we're doing something that has been *tested and proven* and will eventually reap incredible rewards.

Being positive isn't about denying reality or pretending that every technique you apply will generate instant and wild success on your real estate team. Sometimes it can take a while before we start seeing successful results from our daily practices and activities.

Activity-Based Indicators versus Results-Based Indicators

Many of our coaching clients come to us expecting some sort of insider secret or magic formula for their team and, often, a few of them seem perplexed by the very word "activity," as though it must mean something more complicated, elaborate, new, or different than it actually does.

Not to state the obvious, but an activity is simply a thing – any thing – that a person or group does or has done for or within their team. The particular things you personally do each month, week, and day will, of course, depend on the structure of your team, as well as your role within it. Regardless of those factors, within a real estate team, each of us performs a variety of activities on a regular or recurring basis.

Few of us, however, reflect upon, let alone research or record, the value or effectiveness of those activities. All of us perform activities and "do" a lot of "things," but only a handful of real estate teams track and analyze the tangible worth and material effectiveness of those things.

Few real estate teams invest their time and energy into tracking activity-based indicators (ABIs). At best they keep a close eye on results-based indicators (RBIs), though many are not evaluating anything at all.

Indicators signal or gauge the state or level of something. As its name suggests, results-based indicators provide an indication of results or outcomes.

RBIs are things like:

- Gross commission income
- Total sales volume
- Units closed
- Listings taken
- Contracts written

Essentially, RBIs are the final outcome or result following of a period of activity, and are what most real estate teams tend to track, but this is a point that bears repeating:

RBIs gauge the *final* state or level of something – the results – *following* a period of activity. Progress, as indicated by RBIs, can be incredibly motivating. Who doesn't get excited seeing progress, true progress, being made? However, when real estate teams track and follow RBIs exclusively, their focus and energy is centered on something that has already taken place, is situated in the past, and which they no longer have any control or power over. RBIs are set in stone. Good or bad, they simply are what they are.

Activity-based indicators (ABIs), on the other hand, are an indicator of the activities most connected to achieving a goal or desired result.

ABIs are things like:

- Contacts made
- Appointments set
- Database members added
- Open houses conducted
- Content written
- Social media posts made
- Social media messages sent
- Social media ads run
- Recruiting appointments set

Importantly, ABIs not only assess the activities that drive results, they also measure those activities that you have control over and can actively do something about.

As we've discussed, most real estate teams are inordinately focused on results and outcomes when their focus should be centered on activities first. Now, don't get us wrong, there is a time and place for tracking results, and we would rather that you track results than to not track anything at all. However, while an RBI tells you if you've achieved a goal, an ABI tells you if you're *likely* to achieve the goal. And while an RBI is outside your control or is almost impossible to take action on, an ABI is highly actionable and more clearly within your power or ability to influence or regulate.

Returning again to our football game, while a fan in the crowd might look at the scoreboard, see their team is behind, and feel utterly powerless, down by the field a good coach is focused on things within their control. While the frustrated fan is staring at the scoreboard and wondering why they don't just "play harder" (a vague and largely meaningless statement), the coach is focused intently on an offensive lineman whose repeated failure to block during the first two quarters has enabled the opposing team to consistently break through and sack the quarterback. Seeing this, the coach can focus on what is within their control and correct the failure of the lineman with something actionable that has a higher chance of changing the eventual outcome.

Focusing on activities first is a way to take responsibility and exert control or influence over a process or situation.

For example, pretend you're back in those good old student days. While you can't completely control the grade percentage you get on a test (an RBI), it's absolutely within your power and ability to create and commit to a fixed study schedule, practice on old exams, and put controls and systems in place to effectively manage distractions. The more you take action on each of these ABIs – that is, the more you focus your attention and daily practice on activities first – the more likely you are to achieve a great grade and influence the likelihood of success.

However – and this is a super important point – getting a great grade on a test isn't simply a matter of studying in advance and managing distractions. Everyone knows the importance of studying before an exam, but there's a big difference between someone who sits down at their desk and reads a book and someone who measures their grasp of the material in a quantifiable way. What do the practice test scores indicate? Can they recall the information two days later or has the next chapter caused them to forget the things they thought they'd learned? How are they quantifying that? How can they tell?

From the importance of studying before a test to the importance of diet and exercise in losing weight to the importance of brushing our teeth and flossing to avoid cavities and painful dental work, we all *know* what we need to do to achieve (or avoid) certain things in life. However, there's a huge difference between knowing and doing; and there's an even bigger difference between doing and *assessing* what you're doing, doing and *measuring* what you're doing, doing and *quantifying* what you're doing.

Over the next weeks and months (and for as long as you want your real estate team to continue growing), you will devote significant time and energy into activities that drive growth and perceptibly cause you to prosper and thrive. You will know that they drive growth because you will monitor, track, assess, and evaluate these activities, and the ABIs will provide quantifiable, visible proof.

Identifying Activities That "Move the Needle" on Growth

Needless to say, identifying the most effective growth activities that drive your team forward is no easy feat. However, we often find that a real estate team's ABIs – the best and most impactful activities – already exist and are already happening on some level, it's just that nobody has thought to identify, isolate, and track them yet. This is a key point. You should never assume an activity to be valuable or effectual and simply tell everyone to do it. You must justify your chosen ABIs with supporting data that can be tracked.

RBIs versus ABIs on a Real Estate Team

Here are several samples of RBIs and ABIs on a real estate team. There are many great RBIs and ABIs that are not on this list, but hopefully, this will get your brain thinking about which RBIs and ABIs to use for your own team.

Results-Based Indicator Examples

These are all indicators that you cannot change because they already happened.

- Gross commission income
- Total sales volume
- Units closed
- Listings taken
- Contracts written

Activity-Based Indicator Examples

- Contacts made – How many contacts are you making every day/week/month/quarter? (A contact is any conversation you have with another human being that is intentional, where you are at least reminding them that you are in real estate. These contacts are a part of your lead-generation activities, and could include contacts you are making with your sphere of influence (SOI), contacts in your database, expired listings, contacts made from working expired listings, through farming neighborhoods, circle prospecting, or working online leads.)
- Appointments set – How many appointments are you setting each week?
- Database members added – How many people are you growing your SOI by every single day/week/month/quarter?
- Open houses conducted – How many open houses are you holding each week/month/quarter?
- Content written – How often are you writing original content for your blog or social media platform posts?
- Social media posts made – How often are you posting to your social media channels?
- Social media messages sent – How many direct messages are you sending via your social media channels?
- Social media ads run – How many ads are you running across your social media channels?
- Recruiting appointments set/conducted. How much are you recruiting to your team? If you are the team leader or broker/owner, this is a vital ABI.

On a real estate team, ABIs and RBIs exist on a sliding scale. This can make determining whether an action is actually an ABI or an RBI relative to what your goal is. For example, if you are looking at the number of contacts an agent on your team is making that result in appointments set (the desired end result), the number of contacts is an ABI. However, if you are trying to get your agent to make more contacts, then the contact attempts become the ABI and the contacts made are the RBI (the desired end result). Here is a graphic to illustrate the existence of each activity on that sliding scale to help you see this progression more clearly.

ABIs

- **Contact attempted (i.e. call made but not picked up)**
- **Contact made (conversation engaged)**
- **Nurture the lead (stay in touch until you get an appointment set)**
- **Appointment had**
- **Contract signed (a buyer's agency agreement/listing agreement)**
- **Offer written or received**
- **Offer accepted**
- **Transaction closed**

RBIs

FIGURE 6.4　ABI RBI Sliding Scale

We are going to dig deeper into ABIs and RBIs later in this chapter. But for now, this should give you a good sense of the difference between an ABI and an RBI as we continue our discussion on how to prioritize activities.

Pareto's Principle

The Pareto Principle (also known as the "80/20" rule, or the law of "the vital few and the trivial many") states that, for many events, roughly 80% of the effects or results we see can be attributed to 20% of the causes.

In reality, the numbers may not always add up to an exact 80–20 ratio, but the central idea is that the majority of your results will come from a relatively small concentration of efforts. Focus your attention on the few vital elements in your real estate team that indicate the most impactful results. Avoid, at all costs, the common trap of trying to fix issues that may be very visible but improving them will have only a marginal or inconsequential effect.

At most real estate teams, the 80% that occupies our day-to-day lives and actions falls into one of the following areas:

- **The Safety 80.** Those day-to-day tasks and activities that keep you busy and visibly "productive" but are actually keeping you safely in your comfort zone and preventing you from pushing through discomfort and fear of change.

- **The Weighty 80.** Those day-to-day tasks and responsibilities that we imbue with a sense of importance and gravity. They have the appearance or feeling of "weightiness," but they are not as important as we think and are, in fact, only weighing us down and holding us back from success.

- **The Hasty 80.** Those day-to-day tasks and activities that have you running around putting out fires, acting with excessive speed and insufficient thought or consideration about the effectiveness of your actions.

No matter which area you are personally prone to (and it's probably a combination of all three), it's essential that you don't spend excessive amounts of time and energy on the 80% of tasks and activities that don't add much value. It's crucial that you tackle only the most key issues and prioritize the most effective activities.

Providing incredible customer service is important if you want to retain existing clients, but despite its importance, customer service is an 80% activity that only generates 20% of the results in regard to profitability and growth. Customer service has been falsely labeled as a core activity that leads to increased business or growth, when in fact it forms part of the trivial many. If it were a core activity, then customer service should have readily apparent ABIs that allow us to directly measure customer service and its impact on the growth of a real estate team. Yet no such ABIs exist.

Pareto's Principle

FIGURE 6.5   Pareto's Principle

While real estate teams can track things like positive online reviews or average response time to inquiries, these ABIs have a marginal impact on growth and are relatively inconsequential from a growth perspective, though they undoubtedly feel extremely important to both you and the client. This is a crucial point. We're not saying that customer service isn't important and that it cannot be measured in some way. We're saying that its actual impact on profitability and growth is negligible compared to other business-generation and growth-building activities for your real estate team.

ABIs are an indicator of the activities *most connected* to achieving a goal or desired result. Real estate team leaders must find a way to prioritize the more impactful activities for all team members.

It may not be easy, but focusing on the most effective ABIs means refusing to put your most essential tasks on the back burner out of a well-intentioned but misguided concern for pleasing and appeasing your clients. When you put these essential tasks on the back burner, you are focusing on the 80% instead of the 20%. Symbolically, it is the same thing as putting your personal goals and dreams on the back burner. Don't do it!

When thoughtfully and properly applied, Pareto's Principle will allow your team to allocate your precious time effectively, prioritize your activities, and ensure that your real estate team gets maximum returns on its time and energy investments. The challenge lies in identifying the 20% that matter and focusing on them to achieve the greatest value.

The remaining 80% of the causes should not be *completely* ignored. Oftentimes, an activity produces seemingly marginal or inconsequential results because it is not being performed properly or consistently. In other words, the issue sometimes lies in the execution of an activity rather than the activity itself. Performing a Pareto analysis can help real estate teams dial in on problems that impact the achievement of a goal as well as those activities that are most likely to lead to success.

A Pareto analysis is a great way to:

- Provide facts needed for setting priorities.
- Analyze data about the frequency of activities performed in a process.
- Analyze data about the frequency of problems that impact a process.
- Focus on the most significant causes/activities or problems in a process.
- Determine activities that represent the largest areas of opportunity.
- Help team members focus on a small number of really important activities.
- Identify the most critical issues that need to be tackled first.
- Examine the specific components of broad activities.
- Visually communicate your ABIs to others.
- Build consensus when disagreement arises about the best course of action.

Having said all of that, if the thought of spreadsheets and graphs and cumulative percentages is causing you to panic right now, then please don't worry! While Pareto charts are a great way to focus on the most impactful activities of your real estate team – and we promise you'll get the hang of them with just a little time and effort – there are other ways to determine which ABIs are most likely to help you reach your goals.

Activity-Based Indicators Are Not People

We need to remember to put people first. In other words, it is important to not focus solely on the numbers. We don't want team leaders to misinterpret this chapter and put all the focus on the activities and, as a result, lose sight of the people who make up the team, and their struggles to hit their numbers.

Many team leaders who are reading this book will need to be honest with themselves. They have known that they are supposed to create a referral database, contact a certain number of people in their database, and that certain activities need to happen on a regular, consistent basis. These team leaders may expect this of their team members, and yet, they haven't done it themselves. Many successful team leaders have built their businesses through existing relationships and their business has just come to them. They haven't put a whole lot of effort into developing and growing beyond that. This roadblock is a major reason why many team leaders come to us at ICC for help.

Of course, anyone reading this book would like to change that outcome, change those results, and put in the work to grow. And whether you are a team leader or team member, you need to get consistent with your activities to see the results.

Team leaders need to drop the expectation that all agents on the team will always hit their numbers. There's going to be struggle with it. It is very rare for any real estate team to have all their agents always hitting all of their ABIs on the dashboard every single week for any sustained period of time. In fact, if you did have that situation where everyone was always hitting their numbers, I'm not sure those agents would need the team, or the leader, anymore.

Team members must embrace accountability. The relationship between a leader and a team member is a two-way street. Of course, the leader needs the correct mind-set going into setting up ABIs and holding team members accountable to them. On the flip side of the coin, team members must be willing to put in the work. It's vital that team members be "coachable," and be open to being led. Agents on teams must respond positively to being held accountable to tracking their numbers, showing up at team meetings, making their contacts, and so on, since all of these tracked ABIs are put in place in their best interest.

Remember the three biggest things a team provides to its agents are leads, administrative support, and accountability and mentorship. If team members don't need the accountability and mentorship anymore, because the team leader has put so much focus on the importance of hitting numbers, then these team members will realize they don't need you anymore. ABIs are important to focus on, but a team leader must come at it with an encouraging mind-set.

 ## Case Study

Judy from Pittsburgh, Pennsylvania

Judy was a team leader who coached with us for more than four years. She's one of the top agents in her MLS. She was a high-producing agent who would do well over $25 million in sales volume as a solo agent. Then she decided that she was getting to a point in her career where she wanted to spend more time with her family. She wanted to work less. She wanted more time off. Ultimately, she wanted to step out of day-to-day activities and let her team run itself.

So, Judy took a step back in her production in order to move forward and decided to build a team. She let go of a lot of business. She let go of showing buyers properties and brought on other agents. Early on, as she met with her team, she found that the leads she provided to the team members were not being followed up. The team members were not contacting their own spheres of influence (SOIs), and, therefore, not growing their own SOI databases. Judy was moving backward instead of growing through building a team as she had hoped.

Judy was getting frustrated because she had no problem putting in the work as a solo agent. As a result, she began to focus too hard on ABIs in her team meetings. After a while, agents on the team started to fear these team meetings. Team meetings became negative for everyone involved.

For decades, Judy has been a Realtor known well throughout Pittsburgh, with a strong SOI. So, a lot of business came to Judy, and Judy had long ago established a very regimented discipline of contacting her SOI, following up, jumping on leads quickly – her good habits were in place. Judy expected her team members to do the same, but she didn't take into account that her team members did not have this experience. They didn't already have these habits. It was difficult for Judy to understand why her team members could not keep up, and why all of this business was slipping through the cracks. To Judy, the issue seemed to be a lack of effort on the part of the agents.

The culture on Judy's team started to become very negative. Nobody felt like they were doing a good job. Judy questioned whether she even wanted to have and grow a team. She questioned herself as a leader.

This challenge is almost a rite of passage for any real estate team leader. You must feel these emotions and go through this struggle and fight through it. Something that helped Judy work through this challenge was developing a leadership mind-set around ABIs. We worked on this together, and reframed her thinking so that she started to look at her leadership like parenting.

This is not easy. You can get so frustrated. Everyone knows what they are supposed to do, and they feel the urgency. But for some reason, they can't find success and balance. This feeling applies to all real estate agents. In fact, it applies to anyone in any profession. There are so many people who want something badly but just can't seem to achieve the growth they need to get there. For example, how many people want to diet but just can't seem to stick with it? We all know what we should do, but it's very hard to make ourselves do it.

As we mentioned earlier, if all real estate agents did hit all their ABIs every week, they wouldn't need a team. This is where that mind-set of a parent comes in. Parents don't "fire" their kids when they don't pick up their clothes or eat their vegetables. Parents stay with their children to positively encourage them enough times until they start doing what they need to do.

Real estate team leaders must keep giving team members those positive nudges, much like a parent would. Leaders must expect, going in, that team members are going to struggle with a lot of things. They are not going to always hit their numbers. Leaders should be surprised if they do hit their numbers! It's all about shifting the context of the dashboard (which we will dive into in Part Four of this book) and reframing the way we look at our team members. Our context must shift to that of a loving parent/child relationship.

All team members must take this to heart, too. This is not just advice for the team leader. As you know, with growth comes more opportunity for leadership positions on a real estate team. All team members should be trained to have this mind-set because it may apply to them as they grow with the team.

Always stay positive and always be encouraging. However, in the case where a team leader is dealing with an agent with poisonous behavior, it's a little different. If the team member is negative and doing something to harm the culture of the team, a team leader must address the issue and leave ABIs out of the conversation entirely.

Weekly growth huddles (which you will learn about in Part Five) are not a time to come down on team members about not hitting their ABIs. Leaders must pull team members aside for this conversation. As a rule of thumb, always "punish in private, praise in public." In your growth huddles, you must maintain positivity. If a team leader must get down into the real problems that may be the source of the issues for an agent's failure to hit their ABIs, that should be in private. Come from the perspective of trying to help. "Hey, what's going on? I see you're not hitting your numbers. I know how badly you need to hit your numbers because I know what your goals are. So what's going on? How can I help you?" The leader must use a more positive and encouraging approach to talk to the agent more like a parent, or even a coach.

Remember that real estate agents are like independent contractors. If a team leader pushes the team members too hard, they'll just walk across the street to a different brokerage or team. Sometimes the team member that was having issues hitting their ABIs on your team will find success somewhere else. Perhaps the leader of their new team has more patience. Just like a parent, team leaders must possess patience and understanding.

This is exactly what Judy did to save her team. Judy shifted her context, came to her weekly team meetings with an encouraging and positive mind-set, and got less stringent with her ABIs. Instead, she used the ABIs as more of a way to encourage her agents. She became patient with her agents. As a result, they have increased their production dramatically year over year.

An added bonus? Judy is happier. When she goes to look at the dashboard or she walks into her team huddle, it's fun to her. The relationships are better. The culture is positive. She is more patient with herself and more patient with her team members. She made the decision to change her context and reframe her view of the team's performance, and her new view is less focused on the ABIs and more focused on her people.

Up Next: Following a Proven Model

Now that we've talked about ABIs and RBIs, let's shift our focus to the transactional timeline. We also take a look at the Listing Inventory Pipeline, a model we have developed with our clients here at ICC.

CHAPTER 7

Build Your Inventory Pipeline with a Proven Model

From Albert Einstein to Steve Jobs, nobody has ever made a groundbreaking scientific discovery or built a business that would literally change the way the world works all by themselves. Human progress and innovation is shaped and supported by previous discoveries and the cumulative knowledge of those who have gone before us.

At Icenhower Coaching and Consulting (ICC), we strongly believe that modeling creates success. We have developed all our processes from working with the top teams from across North America, seeing what works, and sharing it with our clients.

In practice, the concept of modeling others' success has been around forever, but the technique has been codified and made more widespread through Charles Grinder and Richard Bandler's neuro-linguistic programming (NLP) strategies.

NLP modeling has been described as the process of re-creating excellence. By observing and mapping the successful processes that underlie an exceptional performance of some type, we can achieve a desired outcome by studying how someone else goes about it.

In other words: find someone who's insanely good at doing what they do and follow in their footsteps! In your case, that means choosing a real estate team, or team leader, whose success you'd like to replicate. Whose footsteps do you want to follow in? Whose team model would you like to emulate? Once you've identified a desirable model, you then "model the model" and pass on what you discover to your fellow team members in turn.

Model the Model

In our experience we find that if you want to know how to do something, the best thing to do is to find some people who are good at that thing and ask them what they do.

For every person who strictly guards their secrets to success, you will find 10 others who are more than willing to share their experience and knowledge with you. One great example of this positive, "share what you know" mentality is present in our Facebook group, the Real Estate Agent Round Table. Through creating a community based on collaboration and a desire for learning and continual growth, top team leaders and team members from across North America (including many of our clients) share their own tips and strategies.

Part of being a successful leader is recognizing and respecting the knowledge and experience of those who have gone before you as well as those who are presently out there doing great work. The same goes for successful team members. Real estate teams that want to grow should actively seek input, feedback, and guidance from people in and outside of your professional circles. Mentors, coaches, and fellow team leaders are great people to bounce ideas off. The more you speak to those on successful real estate teams or watch them closely, the better you'll be able to see the clues. And with enough clarity on the clues, you'll be able to reverse engineer a team's success.

Ideally, you should identify and reverse engineer, when possible, a real estate team's 80/20 (see Chapter 6 for more on conducting a Pareto analysis on your team). Don't haphazardly copy your organizational idols in every way. It's highly likely that there were a "vital few" things they gave disproportionate energy, and persistent focus to that made the majority of the difference. Do everything within your power to uncover these 80/20 clues. Don't waste time on another team's "trivial many" or mindlessly model the 80% that produced a mere 20% of their results.

The beauty of modeling someone else's successful 80/20 is that it creates a specific and explicit strategy to follow. Rather than vaguely imitating what another team "sorta kinda" does, it's far better to identify *actionable*, *measurable*, and *trackable* activity-based indicators (ABIs) that you can put into practice where you are. Once you've uncovered the clues to success, it's essential that they are clearly defined and mapped out so that your team members can follow in the footsteps, too.

Pass the Model on to Your Team

Remember that what makes a virus so successful and effective is its ability to replicate and multiply itself. Your real estate team's goals will be achieved by the efforts and activities of each team member. Every single person on your team will be a powerful and active participant in making your growth goals go viral, so it's crucial that the clues you discover in others can be passed on to, and replicated by, your team.

When modeling a real estate team's success, real estate team leaders must be able to describe their system in detail and clearly convey it to all team members. A vital criterion for modeling another leader or team is that the people on a real estate team can also "model the model" and produce comparable results.

What's more, a real estate team's model will not always map neatly or directly onto your particular situation or set-up. Depending on the size and structure of your own team, or the different departments or divisions of people within it, when modeling a team's success you must translate broad clues into specific and measurable activities that relate to everyone on your team.

Whether your chosen ABIs are already happening at your real estate team or whether you're emulating the activities and strategies of others, success depends on collaboration and equal participation. Everyone on your team must be committed to performing specific growth activities. If everyone performs *their* activities and achieves *their* results, the entire real estate team should reach its overall growth goals, so it's essential that any chosen model contain ABIs for everyone on your real estate team.

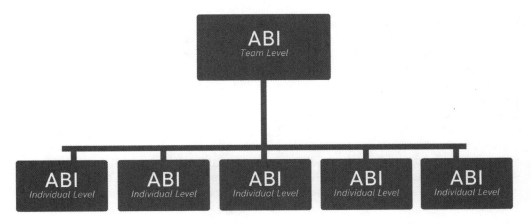

FIGURE 7.1   ABI Chart

Back to Basics

By now, you should have a clear idea about the importance of focusing on activities first, and how to begin identifying specific and measurable ABIs that will demonstrably move the needle on growth. But let's go back to basics for a moment.

Say you don't have anyone to talk to or emulate. Imagine you're the first real estate team in the world. Without anyone to look to, without any strategies to model, principles to follow, or proven activities to replicate, what would your first step be? What is the one thing your fledgling team would need in order to grow?

Sometimes, we overcomplicate what's actually a pretty simple issue. What each team member has in common is the *dependence on the other team members to achieve their own personal growth goals*.

Make the Connection

We've spoken at length about the importance all team members will play in spreading a viral growth goal and realizing your real estate team's success. At the same time, it's the people out there in the public who will play a different but very real part in achieving the growth goal, too – by becoming your client.

When you break it down and take things back to basics, *making contact and engaging other people is the primary activity that underlies any strategy or model*. On some level, making contact and engaging other people will tie into every single ABI that you implement at your real estate team.

Once you've clarified your growth goal and created super-specific, time-bound targets, the next thing you need to do is identify the people out there in the public who will cause you to meet those targets. *Who are your clients?*

You can, of course, use spreadsheets and complex analytics to answer this question, but you can equally go back to basics and apply some good old-fashioned brainstorming. Analyze past interactions. Evaluate the characteristics of your current clients.

Then, having answered this question and identified who your clients are, the next step is to determine how, exactly, you are going to make contact with these people and enter in a conversation with them. What is your sphere of influence (SOI) contact plan? How will you use various methods of communication (phone, email, website, Zoom, social media, in-person appointments, word of mouth, client events) to make contact with them?

Once you've identified your targets and the industry standards for making contact, you are then ready to create measurable and trackable ABIs that will play a critical part in the successful completion of what we will call your transaction timeline. Before we identify specific ABIs in the timeline, let's take a look at the overall timeline itself.

The Transaction Timeline

Remember: deliberate, purposeful, systematic activities produce successful and desired results. You must have a plan. In essence, the transaction timeline is a systematic, repeatable series of steps and actions that map out and track communication and interaction with your clients, from their first point of engagement or contact with your real estate team through to the completion of the transaction.

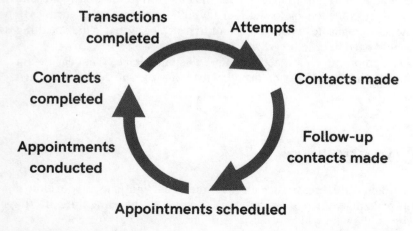

FIGURE 7.2 Transaction Cycle

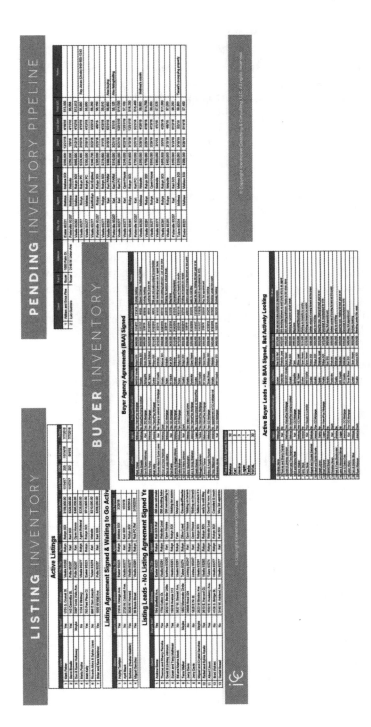

FIGURE 7.3 Inventory Pipelines

Resource   **Inventory Pipelines**

In the online resource appendix of this book, you will find our Inventory Pipelines Excel spreadsheet. This tool helps track your inventory, which in turn will help you stay on top of your current business while pipelining more for future months. There are three tabs within this spreadsheet, labeled Listing Inventory, Buyer Inventory, and Pending Inventory.

All resources can be downloaded from this book's online appendix at therealestatetrainer.com/ teambook.

To set the transaction in motion, drive it forward, and ultimately complete a transaction, real estate team members will need to follow a specific contact plan. As you can see in the cycle, the second-to-last stage in the transactional timeline is "Contracts Completed."

At first glance, the contractual/transactional process on your real estate team may seem like a linear timeline – if you consider your client to be a one-time transaction. There is a checklist of contract-to-close tasks for each client, that is true. However, if you view the real estate transaction as a systematic and continuous circle, you will maintain contact with your client after you close, making you their Realtor for life. It's one thing for a client to buy *one* home through you, but it's another thing for them to come back in five years for your help again. As real estate teams thrive on referral business, we use the circular model to illustrate this concept.

One model that we follow here at ICC is the Inventory Pipeline model. You don't have to re-create the pipeline – we have it for you. We have hundreds of clients across the country that use this to help organize and focus their efforts, and so forth.

Up Next: Implementing ABIs and RBIs on Your Transactional Timeline

Now that you can relate the transactional timeline to your particular real estate team, in the next chapter we take another look at the timeline and try to identify the ABIs and results-based indicators (RBIs) in the cycle.

CHAPTER 8

Your Pipeline – One Step at a Time

Component 2 requires real estate teams to *set end results and outcomes aside* somewhat and *focus on activities first*, identifying and capitalizing on those activities that have the greatest impact and likelihood of helping you and your team members in achieving your goal.

Real estate teams that focus less on results and more on the activities that produce those results are more likely to achieve their goals. Focusing on activities first enables teams to apply their time and energy to those things that are most likely to drive growth and have the greatest impact on hitting your goals.

With this in mind, take another look at the transaction timeline and see if you can distinguish the activity-based indicators (ABIs) from the results-based indicators (RBIs).

Most real estate teams focus on the middle to the end of the cycle, tracking the number of appointments scheduled, or the number of contracts and transactions completed. Chances are this is what your eye is drawn to when you look at the timeline, too, but if you've begun to appreciate the difference between ABIs and RBIs, you'll have correctly identified that "Appointments Scheduled," "Appointments Conducted," "Contracts Completed," and "Transactions Completed" are all RBIs:

- They gauge the final results following a period of activity.
- They measure something that has already taken place and that they no longer have any control or power over.
- They are set in stone – good or bad, they simply are what they are.

As you'll recall, while an RBI is outside your control or is almost impossible to take action on, ABIs are the activities that drive results and that you can actively do something about.

In the transactional timeline, therefore, the activities that you should focus your time, efforts, and attention on are primarily those at the beginning of the process. The trackable ABIs that you and your real estate team members should focus on are:

- **Attempted Contacts**, in which you attempt to call or reach out, but no contact is made – meaning you must attempt to contact them again.

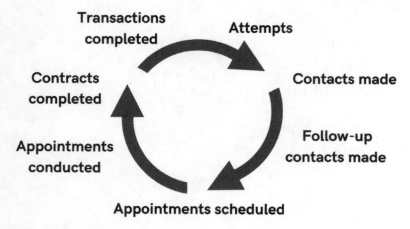

FIGURE 8.1 Transaction Cycle

- **Contacts Made**, in which you make contact and do engage an individual in an actual conversation.
- **Follow-Up Contacts Made**, in which you do something to follow up with an individual to remind them of who you are, deepen rapport, and/or nurture the relationship.

An ABI is anything that is measurable, highly actionable, and exerts an influence on the final outcome. To be clear, however: while "Attempts," "Contacts Made," and "Follow-Up Contacts Made" are the *foremost* ABIs in a typical transaction timeline, they are not the only ones, and you'll find that not all ABIs are readily apparent.

Not All ABIs Are Readily Apparent

The transaction timeline is comprised of seven broad steps, but within each of these broad steps additional actions and activities must be performed in order to move your target audience forward to the next step. Not all ABIs are readily apparent within this seven-step timeline. Oftentimes, you will have to pay attention to the spaces between one step and another in the sequence and identify ABIs that will drive results between one step and the next.

For instance, in the time period between the RBIs "Appointments Scheduled" and "Appointments Conducted," at least one other ABI will typically take place.

The data might confirm, for example, that there is a significant correlation between reconfirming an appointment and the number of appointment no-shows, in which case a measurable and trackable ABI would be "Appointments Confirmed" where you do something actionable and within your control, such as calling or emailing to verify that the target is committed to the time and place you previously scheduled.

This is important: the actual activity you would perform is picking up the phone or sending an email to confirm the appointment, but the ABI that you would measure and

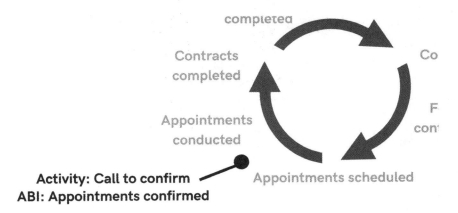

Activity: Call to confirm
ABI: Appointments confirmed

FIGURE 8.2   Appointments Confirmed

track would be the number of appointments actually confirmed. Sometimes you will have to perform a particular activity several times before you can record it as a successfully completed ABI. Below, you will see an example of one of the resources that we will talk in greater detail about in Chapter 11. The Daily Contact Form provides an example of this kind of repeated activity, and a great way to track it.

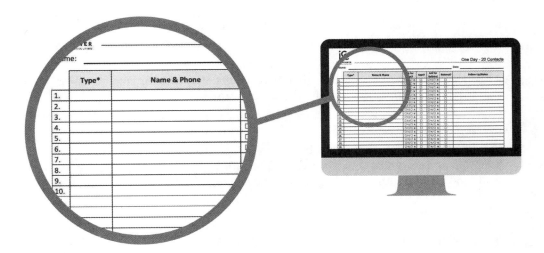

FIGURE 8.3   Daily Contact Form

Not All ABIs Are Necessarily Interactive

While this section of the chapter has placed particular emphasis on communicating and engaging with your target audience, not all ABIs are necessarily interactive. Generally, data tends to show a significant increase in the time and methods spent preparing for an appointment and the successful outcome of an appointment (i.e. contract or transaction completed), so "Appointment Preparation" would be an actionable, measurable, and trackable ABI even though it doesn't involve communicating with the target.

Having said that, diligent preparation hones your communication skills and increases your ability to effectively deliver your message, so the ABI does relate to communication and engagement. As we said before, on some level – either directly or indirectly – engaging other people is the primary activity that underlies every real estate team's strategy or model and will tie into every single ABI that you implement at your real estate team.

When ABIs Are RBIs

Not all ABIs are purely ABIs, and not all RBIs are purely RBIs. Some parts of the process can function as both RBIs and ABIs. For example, "Transactions Closed" is an RBI in that it measures the final outcome following a period of activity. However, Transactions Closed is also an ABI in that "closing" is an activity that involves effort and performing specific strategies or activities that have proven effective in getting your client to close.

Along those same lines, Transactions Closed is the sum of every single activity that precedes that final moment. In a transactional cycle, one event connects to another then another, with each activity and mini-result leading to the overall desired outcome.

To summarize all of this:

- Deliberate, purposeful, systematic activities produce successful and desired results.
- ABIs are an indicator of the activities most connected to achieving a goal or desired result.
- ABIs not only assess the activities that drive results, they also measure those activities that you have control over and can actively do something about.
- Focusing on activities first is a way to take responsibility and exert control or influence over a process or situation.
- The more you take action on each of these ABIs – that is, the more you focus your attention and daily practice on activities first – the more likely you are to achieve your goals and influence the likelihood of success.

From Prognosis to Diagnosis

We've already talked about the miserable effects that someone experiences when they've caught the flu – a sore and scratchy throat, feeling feverish and chilly at the same time. The telltale signs are a clear indication that something is up, and it's usually at this point that a doctor will confirm your suspicions and make an actual diagnosis. And, while they can prescribe something to ease the symptoms and make you feel a bit better, you may still be left wondering how this happened in the first place.

For *results-focused* teams, determining why you didn't hit your targets and achieve your goals looks an awful lot like this. While there may be things you can do to recover and mend the situation, you may be left wondering how this happened in the first place and what went wrong along the way. All too often, real estate teams look for a culprit to blame for a failure that has already taken place. They point the finger in the wrong direction, finding fault with team members rather than the results-focused process. They mentally revisit the past over and over, thinking, "If only this . . ." or "If only that . . ."

We cannot go *back* in time to change results that have already taken place.

FIGURE 8.4 We Cannot Go Back in Time

While it's important to reflect upon our failures and learn from our mistakes, we cannot go back in time to change results that have already taken place. It's far better to diagnose potential problems along the way and identify difficulties activity by activity, rather than at the end of the process when the outcome cannot be altered or reversed. In the absence of component 2 (focus on activities first), those on a real estate team can blame, justify, and make excuses when problems arise and goals aren't achieved. They're able to slide out of responsibility because of how difficult it is to get to the truth of why failures occur.

Component 2 puts an end to all of that. Focusing on measurable and trackable activities produces accurate, objective data, and eliminates interpersonal blame and excuses. If a desired result isn't achieved, neither you nor the people on your team can shrug their shoulders and say "I dunno," or pass the blame to somebody else. Avoiding responsibility may have worked before, but it won't work now.

When you focus on the activities, success is the sum of every single thing that you and your team members do. Each step in the sequence connects to the next, with each activity and subsequent result leading to the overall desired outcome. When every activity is measured, tracked, and connected there is no longer any wiggle room between the end result and what precedes it. In the place of wiggle room, everything is now tied together in a taut, deliberate, systematic, activity-based sequence.

Activity-focused real estate teams are more likely to achieve their goals and less likely to be caught off guard by signs that tell you something serious is up. Focusing on activities enables real estate teams to predict or forecast the likely impact of a specific course of action, and acts as a form of *prognosis*. At the same time, focusing on activities can act as a form of *diagnosis*, enabling teams to detect potential problems and to track where breakdowns or other issues arise in the process.

As previously discussed, in addition to identifying activities that are most likely to lead to success, performing a Pareto analysis can help real estate teams dial in on problems that impact the achievement of a goal, but intricate spreadsheets are often unnecessary.

Many times, retracing your steps and walking back through the component ABIs in the transactional timeline will help you to diagnose what happened (or failed to happen) along the way, and pinpoint where you went wrong. An activity-focused team can remedy a situation by tracing each activity leading up to the result.

For example, let's say for simplicity's sake that your real estate team is comprised of a small sales team of four buyer's agents. One of your buyer's agent's subgoals is to schedule 10 buyer consultation appointments per month. At the end of the month, they have only managed to schedule three appointments.

In a *results-focused* real estate team that has not identified its most impactful ABIs and that does not track specific activities around each step in the sequence, it is almost impossible to accurately identify the reason for the poor result.

In an *activity-focused* real estate team, on the other hand, the team leader or lead buyer's agent could backtrack through the sequence to uncover the source of the problem. They may find, for instance, that while the buyer's agent hit all of their Contacts Made targets, they didn't follow up with any of them between initial contact and calling them again to try to set an appointment. In this straightforward case, the salesperson would clearly need to focus on performing follow-up activities that nurture the relationship and build rapport.

Oftentimes, when a problem occurs it's just a matter of isolating the one activity that precipitated the problem. However, diagnosing issues and implementing solutions is not always so straightforward. For example, the team leader may find that the same salesperson did indeed hit all of their ABI numbers and technically performed all of the activities they were supposed to. Based on previous data, and compared with other people on the sales team, the ABIs on the dashboard should result in more buyer consultation appointments scheduled. However, as we previously mentioned, oftentimes an activity produces seemingly marginal or inconsequential results not because it is a bad activity, but because it is not being performed properly or consistently.

Sometimes, the problem lies in the execution of an activity rather than the activity itself. In this not-so-straightforward case, the leader and the buyer's agent would need to improve their communication skills and practice their initial-contact sales scripts. If "Script Practiced" is already an ABI then that ABI may need to be broken down into further practice-related activities/ABIs that pinpoint the exact nature of the problem.

Whatever the ultimate problem is, tracking your activities and the results you get from those activities will prevent you from becoming complacent and presumptuous about your growth-building techniques and strategies. Tracking and monitoring helps you to identify weaknesses and possible pitfalls in your process and can set you on the path to recovery before the diagnosis becomes fatal.

Up Next: How to Measure Success

Now that we've discussed the pipeline activities that are a part of your transactional timeline, it's time to turn now to the actual metrics that will help you define success and failure.

CHAPTER 9

Plotting Progress – Where Metrics Meet Milestones

As we near the end of Part Two, we would like to emphasize the motivational force of focusing on activities. While it's true that the path to team growth isn't all sunshine and rainbows, it's equally true that the path to success isn't all dark skies and storm clouds. The beauty of being activity-focused is that your attention and awareness encompasses every aspect of your real estate team, good and bad. As well as pinpointing problems and potential inhibitors to growth, focusing on the activities allows you to pay attention to the positive changes that you're making and the steadily increasing progress of your endeavors.

Finding Motivation in the Ratio of Failure to Success

Focusing on activities helps real estate teams to set realistic expectations. When you're intimately familiar with the activities required to produce a certain result – that is, when the data tells you that doing X (specific activity) causes Y (specific result) – it eliminates stressful guesswork, impulsive and chaotic decision making, and allows you to do your work in a composed, intentional fashion.

When you focus on the activities and track quantifiable activity-based indicators (ABIs), you won't have to wonder how many calls it takes to get a single listing appointment, for example. You'll know what to expect in terms of the number of people an expired listings prospector can expect to make contact within one day. Let's say, for every 100 phone calls that a prospector makes to expired listings, they can expect that 25 people will take the call. That's 25 contacts per day. And let's say of those 25 contacts, you know the prospector will set one listing appointment. Further, let's assume you know it usually takes three listing appointments to get two listing agreements signed. Because you are knowledgeable about this data, you can set realistic expectations.

Please understand that this type of breakdown will work with any lead-generation method. Making phone calls to expired listings is just one example of many. Whether it's making contacts to people in your geographic farm, writing handwritten notes to members of your sphere of influence (SOI), or engaging with social media posts made by your friends on Facebook, you can break it down into lead-generation tasks and expected results.

So, if you set the expectation that an expired prospector is making 100 phone calls in a day, you can also expect that they will set one listing appointment per day. Naturally, some prospectors may be able to hit two or more listing appointments made in a shift. This would likely be due to either luck or a team member's own prospecting prowess. The average expired prospector, though, should be more than able to get their one listing appointment each and every shift.

One listing appointment is the expectation. It's what should happen. But will it?

Yes, most likely. One reason, of course, is that this is a realistic expectation, supported by data from specific ABIs you've tracked. Beyond that, your callers are also likely to hit the expectation because they're *motivated*. Their motivation comes from the knowledge that 100 calls are needed before one sale or donation can be gained. With 100 calls as the target, the callers on your team will be motivated to keep calling. They'll fight on for that single *yes*, despite the other *nos* and rejections. Those on the other end may say all manner of dismissive, disheartening things, yet the prospector will persist, driven by their awareness of what it typically takes to get a listing appointment.

When your focus is fixed on results and outcomes, there may be times when your targets seem unachievable, but when your focus is centered on activities first you will develop a motivated mind-set in which you see that there is always something *actionable* you can do to stay on track and achieve things you never thought possible.

There is always something *actionable* you can do to stay on track.

FIGURE 9.1 Always Something Actionable

In time, you will identify your most impactful and effective activities. As long as you track your efforts with measurable ABIs, reliable conversion ratios will emerge and harden into consistent, predictable stats. Eventually, you will reach a state of team nirvana where the data you've obtained acts as a "gas pedal" in driving growth. When you know for a fact that X (activity) produces Y (result), consistently and reliably, you can simply step on the gas pedal and increase that activity, whatever it may be, to accelerate results and drive your real estate team forward, faster.

Finding Motivation in the Day-to-Day Activities

For most of Part Two, we have asked you to turn your attention away from results and outcomes and to focus, instead, on systematically identifying and steadily practicing the "vital few" activities that will generate those results.

For team leaders and team members alike, we expect component 2 to be a significant shift in emphasis for you. Most probably, your day-to-day focus is currently – and chaotically – split between the "trivial many" (the 80% activities that don't contribute much to growth) and the big year-end targets you've been tasked with achieving. Your focus is centered on distant results. Your sights are fixed on long-term plans and goals in the future. A focus on individual activities might seem to be shortsighted and somewhat misguided. It's almost as though we're advising you and your people to think small, take each moment at a time, and not have a larger, long-term vision.

Remember, however, that the principle of focusing on activities first is but one of five important components to team growth, and it is the synthesis and combined application of the five components that creates and causes success. While Part Two has zoomed in and narrowed its focus to the level of individual activities and endeavors, your overall growth goals and ultimate vision is still in place. Focusing on day-to-day activities is not separate from your long-term vision. Focusing on day-to-day activities will bring your ultimate goals to fruition and prevent you from becoming overwhelmed by the big picture.

Understand that what we have been describing in Part Two is a *process*. It will take time to identify your most impactful activities, to determine the 20% that produces the majority of your results, and for accurate conversion ratios to emerge out of your concentrated efforts. However, once you have even a hint of consistent and predictable outcomes, you can apply that data to your overall goal and use those ratios to guide your long-term plans.

Metrics Meet Milestones

Let's use recruiting as an example. For leaders and team members in certain leadership positions on a real estate team, a large part of your focus is on recruiting agents into the team or brokerage.

Though it was uncomfortable at first, you trusted the process and shifted your focus from results and outcomes to performing and tracking the activities that drive those outcomes. After some research, experimentation, and feedback from industry peers, you have determined that the most successful recruiters are those who make outbound contacts. You found that your first move is to call or text real estate agents to set in-person appointments or video conference meetings. The key is to get face to face – an in-person meeting is most desirable, but video conferencing is better than a phone call.

Over time, the ABI data is showing that for every 10 phone calls you make to real estate agents, three will likely pick up. So, you can approximate that you will speak with 30% of the agents you call. The data also tells you that for every four agents that you actually speak with, only one will likely agree to an in-person or virtual meeting.

From this data, you can make this calculation. If you make 100 recruiting phone calls, you will probably speak with 30 real estate agents. Of the 30 real estate agents you speak with, only 25% (let's say eight, for the sake of this example) are likely going to agree to making an appointment to meet with you in person or virtually.

PHONE CALLS   CONNECTIONS   APPOINTMENTS SET

FIGURE 9.2   Recruiting Example

Additionally, the ABI data shows that of those eight agents that you have an in-person appointment with, we can calculate, based on the agents' experiences, approximately how many of those will probably accept your offer to join the team. Depending on the experience level of the agents you are meeting with in person, your conversion rate will be higher or lower.

If you are meeting with a newer agent who has less experience under their belt, your conversion rate will be fairly high. You can expect that for every two in-person appointments you have with a "newbie" agent, you will likely add one of them to your team.

If you are meeting with a lower-producing agent who has had their license for several years and has been working with another team, your conversion ratio will be a little lower. For every five low-producing agents you set recruiting appointments with, you will likely add one of them to your team.

Now, if you are having your in-person appointment with a high-producing agent, you will experience the lowest conversion rate. Depending on how attractive your team or brokerage is to high-producing agents, your conversion rate will go up or down. Anywhere from 10:1 to 30:1 would be normal. So, for every 10–30 high-producing agents you have a recruiting appointment with, you can probably expect at least one hire.

For the sake of this particular example, let's say that you are focused on recruiting high-producing agents to your team. Your team currently contains several high-producing agents, and you have set yourself up with a great training program. You're coaching with ICC and you have a lot to offer a high-producing agent in terms of team culture and support. For that reason, your conversion rate reflects that for every 10 high-producing agents you meet with in person, you will likely hire one of them.

As the team leader or team member in a leadership position on the team, you know that recruiting is essential to organizational growth. Looking at last year's performance, you're eager to soar even higher this year. Instead of bringing on six more real estate agents to your team, you envision doubling that number and recruiting 12 in the year ahead. That's your ultimate, long-term growth goal.

However, applying what you've learned from component 1, you understand that time creates a *When* to balance against the *What* of your viral goal. Every goal needs a target date so that you have a concrete deadline to focus on, and something to work toward on a quarterly, monthly, weekly, and daily basis. Time gives you a means for plotting your progress and determining if you are ahead, behind, or on the predicted track to achieving your goals.

Knowing this, it's clear that to hire those 12 new team members, you'll need to break things down into smaller, time-bound steps. After dividing your overall annual goal into quarterly goals, you further divide it into more manageable monthly goals. During each of these 12 months, you determine that you'll need to recruit one real estate agent to your team.

As you work to recruit new team members, you'll need to make approximately 10 appointments per month. With four weeks in a typical month, you'll need to have two or three appointments per week in order to get those 10 total per month.

Do some simple math here and you'll realize how many contacts are likely needed to get 10 recruiting appointments per month. The requisite number of contacts is 125. Break that out on a per week basis and it's approximately 31–32 contacts per week (from 125 divided by four weeks in a month). Break that out on a daily basis and it's six to seven contacts per day in a standard Monday to Friday working week.

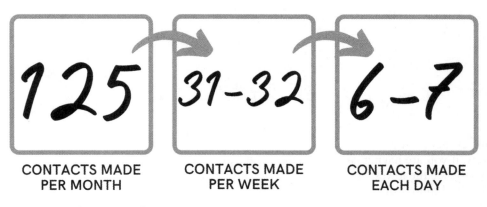

CONTACTS MADE PER MONTH   **CONTACTS MADE PER WEEK**   **CONTACTS MADE EACH DAY**

FIGURE 9.3 Contacts Broken Down

If these numbers are understandably making your head spin, don't worry. The key takeaway here is that you can take the various data, metrics, and ratios you uncover from tracking measurable ABIs and apply them to your long-term goals. Long-term plans can coexist with ABIs, provided that any detailed long-term plan is broken down into short-term steps with metrics (ABIs) applied at every step of the way

One thing to keep in mind is that whether you are selling houses or making recruiting appointments, the ABIs can be categorized the same: calls, contacts, appointments, and contracts.

Once again, you can see how we've broken down a long-range plan into bite-sized chunks. It makes no difference how many people are on your real estate team or how large the plan is. Breaking plans down into more manageable pieces applies at both an individual level and at the group level, too.

In all such instances, the key to successfully crunching plans into those bite-sized chunks is to focus on the daily and weekly activities. You can let the end result inspire you, but then you need to keep going and identify the activities, along with the ABIs involved in achieving your target outcome. These activities and ABIs will be connected to one another in perfect alignment. Together, they'll form a seamless, logical sequence that takes you step-by-step, one activity after another, toward your ultimate final goal.

Up Next: Who Does What?

Coming up next, we're going to discuss the job descriptions for each member of a real estate team. This includes the tasks each member should be delegating to other team members. We examine the duties of the team leader, the team's sales agents, and the administrative staff members on the team.

CHAPTER 10

Which Activities Should Agents Delegate to Administrative Staff to Improve Sales?

But First, Let's Recap!

We have covered a lot of ground in Part Two. We talked about the activities that team members should be doing to grow their pipeline. We touched on various tracking tools and resources that provide a great jumping-off point so that you can start to see your pipeline grow.

In this chapter, we break it down a little further and talk about what each person on a real estate team should be doing, and what tasks they should be delegating to other team members. In order to do this, we need to examine the duties of the team leader, the team's sales agents, and the administrative staff members on the team.

We also look at how the workflow between administrative staff and sales team members is handled with clients from listing-to-contract and from contact-to-close. When it comes to servicing clients, both administrative staff and sales agents have their part to play. For a real estate team to run efficiently while also providing a high level of customer service, a frequent amount of delegation must occur while servicing clients in transactions. Let's dive in and talk about the duties of every member of your team, and how each member can play their part in your client's experience.

Duties of the Team Leader

The duties of a real estate team leader are fairly straightforward. Lead generation, taking listings, negotiating contracts, and recruiting are the four primary jobs of a good team leader. Let's break each of them down.

Lead Generation

First and foremost, a real estate team leader's job is to get more leads. The leader must do the activities to generate more leads, whether that's spending more money on marketing or strategizing over which lead-generation methods work best for their team. It is the team leader's responsibility to ensure that there are enough leads for the team (ultimately, clients) so that everyone can continue to grow and earn income. Just to be clear, sales agents on real estate teams must also perform activities to generate leads themselves. However, the team leader should provide agents with additional leads to help supplement everyone's individual sales production.

Take Listings

In most cases, the team leader of a real estate team takes listings and goes on listing appointments. Not only do they generate the listings through performing their lead-generation duties, they also go on the listing appointments and get listing agreements signed by sellers.

Generally speaking, team leaders should not service buyers. Working with a buyer is four times more time-consuming than working with a seller. With a home seller, you are going to the house once or twice to meet with the seller and list the property for sale. To work with a home buyer, you are showing multiple homes and potentially writing multiple offers until you get one offer accepted. Of course, that may fall out of contract so you may need to write more than one offer on more than one home for your buyer. Because working with a buyer is more time-consuming, it is very important that the team leader not focus their energy here, because the team leader has so many other responsibilities.

It is important that the team leader is confident in letting go of the majority, if not all, of their buyer side business to the other agents on the team. This way, the leader can primarily focus on listings (seller side transactions) and managing the team.

There are real estate teams that we have worked with here at Icenhower Coaching and Consulting (ICC) who become very successful, very large, and highly profitable, where the team leader stops taking listings themselves altogether. The team leader pulls themselves out of production completely on the team and allows other agents on the team to take the listings. Of course, in order to do this, there needs to be enough production generated by the team's agents to create a large enough profit margin so that the team leader is able to step out of the role of taking listings. Know that this case is not very common, however, and for the most part, team leaders still take listings.

TEAM LEADER DUTIES

① **Lead generation**

② **Take listings**

③ **Negotiate contracts**

④ **Recruiting**

FIGURE 10.1   Team Leader Duties

Negotiate Contracts

The third duty of a team leader is to negotiate contracts. The team leader should step in and negotiate offers on their listings to acceptance. As you know, in a contract, we have to have an offer and an acceptance made to have a valid contract. When offers come in on the team leader's listings, the team leader will step in and get involved with the assistance of administrative staff members.

We are going to cover this more when we talk about the duties of administrative staff members later in this chapter. However, with regard to prelisting to listing, listing to contract, and contract to close, the entire client workflow process (from preparing for that first listing appointment in the prelisting, the listing appointment itself, all the way to when we get offers at contract, and offer acceptance and we go from contract all the way to closing) must be managed by administrative staff members.

Successful teams ensure that their agents are involved in this process on a very limited basis. Sales agents must be out selling property! A team wants the experts, the seasoned professionals, the transaction coordinators, and listing managers, to be servicing the clients.

This is why the team leader's job is to go on the listing appointment, and then negotiate the offers that come in to acceptance. Now, in some instances, negotiating contracts can also include negotiating inspection repairs. After the inspections are done, typically there is a lot of negotiation back and forth on who has to pay for what, what work must be done, and that's kind of like the second round of negotiating in a contract. Negotiating inspection repairs is something that the team leader might also do. With some of the highly successful real estate teams that we coach, we see the team's highly skilled and experienced transaction coordinators negotiating inspection repairs themselves. When a team can get to this level, it frees up a lot of time for the team leader.

Recruiting

The fourth and final duty of a team leader is recruiting. The team leader is in charge of growing the team. Team leaders must become proficient at recruiting. This is typically what separates the highly successful teams from the rest. Team leaders should not take their eyes off talent acquisition – ever. Their radar is always on for recruiting, and they should always be looking for new recruits.

Quick Tip   Let It Go!

It is normal for team leaders to feel nervous about letting go of many of their transactional duties. The top agents and top team leaders all have made it over this speed bump on the pathway to success.

Everyone wants to make sure their clients are taken care of and that everything is done correctly. The idea of letting go of many of the responsibilities and duties involved in servicing a transaction to another person on your team (who may or may not have a personal relationship with the client) can be really tough.

This same issue exists in just about every other industry in the world. For example, when you go to the dentist's office, oftentimes you will see several people who help you throughout your visit. Dentists have hygienists, X-ray lab technicians, front desk receptionists, insurance specialists, and so on. Often, you won't even see the dentist – even though you are his/her client! You are being serviced by multiple people who are all experts and specialists in doing exactly what they do so the dentist can be focused on the more high-level (and high-paying) procedures. Because of this structure, the dentist will have a better work/life balance.

The key takeaway is for sales agents to let go of administrative work.

The same is true with many other professions. Letting go of these tasks will allow sales team members to focus on the sales side of the real estate business. The Pareto Principle comes into play here. The sales side of the business is where your team's 20% exists. The 80% is the client servicing. If you as a team leader or sales agent want to earn more income, you must let go and delegate to administrative staff members. All prelisting, listing-to-contract, contract-to-close work must be delegated. And, once the tasks are delegated accordingly, it is crucial that administrative staff members and sales agents stay in their lanes!

A good team leader is growth-oriented and is not focused on being a problem solver for the team. Team leaders that concern themselves with always putting out fires for their team members will find that they can get nothing else done. Instead, a team leader that is focused on growth and recruiting ignores the vast majority of problems that exist on their team and they adopt a mind-set where they "go forward sloppy" by continually generating more business and recruiting top talent.

Team leaders often complain that the real estate agents on their teams don't work. "They won't lead generate." "They won't make their daily phone calls." "They won't make the contacts required each week." "They won't grow their sphere of influence (SOI) database." "They won't do the hard work."

The National Association of Realtors has repeatedly reported that one in three real estate agents quit after their first year in the business. In addition, 87% of all agents quit after their fifth year. The reason these agents are quitting is often the same. It's because they don't have enough income. However, when you ask these agents what activities they did to generate more business in the last week/month/year, they'll tell you they have done very little. These agents typically are not willing to put forth the effort to do the essential activities.

Of course, joining a real estate team greatly improves the likelihood of success as a real estate agent because of the team's support. The team provides leads, administrative support, as well as mentoring and accountability. In fact, in ICC's experience consulting many of the top real estate agents, teams, and brokerages in North America, agents who join teams have an eight-times better chance of succeeding in real estate than solo agents trying to find their way alone.

A good team leader knows this, and the leader knows that the systems on the team must do the work. The team leader brings the agents on the team, onboards them through the training systems, mentors them, meets with them on a weekly basis (which we will talk about in greater detail in Part Five), and ensures that all the systems that we talk about in this book are implemented.

A good team leader is going to bring on a larger number of new recruits with the understanding that not all of them will work out. All of the agents that they bring on will get the same chance to succeed. The team leader will do their part to meet the agents halfway and provide the systems, tools, models, and support, but then, the team leader has to sit back and see which agents will do their part. Many of them won't. If you look at any Multiple Listing Service (MLS) in any location across North America, you'll see that typically 50% of the agents in a given MLS have not even closed on transaction in the last year. You'll also see that only 10% of the agents in a given MLS do 90% of the business. So, 90% of the agents out there are floundering on their own. It is a very low success rate for real estate agents making it in the real estate industry.

Team leaders must understand that even with the support of the team and an increased chance of success, many agents will still fail. They won't show up, they won't make the contacts, they'll say they're uncomfortable, and they'll make excuses. If the team leader gets too frustrated, they may give up on the idea of growing a team at all. The team leader must shift their focus away from the problems, issues, and fires to put out on the team. Instead, successful team leaders know when agents don't do their part – they will either start doing their part or they will eventually self-select themselves off the team, or even be asked to leave the team. It's a constant cycle of recruiting, hiring, and seeing which team members will be a good fit.

Coming from decades of experience in recruiting and coaching recruiters, it is impossible to read a book by its cover. It is very difficult for a team leader to tell if newly recruited agents are going to succeed based on first impressions. Until you bring them onto your team or into your brokerage and give them work to do and see if they do it, it is extremely difficult to predict which agents are going to show up and do the work. Sure, there is plenty a team leader can tell about a recruit through a first impression; however, there is a process to follow that will help a lot. Our ICC recruiting process is a very detailed process that will help you assess the recruit.

Do not mistake the message here. We are not telling team leaders to compromise their standards on recruiting. We are simply instructing team leaders to recruit more. For example, if a team leader would like to add four team members this year, they should be recruiting eight. This number, of course, is different for every team and will fluctuate, but the point is clear: recruit more because some will not pan out. The reasons that four of the recruits won't work out could be a million different reasons under the sun. One of the four might get a divorce. One of the four might move across the country. One of the four might decide they don't like real estate. They might get sick. Their spouse might get sick. There are endless examples of how life gets in the way with real estate agents and they don't work out or produce for your team.

If a team leader is constantly obsessing over recruiting the perfect real estate agent with each hire, the team's growth will be stunted. A team leader must play the numbers with recruiting. As in our example, if the team leader wants to grow the team by four, they must recruit eight. Everyone has slightly different recruiting ratios, but a team leader must understand there is a difference between net recruiting and gross recruiting. If the team leader wants to net four, they must gross eight, with the understanding that four will likely not work out by the end of the year. This is why constantly recruiting is so crucial.

Duties of Sales/Buyer's Agents

For sales agents on a real estate team, there are four crucial duties: lead generation and follow-up, conducting buyer consultations, showing property, and negotiating contracts.

Lead Generation and Follow-Up

As we mentioned when talking about a team leader's duties and delegation to administrative staff members, it is also crucial that the sales agents on a team let go of all contracts-to-close work to administrative staff. Sales agents on the team must be focused on lead generating. The first duty of all sales agents on a team, including the team leader, is generating leads. Sales agents must devote time on their daily calendar to lead generation and follow-up.

Buyer leads typically come to teams as home buyers looking for a house to purchase. So, an agent may initially generate a lead, but still needs to nurture them and follow up with them as well. Some leads will not be ready right away. The sales agent must continue to reach out to them until they are ready to meet for a buyer consultation. That follow-up and nurturing process can last anywhere from a week to a year. The sales agent is nurturing the lead until they are ready to buy. The sales agent must reach out by a variety of methods (phone, social media, email, etc.) to try to move leads from an initial contact phase to an appointment when the sales agent meets them one-on-one.

We have found that a sales agent's number-one excuse for not doing lead generation and follow-up activities is because they are too busy handling issues with their current transactions that are under contract. But here's the kick – they should not be doing any work on existing transactions! That should be handled by the administrative team! The sales agent should be letting go of these tasks to the administrative staff members. A good sales agent learns to let go of transactional operations so they can focus more on sales. It is crucial that everyone on the team lets go of tasks that are not in their job description and stay in their prospective lanes.

Conduct Buyer Consultations

A buyer consultation is an appointment when a sales agent meets one-on-one with a client in a format where expectations are presented, client questions are answered, and the sales agent learns about what the client is looking for in a home. This is where the sales agent cements their relationship with the client and establishes the expectation that they are going to work together to find the client a home.

Sales agents should never skip this crucial step. A lot of agents want to skip the buyer consultation and just get out there and start showing property to buyers. The consultation allows the sales agent to follow a procedure, set expectations, and act professionally. The sales agent has the opportunity to explain to the client what expectations to have based on the current market. If the sales agent does not have a buyer consultation, the buyer will assume that they are not beholden to the sales agent, and that they are only obligated to use the sales agent if they happen to show them the home that they ultimately buy. Otherwise, because the sales agent hasn't laid out any expectations about the relationship going forward, they will continue to go to open houses held by other agents, they are going to talk to new home builders and developers, and they may even call another agent to see another house. The buyer isn't going to think they did anything wrong because the sales agent never had a buyer consultation and outlined all the expectations for working together. This is a crucial step that top teams implement. It's very uncomfortable for agents who are not accustomed to it. However, again, we go back to our examples with dentists, or any business professional – it is very common to have a consultation before engaging in a client/professional relationship going forward.

SALES/BUYER'S AGENT DUTIES

1 Lead generation and follow-up

2 Conduct buyer consultations

3 Show property

4 Negotiate contracts

FIGURE 10.2 Sales/Buyer's Agent Duties

Show Property

This is the most time-consuming part of any sales agent's job. A sales agent will spend a lot of time going out and showing property to their clients. This is where a Showing Assistant might come in down the road for larger teams that are training new agents that just joined the team. We discuss Showing Assistants in greater detail in Chapter 5. Otherwise, this is where a sales agent spends the bulk of their time. However, because the top teams provide their agents with administrative support from contract to closing, buyer's agents can spend more time showing property with clients since they do not have to service their own transactions.

Negotiate Contracts

Just like the team leader, a sales agent steps in to write the offer on the buyer side and assists in negotiating back and forth with counter offers. Again, we are getting the help of the administrative staff members here. The minute we have offer acceptance, the client file immediately gets transferred to the team's administrative staff member, in particular the Transaction Coordinator on the team, and they take it from contract to close. The agent then might step back in and get involved, much like the team leader, when inspection repairs are negotiated.

Duties of Administrative Staff Members

Real estate team administrative staff members must own and protect their roles. Although it may defy common business logic, real estate agents do not naturally delegate their administrative tasks to the team's administrative staff. Agents tend to cling to transactional tasks to ensure that everything goes smooth up to closing. However, administrative staff must continuously encourage sales agents to delegate business servicing tasks so that they can focus more on income-producing activities. Agents must trust their administrative teammates to increase their sales and income. They must force themselves to let go of servicing tasks while administrative staff members are simultaneously trying to take them away. Remember that delegation rarely comes naturally, so everyone involved needs to commit to sticking with it until everyone is properly in their lanes.

When a real estate team first starts out, just one person might be performing all of the administrative duties all by themselves. As the team grows (maybe you have five or six sales agents on the team), the team may need two administrative staff members to handle the increased workload. With more on your sales team, now you can afford to hire a second person. Maybe one of the administrative staff members performs three roles at once as the Listing Manager, Marketing Director, and Runner, while the other administrative staff member acts as both the Transaction Coordinator and the Administrative Manager at the same time. (Remember, we talked in greater detail about these individual administrative roles in Chapter 5.) Once the team has grown more and perhaps is closing 300 deals a year, for example, a third administrative staff member may need to be hired. Perhaps at this point, the team would split off the Transaction Coordinator so that we have an Administrative Manager as its own role and the third administrative staff member is still the Listing Manager, Marketing Director, and Runner. This type of growth and shift will continue as the team grows and makes more room for new administrative roles.

Whether you have one administrative staff member or seven, the same duties and workflow will apply. Please understand that the workflow we are about to dive into can work with any size administrative team!

ADMINISTRATIVE STAFF DUTIES

1. **Prelisting**
2. **Listing to contract**
3. **Contract to close**
4. **Lead generation**

FIGURE 10.3   Administrative Staff Duties

Prelisting

When you start working with a new client at the very earliest point, it may be when the client first calls to list their property. The team leader then might give the Listing Manager the address, and the Prelisting Checklist would be used. The Listing Manager does all the items on that checklist to get the team leader ready for that initial listing appointment. Figure 10.4 provides a good example of what a typical Listing Manager's Prelisting Checklist might look like.

PRELISTING CHECKLIST

Days Prior to Listing Appt	Date Completed	Description
3		Create new listing file with all forms and templates
3		Schedule listing appointment in agent's calendar
3		Locate and save old MLS listings for subject property
2		Obtain property profile, assessments, and taxes
2		Call title and request legal description and deed
2		Obtain parcel map and survey info
2		Print agent's prelisting presentation materials for consultation
2		Prepare seller net sheet(s)
2		Prepare CMA for agent's review
2		Prepare map and directions to property
2		Fill out and print seller's disclosures for listing consultation
1		Prepare listing packet
1		Fill out MLS input sheet w/ missing info still needed
1		Input client into CRM database
1		Prelisting packet hand delivered to client
1		Prelisting packet and video emailed to client
0		If listing is NOT signed, schedule a follow-up call for agent
0		If listing IS signed, start "Listing to Contract Checklist"

FIGURE 10.4   Prelisting Checklist

Listing to Contract

Then, the listing agent or team leader would go on the listing appointment, get the listing agreement signed, and turn it back over to the Listing Manager. The Listing Manager then would take it all the way from listing to contract when offers to purchase the property come in. To start this process, the Listing Manager should reach out to the client to introduce themselves immediately after the initial listing appointment is done. On this phone call, the Listing Manager explains their role on the team and completes the initial intake questions on the Assistant's First Call Checklist as shown in Figure 10.5. The listing agent or team leader will have prepared the client for this call from the Listing Manager, so the client will be expecting it.

ASSISTANT'S FIRST CALL CHECKLIST

Checklist	Notes
☐ Confirm business card received	
☐ Office hours	
☐ Confirm phone (H)	
☐ Confirm email (H)	
☐ Confirm phone (W)	
☐ Confirm email (W)	
☐ Communication preference (H)	
☐ Communication preference (W)	
☐ Showing notice	
☐ Showing notice communication preference	
What to Expect from Me	**Notes**
☐ Send copy of Listing Agreement	
☐ Seller net sheet	
☐ Confirm HOA fees	
☐ Confirm loan amount	
☐ MLS listing	
☐ Website creation	
☐ Install sign	
☐ Weekly progress report	
☐ Finish disclosures	
☐ When can we receive those?	
☐ Smoke detectors, CO_2, water heater straps	
Preferred Vendors for Inspections	**Notes**
☐ Roof:	
☐ Termite:	
☐ Septic:	
Closing	**Notes**
☐ How can I ensure this is a positive experience?	
☐ Referrals	

FIGURE 10.5 Assistant's First Call Checklist

The client can get a sense for the organization of the team, as well as the support that will be provided and the standard of customer service on the team. It makes everyone look good. The Listing Manager explains that they will work to take care of all issues the client might face, and tries to take over and own the administrative side of the job. That way, when there are problems, questions, concerns, or anything comes up, the seller will reach out to the Listing Manager and not the listing agent. That's the goal! The Listing Manager will take over communication with the sellers and own the listing side of the job. This does not happen overnight. It takes a lot of purposeful work and effort by both the listing agent and the Listing Manager to build confidence and establish this relationship.

The Listing Agent may tend to want to hang on to control and swerve out of their lane and do all that work on the listing side so they look like a hero to the client. In doing so, they undermine the Listing Manager, and make more work for themselves. The Listing Manager is there to help with this so that the Listing Agent can go out and get more business and do other things to increase their income and keep the team moving forward!

Next, the Listing Manager then arranges for the lockbox to be put on, the sign to be installed, the photos to be taken, the staging, putting the listing on the MLS, scheduling showings, coordinating open houses, and so forth – all the way until offers to purchase the property are received.

Contract to Close

This is when the Listing Manager will notify the listing agent so the listing agent can step back in and help negotiate the contract to acceptance. After acceptance of an offer, the client and the transaction now pass on to the Transaction Coordinator who handles things from contract to close. As before with the Listing Manager, now the Transaction Coordinator reaches out to the client and introduces themselves. The baton is passed fully to the Transaction Coordinator.

The Transaction Coordinator usually has double the workload of the Listing Manager. If you think about it, every offer (buyer or seller) goes from Contract to Close but only the sellers go from Listing to Contract. For clients who are buyers, they make an offer on a house and they go from Contract to Close. However, on the listing side, your team might represent them to list their property for sale, and then when that house gets sold, the team will continue to represent them from contract to close. All listing side deals go from contract to close, too. That's why contract-to-close tasks get approximately twice the transactional traffic as listing to contract tasks. Not to mention, the contract-to-close side is extra stressful because there are a lot of unexpected problems and fires to put out in real estate transactions. This is a big reason why agents have a tendency to swerve out of their lane and do the administrative staff member's job. Yes, problems are going to happen, but agents must let the administrative staff do their job.

LISTING-TO-CONTRACT CHECKLIST

Days After Listing Agmta	Date Completed	Description
0		Admin intro call lo sellers - immediately after listing signed
0		Receive signed listing agreement
0		Did Agent ask for referrals at listing appointment?
1		Schedule Open House(s) with Sellers/Agent
1		Create property file and/or upload all prelisting documents
1		Obtain all signed & completed sellers disclosures
1		Obtain showing instructions from agent/sellers
1		Obtain seller mortgage statement or loan info
1		Put seller on MLS listing auto-alert email drip for home(s) to buy
1		Put seller on MLS listing auto-alert drip - MLS status changes in neighborhood
1		Get seller prequalified for loan to purchase next home
1		Order preliminary title report, HOA Documents & CCRs
1		Call stager to schedule staging consultation
1		Call photographer to schedule photo shoot
1		Order & schedule yard sign
1		Add sellers to admin weekly update call list
1		Add sellers to agent's weekly update call list
1		Enter listing into MLS as incomplete for agent to proof
1		Assign lock box to MLS listing
1		Add client to CRM database
1		Add new listing to Team Scoreboard
1		Turn listing contract/disclosures in to brokerage compliance
2		Get MLS listing edits/approval from Agent
2		Upload MLS Client Detail Report to property file
2		Email MLS Client Detail Report to all team members
2		Add/Enhance Listing on all other websites
2		Add listing to broker tour/caravan
2		Calendar Listing Expiration Date
2		Prepare property flyer template (& Open House flyer)
2		Create "Just Listed" Facebook & social media posts
2		Obtain Neighborhood Contact Information
2		Get 2 sets of keys made - for lockbox & office
2		"Just Listed" mailers/flyers created & ordered
2		"Open House" mailers/flyers created
2		First Open House day/time scheduled with sellers/agents?
2		Add clients as friends on Facebook/Social Media
2		Order Seller Coverage Warranty
3		Claim listing on Zillow/Trulia & set up reporting
4		Sign up at property
4		Lockbox on at property
4		Flyers delivered to property

5	LISTING GOES ACTIVE on MLS
5	Send Thank You/Gift Card to Person who Referred Listing
5	Start agent prospecting calls around new listing
5	"Just Listed" email to neighborhood & SOI
5	"Just Listed" posted on Facebook & social media
7	Email Activity Report to sellers
7	Weekly Activity Report Call to sellers
7	Agent ask for referrals on weekly call?
8	Order "Open House" Mailers/Flyers for neighborhood
8	"Open House" email to neighborhood & SOI
8	"Open House" posted on Facebook & social media
14	Email Activity Report to sellers
14	Weekly Activity Report Call to sellers
15	Schedule 2nd Open House?
21	Email Activity Report to sellers
21	Weekly Activity Report Call to sellers
28	Email Activity Report to sellers
28	Weekly Activity Report Call to sellers
35	Email Activity Report to sellers
35	Call to sellers for PRICE REDUCTION APPOINTMENT?
42	Email Activity Report to sellers
42	Weekly Activity Report Call to sellers
49	Email Activity Report to sellers
49	Weekly Activity Report Call to sellers
56	Email Activity Report to sellers
56	Weekly Activity Report Call to sellers
63	Email Activity Report to sellers
63	Weekly Activity Report Call to sellers
70	Email Activity Report to sellers
70	Call sellers for RELISTING APPOINTMENT? Price Reduction?
	Once Offer(s) Received
71	Prepare summary(s) of key offer terms to present to sellers
71	Prepare net sheet(s) for offer(s) to present to sellers
72	Draft response(s) to offers for sellers to sign acceptance/counteroffer
72	Send counteroffer (or acceptance) to buyer's agent
	Once Offer Accepted -Start Seller Closing Checklist

FIGURE 10.6 Listing-to-Contract Checklist

SELLER CLOSING CHECKLIST

Days After Acceptance	Date Completed	Description
0		Upload signed contract, forms & contact info to property file
0		Calendar all key contract dates & deadlines – see below
1		Email signed contract & contact info to lender; title & buyer's agent
1		Email signed contract & contact info to seller w/ title contact info & next steps
1		Call seller with next steps, key dates/deadlines & inspection info
1		All utilities are on, and to be left on?
1		Change MLS status to pending
1		Sale pending rider on sign at property
1		EMD-Earnest Money Deposit received & deposited/logged
1		Request Preliminary Title Report
1		Obtain/Order neighborhood contact information for mailers/calls
1		Submit all documents/forms to broker compliance
1		Update Team Scoreboard
1		Listing agent "congratulations" call to seller – ask for referrals
2		Order all seller-required inspections – see inspection checklist below
2		Order Home Warranty (if applicable)
2		Order Natural Hazard Disclosure (if applicable)
2		Friend request to buyers on Facebook & social media
2		Send/Request disclosures to/from buyer's agent
2		"Sale Pending" mailer/flyers to neighborhood ordered
2		"Sale Pending" Facebook & social media posts
3		Start agent circle prospecting "sale pending" calls/door knocking
3		Confirm Earnest Money Deposit (EMD) is deposited
3		Submit commission disbursement/disbursement authorization
3		Contact buyer's lender to ensure all docs recvd (tax info pay stubs, etc.)
7		Has appraisal been ordered? Contact buyer's agent/lender
7		Call seller with update – what's been done & next steps
14		Call to check loan status with lender
14		Call seller with update – what's been done & next steps
15		Request for inspection repairs received? Remind buyer's agent
15		Appraisal In? Contact buyer's agent/lender
17		Home Inspection repair request received? Respond to Request?
17		Appraisal contingency removed?
17		Agent call seller to congratulate on property appraising
18		Contact lender – File submitted to underwriter? Still needed?
19		Request loan contingency removal from buyer's agent
19		All other inspection reports received? See below
20		Get client's new address & update SOI database in CRM
21		Loan contingency removed?
21		Call seller with update – what's been done & next steps
22		Contact lender – Underwriter approval? Any conditions?
23		Are all contingencies of the sale removed? Still needed?

Five Days Before Closing

25	Call seller five days before closing to explain closing process
25	Have staging furniture removed
25	Schedule buyer's final walkthrough inspection
25	Schedule sellers to sign at closing
25	Request & review estimated closing statement
25	Submit any final invoices to escrow/title/attorney
25	Loan Documents in and signed by Buyers?
25	File Housekeeping – contact other agent to ensure file is complete
25	Oder closing gift for sellers
25	Contact sellers to get utilities list
26	Signed loan documents sent to lender for loan funding?
26	Send utilities list to buyer's agent to switch names at close date
27	Contact escrow/title/attorney – Still needed to close (buyer funds up?)
28	Buyer walkthrough inspection conducted?
28	Loan Funded? Has escrow/title/attorney received funds to close?
29	Request & review final estimated closing statement

Day of Closing

30	Confirm Recording
30	Keys delivered
30	Agent to call seller w/ "congratulations" – ask for referrals
30	Receive closing documents from escrow/title/attorney (upload to file)
30	Change MLS status to "Sold" on MLS
30	Change Zillow Status to "Sold"
31	Commission check(s) received/deposited
30	For sale sign removed from property
30	Lockbox removed from property

After Closing

31	Input "adopted" buyer contact information into CRM database
31	Update new seller notes in SOI database w/ new address
31	Start seller on past client email/mailer drip campaign
31	Send seller congratulations email w/ online review request links
31	Send seller congratulations letter
31	Send adopted buyer congratulations letter
31	Send "Thank You Colleague" letter to co-op agent
31	Send "Thank You" letter to lender
31	Update closing on team scoreboard
32	Calendar Home Anniversary & 30/90 day agent calls (referrals)
32	Create/save PDFs of all file documents & emails
32	Start agent "Just Sold" calls to neighborhood
32	"Just Sold" mailers/flyers to neighborhood & SOI
32	"Just Sold" – FB & other social media posts

FIGURE 10.7 Seller Closing Checklist

Key Contract Dates and Deadlines

Description	Dates
7th Day – Disclosures Delivered	
7th Day – Preliminary Report Received	
15th Day – Inspection Repairs Request Received?	
17th Day – Inspection Contingencies Removal Deadline	
17th Day – Appraisal Contingency Removal Deadline	
21st Day – Loan Contingency Removal Deadline	
5 days till close – walkthrough, funding, etc.	
Other:	
Other:	
Closing Date	

Inspection Information Checklist

Type	Company & Contact Info	Date & Time	Report Received?
Termite/Pest			
Home Inspection			
Pool Inspection			
Roof Inspection			
Septic Inspection			
Appraisal			
Well Inspection			
Flood Zone Insp.			
Other Inspection			

FIGURE 10.8 Seller Closing Checklist Part 2

Quick Tip   Weekly Proactive Client Calls

It is crucial for both the Listing Manager and/or the Transaction Coordinator to conduct weekly calls to all active clients. A Listing Manager should be calling home sellers every single week to give them an update. They must update the seller on everything that has been accomplished during that week, and they can go right down their listing checklist.

The Listing Manager must also tell the seller what to expect in the next week. This is easily done when referencing a listing checklist, because the Listing Manager can just work their way down the checklist and know exactly what is to be done next. In addition, the Listing Manager should be sharing feedback with the client during these weekly update calls. This would include an update on how well the open house went, and what marketing activities are coming up. It could also include how many views their listing is getting online.

These weekly updates must be done by phone! The Listing Manager may choose to follow these phone call updates with a supporting email. It is important that these phone calls happen every week at the same time, and that they go out to all active listings.

This same principle holds true with reaching out to clients from contract to closing. The Transaction Coordinator should be calling all clients under contract each week while referencing the Contract-to-Close Checklist. This applies to both buyers and sellers that the team is servicing. These phone calls are similar to the calls the Listing Manager will make in that they provide an update on things that were accomplished this past week, as well as upcoming items. It is important for the Transaction Coordinator to remind the client of important upcoming dates, like the date the inspection contingency will be removed, the dates of any inspections, the closing date, and so on.

Administrative staff members must not sit back and wait for clients to call! If your clients are calling you all the time, you have a big problem. That means your customer service is failing, They should not have the need to call you because you should always be beating them to it and keeping them updated. These weekly proactive phone calls are necessary for the team to grow and succeed.

Resource   Listing and Closing Checklists

In the online resource appendix of this book, you will find our listing and closing checklists. This Excel spreadsheet will provide you with a template for devising your own checklists, which will contain the essential activities that administrative staff must complete during each part of a transaction.

All resources can be downloaded from this book's online appendix at therealestatetrainer.com/teambook.

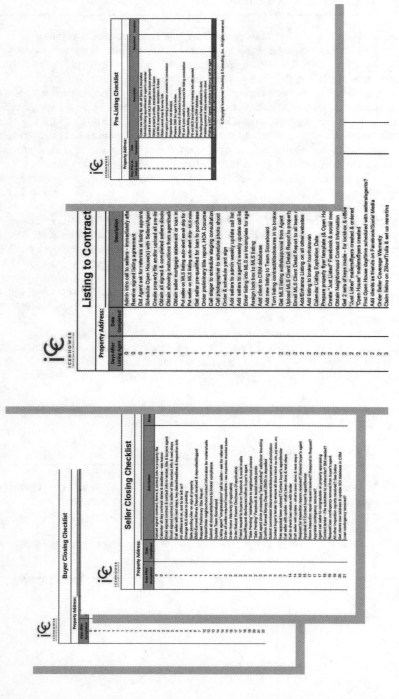

FIGURE 10.9 Listing and Closing Checklists

Lead Generation

Administrative staff members have the additional responsibility of lead generation, just like everyone else on the team. Sure, lead generation is mostly left up to the sales agents of a team, but that doesn't mean that administrative team members are completely relieved of this obligation.

Administrative staff members primarily lead generate in two different ways. First, they can conduct postclosing client follow-up phone calls. These calls happen 30 days, 90 days, and on the one-year anniversary of the closing of the home. Typically, these phone calls are a customer service call where the administrative team member is calling to follow up with the client to ensure that everything is going alright with the home. This is when the administrative team member can provide recommendations for local contractors and other vendors that the client might need to make improvements or repairs on the home. The administrative staff is ensuring that the client knows that the team's customer service does not stop at closing. If the client has any issues or needs with their home, the goal is to have them first call the administrative staff member first so the team can help the client by referring trusted contacts so the client can be assured that they'll get the fairest price and the highest quality of work for their home. Inside this customer service message, the administrative team member is also embedding a little bit of lead generation, too, where they will ask the past client for referrals.

> *On the ABC Real Estate Team, most of our business comes by word of mouth from our past clients. So, if you came across anyone that was looking to buy or sell a home, would you have any problem referring our services to them in the future? [wait for answer, then respond with . . .] Great! By chance can you think of anyone that you know who is planning on moving this year?*

This is how to ask a past client for referrals. This is a lead generation activity disguised and weaved into customer service in your past client follow-up phone calls.

The second primary type of lead generation activity that administrative team members can perform is simply growing and maintaining their own SOI databases. Admin should also be encouraged to build their own SOI database, which should include their family, friends, Facebook friends, coworkers, and so forth.

It is important that administrative team members have this as a goal. They will be tracked on the team's dashboard to monitor their SOI database growth, which is how many people they add to their SOI database throughout the year (we talk dashboards later in Part Four). By maintaining and growing their own SOI database, the team can market to the members of their SOI, too, through email, mailers, social media, client event invitations, and so on. Marketing to the administrative staff's SOI is a more passive form of lead generation – these administrative team members are not being asked to make phone calls by any means! They have enough on their plate and must stay in their lane to some degree with lead generation.

Along with bringing in leads to the team comes compensation. Administrative staff members that bring in leads that end up as clients will make more money through bonuses. Some teams pay referral fees to their administrative staff who bring in leads. Other teams go the route of paying a percentage of commission or set a flat amount per referral. When administrative staff members generate business and bring it into the team, they should be rewarded and encouraged to generate more.

It is very common for successful teams to have goals for their administrative staff members to bring in two to five transactions from their own SOI databases each year. As long as all SOI members are marketed to consistently, this isn't a difficult task. Administrative staff members can make a lot more money by participating in lead generation through growing and maintaining their SOI database, and they are really boosting the team this way. Everyone succeeds and everyone gets more income.

It is important to note that different states, provinces, and local governments have varying rules with regard to licensing requirements for earning commissions. Oftentimes, real estate team leaders will encourage admin team members to get their license so they can do more of the duties that require a license (show a house, set up a lockbox, etc.). In some areas, an administrative team member is able to take a percentage or commission split like a sales agent would. Local laws do vary, so check with your managing broker or government department of real estate for information on local regulations governing compensation for licensed and unlicensed administrative staff members.

Delegation Diagnostic

Again, it is essential that administrative staff continuously encourage agents to delegate more and more business-servicing duties their way. If agents focus more on lead-generation activities and force themselves to let go of transactional issues and tasks, the team's sales and efficiency will dramatically increase. Conversely, if agents cling to client-servicing tasks and use them as an excuse for not having time to generate new business, the whole team is negatively impacted by the resulting decrease in sales production.

Teams can always get better in this area as well. As a result, smart teams continuously perform delegation diagnostic tests on themselves to determine how many tasks their agents are conducting other than: lead generation, buyer/listing consultations, showing properties, and negotiating contracts. If agents are spending time doing anything else, the team should take immediate steps to start shifting those duties to the administrative side of the team.

Next Steps

As we proceed to Part Three of this book, we turn our attention to the third component of team growth: Cultivate Personal Responsibility Through Team Accountability.

As before, if you're reading this book as a leader of your real estate team, we advise you to continue reading each chapter from start to finish.

However, if you're reading this book as a team member, then your next step is to get ready to attend the second of your five book club sessions. The following section helps you to prepare and to give you a sense of what to expect. When the first book club is over, you can then pick up where you left off and continue on to Part Three.

The Team Book Club: Part Two Discussion Guide

Remember, team members and leaders, the purpose of the first five book club meetings is *not* to come to a particular conclusion or decide on what your real estate team's overall growth goal will be. Part Two explored a lot of detailed and multifaceted material. There is a lot to digest, and it's likely that you will need to refer to this chapter again and again when you begin the actual process of identifying your team's activity-based indicators (ABIs) and incorporating them into your transactional timeline.

This second book club gathering provides you with the time and space to start talking about activities that impact growth and how the material in Part Two relates specifically to your team.

We particularly encourage facilitators to continue the process of "making it about everyone," and have team members brainstorm the growth-building activities they might personally perform. While Part Two discussed ABIs in a general way, you will need to apply these principles to everyone on your real estate team. Everyone on your team must be committed to performing specific growth activities. If everyone performs *their* activities and achieves *their* results, the entire team should reach its overall growth goals.

Hold Each Other Accountable

Begin this week's book club by asking the group who did and didn't read Part Two and, if necessary, ask the four key accountability questions to anyone who did not manage to complete this week's reading:

① How do you think you did?

② What got in the way?

③ What do you need to do differently next time?

④ Is there any way we can help?

FIGURE BC.1 Key Accountability Questions

Don't become overly distracted or derailed by those who haven't prepared in advance. Keep the accountability section to a minimum and keep your sight on the real purpose and subject of the book club meeting. As before, distributing a chapter summary helps refresh people's memories, or helps any nonreaders get up to speed so that they can't opt out of participation.

As before, book club facilitators can use the provided chapter summary to guide the conversation in addition to, or instead of, the questions below. As you read through each bullet point in the summary, ask your people, "Did this point resonate with you?" "How?" "Why?" "Tell me more," and so on.

Part Two Summary, Component 2   Focus on Activities First

Deliberate, purposeful, systematic activities produce successful and desired results. The second component of organizational growth requires real estate teams to set end results and outcomes aside somewhat and focus on activities first, identifying and capitalizing on those activities that have the greatest impact and likelihood of helping you and your people in achieving your viral goal.

While a results-based indicator (RBI) measures what you've already accomplished, an ABI tells you if you're on course to achieve a goal. ABIs are predictive actions that drive specific results. ABIs are predictive, because if an ABI changes you can predict that the RBI will also change. While an RBI is outside your control or is almost impossible to take action on, an ABI is highly actionable and more clearly within your power or ability to influence or regulate.

Key Points:

- ABIs must be measurable and trackable. The activities you focus on must be worthy of your time and efforts, so it's essential that you can justify an activity's value with measurable and trackable supporting data. You can't just do. You have to do and assess the effectiveness of what you do.
- Focus on the 20% that drives results. The Pareto Principle states that when several factors affect a situation, just a few of those factors will account for most of the impact. In most situations, 80% of effects or results can be attributed to 20% of the causes. Don't waste your time and energy on the 80% that doesn't make much impact. Instead, focus on the 20% activities that tangibly and exponentially move the needle.

(continued)

Part Two Summary, Component 2 *(continued)*

- Success leaves clues. Choose a real estate team whose success you'd like to replicate. Once you've identified a desirable model, you then "model the model" and pass on what you discover to your people.
- Make the connection. Making contact and engaging other people is the primary activity that underlies every real estate team's strategy or model. On some level, making contact and engaging other people will tie into every ABI that you implement at your team.
- Diligent application brings success. When you focus on the activities, success is the sum of every single thing that you and your teammates do. Each step in the transaction timeline sequence connects to the next, with each activity and mini-result leading to the overall desired outcome.
- Activities for agents versus administrative staff. It's important to delegate tasks across the team and allow each team member to do their job! Understand your role on the team and learn your responsibilities.

Notes:

_____

_____

_____

_____

Questions to Spark and Stoke Conversation

The following questions are simply a starting point for sparking conversation and ensuring that everyone participates. Leaders and book club facilitators are free to create questions of their own, and we highly encourage you to do so now that you're a bit more practiced in guiding your real estate team's book club.

Book Club Conversations for Component 2   Focus on Activities First

- What ideas was the author trying to get across in Part Two?
- How did you feel reading Part Two compared to reading Part One?
- How do the ideas presented in Part Two apply to us at _____ (insert the name of your real estate team)?
- How does an activity-based indicator (ABI) differ from a results-based indicator (RBI)?
- Do you agree that an ABI focus would be better than an RBI focus at our team? Why? Why not?

(continued)

Book Club Conversations for Component 2   (*continued*)

- How might we start applying some concepts around ABIs at our team?
- In your role on the team, what do you think your most impactful activities are? Why? Can they be turned into measurable and trackable ABIs? How?
- What are some potentially impactful activities that we might consider doing that we don't already do?
- Do you think the Pareto Principle (the 80/20 rule) applies to our team? Why? Why not?
- At our real estate team, how does the idea of "the vital few and the trivial many" apply?
- Which is more useful or accurate: "the vital few and the trivial many" or "the vital few and the useful many"?
- If success leaves clues, where and who can our team look to? Who do we aspire to emulate and learn from?
- What new things did you learn in Part Two?
- What questions do you still have?
- Are there any quotes, passages, or ideas you found particularly compelling?
- Do you have a new perspective as a result of reading Part Two?
- Did you learn something you didn't know before?
- How has your attitude or behavior changed?
- How does Part Two relate to your role or experiences on our team?
- Did you connect with the subject matter? Did it make you nervous or excited?
- What did you like best about Part Two?
- What did you like least about Part Two?
- Which topic(s) of Part Two stood out to you?
- If you had the chance to ask the author one question, right now, what would it be?

    No matter what questions you decide to ask, at the end of each book club session, you (or each book club's leader/facilitator) should ask yourself the following questions:

- Does everyone understand the material?
- Have we discussed ways that the material relates to us?
- Are my people excited and engaged? Is there buy-in?
- Did we focus on *activities* rather than results?
- Did we make the concept of ABIs *about everyone*?

    If the answer to these questions is a resounding "Yes" then you are well on your way to devising a viral goal on your real estate team, and identifying the activities that are most likely to drive growth and achieve success.

PART 3

Cultivate Personal Responsibility Through Team Accountability

CHAPTER 11

All the Tools You Need to Keep Yourself and Your Team Accountable

For your biggest goals to go viral and spread like wildfire throughout your real estate team, you must capture the imagination of all team members. The goal-setting process must make it about *everyone*, or it will not inspire or compel each member of the team to perform the daily activities required to reach their – and the team's – goals.

Whatever your chosen ABIs are on your team, success depends upon collaboration and equal participation. Everyone on your team must be committed to performing specific growth activities. If everyone performs their activities and achieves their results, the entire real estate team will reach its overall growth goals.

Component 3 cultivates personal responsibility by practicing public accountability. In doing so, real estate teams create a culture in which people feel personally responsible for their part in achieving the goal and are also held openly accountable for performing their activities and hitting their targets. When team members are instilled with a sense of personal responsibility – and when leaders conduct respectful and responsible accountability gatherings – no one will resist or have reason to fear being held accountable. Rather, everyone will embrace it enthusiastically with a sense of ownership, purpose, pride, and a concern for others as well as respect for themselves.

There are three key values that real estate teams provide to their team members: leads, administrative support, and accountability, in no particular order. Accountability is often the underrated value that real estate teams provide to members.

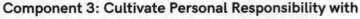

FIGURE 11.1   Component 3

THREE KEY VALUES OF BEING ON A TEAM

1 **Leads**

2 **Administrative support**

3 **Accountability**

FIGURE 11.2   Three Key Values

Accountability Is an Underrated Key Value of Being on a Team

Usually, real estate agents will join a team because they want more real estate leads. They want to get more business, and they hope that the team will give them more leads so they can earn more money. The problem with this mind-set is that it isn't a long-term benefit. Simply providing a team member with more leads is not going to help them become a better agent.

If you want more fish, you're better off learning how to be a better fisherman than to go fishing with someone who will just give you some of their fish. Good teams will help their people learn how to generate leads on their own. And they do that by holding them accountable.

Another reason an agent may join a team is because they need administrative support. Most real estate agents don't want to spend so much time doing the paperwork, including all the contract-to-close tasks, as they would rather spend more time generating business. Most agents would rather be out working with clients and showing them properties.

In general, real estate agents are very aware that teams can help in the two areas of leads and administrative support. They want to get more business and they want assistance in handling that increased business. It's the accountability that they don't assign a lot of value to. One of the reasons why accountability is so underrated is because it is usually painful. It's not something most agents think they need, or it's not in the forefront of their mind when they consider how they would like to grow their business.

Because it is a painful thing to do, leaders usually don't hold their agents accountable. Leaders are human, too, and tend to be people-pleasers. Leaders don't want to be the "bad guy" and hold their team members accountable for activities that they don't naturally want to do, even though doing so would help them attain the results they want. Accountability on a team is so important for this very reason. Having someone that gives you a little tough love when you need it is indeed very valuable.

At Icenhower Coaching and Consulting (ICC), we work with many of the top team leaders and brokerage owners in North America. These real estate leaders come to us wondering what is missing in their team or brokerage. These leaders may question whether they are giving their team members enough leads. They may wonder if their administrative support is strong enough. Though these issues may be present, often the underlying issue is a lack of accountability, resulting in low-producing team members.

Resource   Prospecting Accountability Chart

In the online resource appendix of this book, you will find our Prospect Accountability Chart. This tool helps track monthly prospecting activities and is a very useful, fillable PDF form that provides accountability to getting those activities accomplished month by month.

All resources can be downloaded from this book's online appendix at therealestatetrainer.com/ teambook.

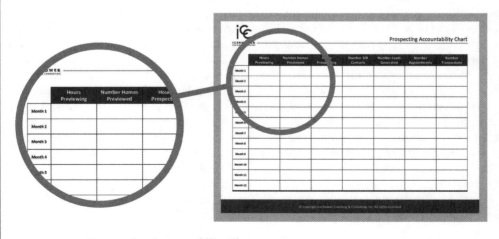

FIGURE 11.3   Prospecting Accountability Chart

A Better Way

While we've been conditioned to associate accountability with pain or a negative consequence, authoritarian or punitive approaches to accountability are not only despised, but they also do not work. Modern cognitive psychology understands that people are motivated to do their best not by humiliation and punishment, but by a sense of purpose, professionalism, self-respect, and autonomy.

However, the opposite of a nonpunitive team is not an *absence* of accountability or responsibility where people do whatever they want, whenever they want to. When an absence of accountability is the status quo, real estate teams struggle with:

- Apathy.
- Disengagement.
- Low morale.
- Frustration and confusion due to shifting or unclear priorities.
- Ineffective and unsuccessful execution of activities.
- Low levels of self-belief, and high levels of turnover.

When properly understood and implemented correctly, accountability and responsibility can be a *collaborative* and *creative* process that inspires all team members to stop making excuses, author their own solutions, believe in their abilities, and be personally invested in contributing to the collective goal.

With this better way, accountability is neither retaliatory nor retributive. Consequences are not harsh reprimands, accusatory outbursts, demoralizing punishments, or coercive threats. Consequences are neither immediate nor guaranteed and, what's more, consequences are rarely referred to explicitly. Rather, consequences are implied. If people fail to take responsibility, and continuously fall short of their daily and weekly targets, there will be no need for harsh words or pressuring lectures: the data on the ABI dashboard will speak volumes. Without saying a word, team members will feel the prospective pain and disappointment of not reaching their goal, and this potential outcome will be consequence enough.

However, this potential consequence is always framed positively as something that can yet be avoided or turned around. Accountability should never be defeatist, despairing, or pessimistic. There is always something we can do to take action or, in other words, to take responsibility for achieving the goal. Both accountability and responsibility are motivating influences that encourage people to tap into an internal locus of control in which we believe in our ability to consciously choose and control our own destiny.

Accountability and Responsibility

The words "responsibility" and "accountability" are often used interchangeably, but while they're on the same spectrum of professionalism and answerability, they actually have slightly

RESPONSIBILITY

- involves implementing a response to designated tasks and activities
- internal
- personal obligation one takes upon oneself and stems from a sense of intrinsic motivation

ACCOUNTABILITY

- involves providing an account or an answer of what did and did not actually happen at the time, or by the time it was supposed to
- external
- more of a social contract or social obligation

FIGURE 11.4   Responsibility versus Accountability

different but important meanings. While both mean "answerable," the main difference between responsibility and accountability can be seen in Figure 11.4.

Before we delve into these differences in detail, please understand that we are not promoting an "accountability *versus* responsibility" perspective. We are not arguing in favor of one over the other or asking you to choose between them. Rather, our hope is that by illuminating their subtle differences, we will exemplify the positive attributes of both, and illustrate how one informs the other when public or external accountability fosters and promotes a sense of personal or internal responsibility.

The science and psychology of procrastination is fascinating, and many a book has focused its attention on why we fail to take action or avoid our responsibilities. From fear of failure to fear of success, and good old-fashioned laziness, there are endless reasons why we fail to take action and do the things we know we need to do. However, our focus is not on the *causes* of our tendency to procrastinate and sidestep our responsibilities; our focus is on solutions and alternative approaches. No matter the reasons behind our innate tendencies, accountability combats the natural human instinct to avoid doing what we know we need to.

In the absence of accountability, it becomes easier and easier to avoid our responsibilities or create excuses about the lazy or sloppy execution of our tasks and duties. Knowing that a moment will come when we will be answerable, one way or another, for our actions increases our moment-by-moment commitment to fulfill our responsibilities. We all *have* responsibilities but we *take* responsibility when we implement actions and systems to ensure that the things we will be held accountable for actually take place.

When holding ourselves accountable, or being held accountable by those around us, we take responsibility and ownership for our actions; we don't tell half-truths or twist what happened to make ourselves sound better; and we implement tangible strategies for how we will do things differently – and better – the next time.

Accountability balances our natural and inevitable shortcomings, reminds us of our responsibilities, intensifies our internal resolve, and ensures a positive outcome despite our natural and normal tendency to slip up now and then.

Responsibility is remarkably similar to activity-based indicators (ABIs), which are highly actionable and more clearly within your power or ability to influence or regulate. However, the similarity between responsibility and ABIs should not be taken to mean that accountability must therefore be the equivalent of a results-based indicator (RBI). As you'll recall, RBIs are outside your control and are almost impossible to take action on. RBIs are situated in the past and set in stone.

Accountability is retrospective in that it looks back on or deals with past events or situations. You can't be held accountable first thing on a Monday morning for that day's activities. You can only be held accountable after a task or activity was supposed to be completed. However, this is not to say that accountability is an ineffective or unproductive navel-gazing process that focuses excessively on a past over which you no longer have any control. Accountability may be retrospective, but it is nonetheless proactive. Accountability huddles provide a safe space for you and your team members to reflect upon the past and discuss what works well (and what doesn't) so that you can take necessary steps to improve. Accountability is a process of looking at completed actions in order to take better immediate and future actions.

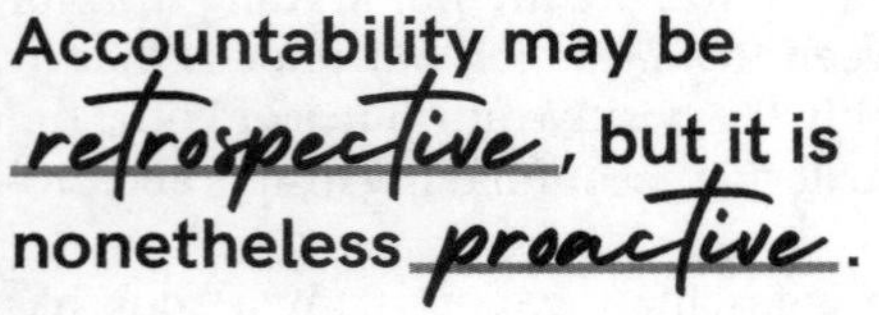

Accountability may be *retrospective*, but it is nonetheless *proactive*.

FIGURE 11.5 Accountability Is Retrospective

Both accountability and responsibility produce action and results-oriented behavior but in different ways. When we take responsibility and act responsibly, we create or control a situation by causing something to happen. When we're held accountable for our actions, we reflect upon the efficacy and actual outcomes of those actions and address any problems with a view to doing things better or differently the next time.

Additionally, unlike RBIs that gauge the *final* state or level of something, accountability does not take place at the end of the year or following a prolonged period of activity. Rather, accountability is implemented from the very beginning and upheld every step of the way. Accountability huddles are sacrosanct and take place on a frequent and regular basis, so that the "past" that you are dealing with is never the distant past. Meeting on a weekly, or sometimes daily, basis ensures that time doesn't run too far away from you, and that there is always something you can do to take control, redirect, and remedy a potentially adverse outcome. We tackle these weekly huddles in Part Five. What's more, regular public accountability produces and promotes a sense of personal responsibility that team members will bring into each and every moment of their day.

Resource   Daily Contact Form

In the online resource appendix of this book, you will find our Daily Contact Form. This fillable PDF form helps track daily contacts. It provides accountability to getting those activities accomplished on a daily basis.

All resources can be downloaded from this book's online appendix at therealestatetrainer.com/teambook.

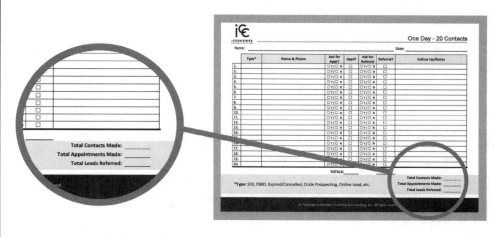

FIGURE 11.6   Daily Contact Form

Accountability Is External, Responsibility Is Internal

Being accountable involves *providing an account* or an answer of what did and did not actually happen at the time, or by the time, it was supposed to. People often talk about "holding myself accountable," but, in practice, this is very difficult and largely ineffective according to most research.

Most of us would agree that when a team member says they will hold two open houses each weekend this month, the team member is more likely to take responsibility and do what needs to be done to successfully hold the open houses. Whether written or verbal, concrete commitments between two or more people create a shared expectation, and that expectation alone is enough motivation to make you focus and fulfill your promise or obligations.

However, when you tell yourself – and nobody else – that you will lose weight, quit smoking, or write the novel you've always dreamed of writing, you are far less likely to follow through on your commitment. It's easy to make excuses or avoid uncomfortable activities when your goals are a secret. When you are accountable to someone or to a team of people, you are motivated by the power of social expectations, which – for better or worse – tend to be more influential and persuasive than our personal expectations alone.

Effective accountability is public, shared, or external.

In their investigation of willpower, psychologist Roy F. Baumeister and science writer John Tierney noted that the mere presence of a mirror (people watching themselves as they walked past) made people more likely to resist bullying, to work harder, or to resist temptation. Numerous other studies have confirmed that if we believe someone is watching then we behave differently. However, it's definitely unwise to create a culture where your people feel as though their every move is being watched.

The American Society of Training and Development completed a study on accountability and discovered that you are 65% likely to achieve a goal if you commit to another person. And, your chances of success increase up to 95% when you commit to ongoing accountability appointments with your partner(s) to provide an update and check in on your progress.

65% of people

are likely to achieve a goal if they commit to another person

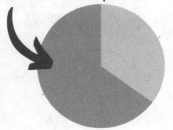

95% of people

are likely to achieve a goal if they meet regularly with accountability partner(s)

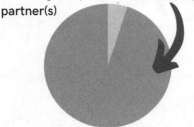

SOURCE: American Society of Training and Development

FIGURE 11.7 Study Chart

Similarly, a study from the Dominican University of California investigated various strategies for successfully realizing goals and measured the results. The findings provided empirical evidence for the effectiveness of three strategies: accountability, commitment, and writing down one's goals.

Commit to Action: Rather than simply writing down a goal, your team should *commit to an action*. Maybe complete a survey to guide you all through a thorough thought process on your goals and setting concrete *action commitments*. Make a commitment, on paper, to achieve the goal activity by activity.

Accountability to Peers: Your team should follow up concrete goal planning and action commitment by enlisting the team as a whole to hold each team member accountable. This will happen at your weekly team growth huddles. Your team members must write these commitments down and present them at the weekly huddle, making them more accountable. Those who bring their written action commitments to the group will accomplish significantly more than those who simply write down their commitments.

Regular Updates: Your team members must update the team on their progress toward reaching their goal on a weekly basis. This will keep everyone focused on their progress. The *positive effect of regular accountability* is supported. Teams that conduct weekly progress reports during their weekly growth huddles accomplish significantly more than teams that don't.

Implementing all three tactics yields the best results. Identifying and committing to specific activities is crucial, but regular and recurring accountability between two or more people is the key to long-term success.

It's fair to say then that public or shared accountability is all that's technically *necessary* for achieving a desired outcome. If a real estate team has a system of accountability between individuals, then its team members may very well perform their activities and hit their targets. So, technically, simply holding people accountable and making them answerable to each other could be enough to achieve your goal.

However, ideally we want people to be intrinsically motivated to do things out of a sense of personal pride and satisfaction, and not just because they're concerned about being called upon to explain themselves in front of others. Accountability is fantastic for getting things done, but it doesn't necessarily mean that your team members will have a *positive attitude* about getting things done.

Whereas accountability operates like a social contract or communal obligation, responsibility is a feeling of ownership, and when people take ownership of the tasks they perform, they look at activities with new eyes and begin to see solutions instead of problems.

When team leaders create a deep-seated culture of accountability, eventually the action of taking repeated responsibility transforms us into responsible people. While external and shared accountability will always be necessary and can never be done away with, in time your accountability sessions will produce automatic and unconscious behaviors where being responsible is simply *who we are.*

At the same time, you can't ever really know how someone feels inside, or whether someone is operating with a true sense of responsibility. Though their actions and their attitude will give you a good idea, emotions and attitudes are not something you can easily quantify. Accountability, on the other hand, *can* be quantified or measured when accountability is focused on each team member's activities.

From One Component to Another: Focus Accountability on Activities

Oftentimes, we find that as we move from component to component, it's easy to lose sight of what has come before and begin to view each component in isolation. However, team growth and success is a *synthesis* of each component where each informs and depends upon the other.

For example, in Part Two, we discussed how component 2 asks you to build upon lessons learned in component 1.

As you'll recall, component 1 transforms the personal motivations of all team members into a unified and concrete viral goal that is then broken down into yearly, quarterly, monthly, weekly, and daily milestones with related activities that tie into the real estate team's overall growth goal. Building upon those principles, component 2 requires teams to identify and capitalize on those activities that have the greatest impact and likelihood of helping the team in achieving its goal, and to set end results and outcomes aside somewhat and *focus on activities first*.

Similarly, component 3 asks you to build upon lessons learned in component 2. To do that, let's recall the Pareto Principle.

The Pareto Principle says that roughly 80% of the effects or results we see can be attributed to 20% of the causes. That is, the majority of your results will come from a relatively small concentration of efforts, so don't spend excessive amounts of time and energy on the 80% of tasks and activities that don't add much value.

FIGURE 11.8 Pareto Reminder

This is undeniably difficult, and it will require a concerted effort to recalibrate your focus and resist the temptation of endlessly fine-tuning the trivial and unimportant aspects of your team. Nonetheless, it's essential that you tackle only the most key issues and prioritize only the most effective activities.

When it comes to accountability, the reality is that you cannot monitor every little thing that happens within a real estate team. While we would hope that a person's sense of responsibility would extend to everything they do, and that all team members take pride and satisfaction in even the smallest aspects of their work or role, the fact is that you cannot – and should not – be held accountable to the 80% of tasks and activities that don't add much value.

Of course, the day-to-day show must go on, and these things will still need to be done, so we're in no way saying that they're unimportant, or that people can abdicate responsibility for the everyday operations on the team. However, it's both inefficient and counterproductive to hold people publicly and systematically accountable to the 80% activities whose impact on profitability and growth is negligible compared to other business-generation and growth-building activities.

When we talk about accountability, therefore, the intention is that you apply it specifically in relation to your growth goals and growth-building activities. For all their importance, ABIs are often neglected by real estate teams during their weekly or monthly meetings. Instead, most teams structure their meetings around day-to-day operational ideas, generic updates, crisis management, and putting out fires – in other words, running the team by default rather than by design. This approach bores people to tears and rightly gives meetings a bad name. More often than not, your team members are more focused on their cell phones than their goals.

There is a time and place for operational updates, but your accountability huddles are not that time and place. Select core ABIs and make those the focus of your accountability gatherings. Don't focus on the "trivial many" that only slightly impact growth; and don't focus on RBIs that are situated in the past and are outside your control. Shift your focus away from results and hold everyone accountable to the most impactful activities that will most likely lead to that result.

When all eyes are on the ABIs, weekly huddles will be more productive and your team will experience greater overall productivity, too. As you'll recall from the previous chapter, when it comes to your own "transaction timeline," the specific ABIs (and ABI methods) that you select and employ will differ slightly from team to team and from goal to goal, but for real estate teams, the most impactful activities are:

- **Attempted Contacts**, in which you reach out to your database contacts.
- **Contacts Made**, in which you have a conversation with one of your contacts and remind them that you are in real estate.
- **Follow-Up Contacts Made**, in which you do something to follow up with one of your contacts to come from contribution, deepen rapport, and/or nurture the relationship.

Whatever your team's particular ABIs are, it's crucial that everyone is held accountable to the most impactful and most effective activities. Focus your time and energy on those things that are most likely to drive growth and have the greatest impact on hitting your goals.

Weekly accountability huddles are not interrogations where each team member is evaluated based on their sense of personal responsibility. But, personal responsibility will nevertheless be a natural and eventual by-product or consequence of those accountability huddles.

In fact, the very format and structure of those accountability sessions will cultivate that sense of responsibility without explicitly discussing or trying to measure it in some way. While the only thing everyone is held accountable for is the performance of each team member's daily and weekly ABIs, the very act of conducting public accountability will cultivate a growing sense of personal responsibility that impacts everyone on a deeper level.

Up Next: The Questions to Ask

The four key accountability questions provide a framework for the practical implementation of accountability and responsibility in your real estate team. What's more, the questions are designed to promote personal responsibility, independence, and autonomy, while also encouraging collective, creative, and collaborative problem solving. We dive into the four key accountability questions in the next chapter.

CHAPTER 12

The Four Key Accountability Questions: Consistently Checking In with Everyone

We're officially at the midway point in our analysis of the five components of team growth. While the final two components have yet to be examined, and you're not quite ready to officially implement the process just yet, we hope you've been practicing component 3 for the past few weeks.

As you know, at the beginning of each book club, a leader or facilitator should take a moment to ask the group who has or hasn't read that week's chapter. When necessary – i.e., when someone has failed to read the chapter or didn't quite manage to finish it – individuals should be asked to explain themselves or to provide an account of their actions in the presence of their peers.

Now, perhaps the people on your team are a responsible, dependable bunch, and there has been no need to hold anyone accountable. But we'd wager that at least some of you have been asked to answer the four questions in Figure 12.1 (in fact, we'd bet that some of you could recite them with your eyes closed!).

When implementing the five components of team growth with our coaching clients and their teams, we generally find that accountability takes up quite a few minutes in the first book club session, and perhaps a bit of time at the second book club, too. However, after the first couple of book clubs, we notice that the accountability portion takes up little to no time at all, and the book club can proceed smoothly and productively.

Nobody wants to be *that* person who is unprepared to contribute to the conversation.

As we've said before, we all *have* responsibilities, but we *take* responsibility when we implement actions and systems to ensure that the things we will be held accountable for actually take place. Whether that's implementing a simple system where you read a few pages of the book every night before bed, or whether it's implementing a more detailed system for hitting your most impactful activity-based indicators (ABIs), public

1 How do you think you did?

2 What got in the way?

3 What do you need to do
   differently next time?

4 Is there any way we can help?

FIGURE 12.1 The Four Key Accountability Questions

accountability induces and endorses personal responsibility, and gives rise to an internal sense of ownership.

The four key accountability questions cultivate a growing sense of personal responsibility while holding all team members publicly accountable at the same time. Long after the Team Book Club has ended and you are taking tangible steps toward team growth, these very same accountability questions will continue to structure your weekly "growth huddles" (which we'll elaborate on in Part Five).

At each growth huddle, an accountability leader will ask those gathered to provide an "account" of their activities (or inactivity, as the case may be). For those who have hit their weekly ABI targets, the data on the dashboard will speak for itself. There is no need to hold those people accountable or ask them the four accountability questions, as they have clearly taken responsibility and achieved their daily and weekly goals.

When an individual has not met their ABI commitments, the accountability leader will not react negatively or punitively. In fact, they will refrain from comment, and simply run through the four key accountability questions.

These questions are designed to keep everyone at the meeting thinking and talking about the ABIs while eliminating irrelevant or unproductive discussion. Each question plays a particular part in cultivating both a sense of personal responsibility and of collective and collaborative accountability. The questions asked are designed to help team members through a process of self-discovery where everyone thinks for themselves, identifies their stumbling blocks, and authors their own solutions.

At the end of the process, individuals will have a clear picture of the problems and their roots and an even clearer picture of how to proceed. Their solutions will have come from within and be further strengthened by the support and feedback of an increasingly bonded team. When conducted correctly, accountability produces a harmonious state where people feel that they have personal control over their life and choices, while also knowing that you're all in this together.

Make It About Everyone (With One Exception)

As we've emphasized again and again, team growth is a coordinated *group effort*. You cannot do this alone, so it's important that all team members have ambitions for growth and are behind the team leader's goals 100%. The best way to do this is with a viral goal that *makes it about everyone.*

"*How do you think you did?*" cultivates personal responsibility by making it unequivocally about each team member.

The question: "How do *YOU* think *YOU* did?" puts the spotlight on their actions and nobody else's. It also privileges their perspective and allows team members an opportunity to express themselves in their own words.

Holding people accountable is not an occasion for either a team leader or for others to express their opinion on another person's activities. Collaborative problem solving will come later, but assessing and evaluating an individual's performance is not a collective affair. Nobody but the individual in question should be voicing a viewpoint or forming an evaluation of that team member's actions or inactions.

This may sound simple but, in fact, it is enormously difficult to simply listen without forming our own opinion or articulating a reproach or counterperspective. Yet, regardless of what you hear in response to the first few questions, neither the team leader of the accountability session nor the other team members present should respond.

Certainly, you should not respond in frustration or ridicule; but, interestingly, studies show that we should also be mindful about responding with praise, or at least consider the *type* of praise that we express.

When a team member is doing a great job performing their daily activities and hitting their weekly targets, in the long run it may be better to *praise the process, not the person.* This may sound contradictory. After all, we've repeatedly emphasized that you must "make it about them" and cultivate a sense of internal, personal responsibility in your team members.

Praise the _process_
not the person.

FIGURE 12.2   Praise the Process

However, in a Reed College study, results showed that receiving "person praise" versus "process praise" might *decrease* an individual's motivation. When researchers set out to gauge the effect that certain types of praise have on our motivation, they assigned 111 college students to one of three groups:

- **Person praise**: Feedback was related personally to the individual.
- **Process praise**: Feedback was related to the method or particular strategy taken.
- **No praise**: No feedback was given either way.

These results led researchers to infer that "all age groups beyond preschool appear to be more positively affected by *process praise* than person praise after encountering failure."

While it's reasonable to praise a team member for their successes, if we overly personalize the praise and make the success about their natural abilities or innate identity, they might feel wonderful in the moment, but personal praise may backfire when they encounter failure. They may think that they are fundamentally flawed, or that their lack of success was unavoidable or inevitable because of who they are as a person.

So, for example, when a team member hits their targets one week, and everyone responds with "Wow, you're so amazing!" but then that same person fails to hit their targets the next week, that setback could negatively impact their motivation to achieve their goal because both success and failure are too closely linked to their sense of self-worth. It's more helpful if team leaders respond with praise focused on the *process*, such as, "That's awesome that you practice your scripts with a partner before making your morning calls," or "I love how you block out the first two hours of your day for your most impactful ABIs."

While it's important to make it about them, and we encourage you to encourage each other, it's equally important to focus on activities first and foremost. By praising the process and not the person, we encourage team members to center their focus on activities and remind them that there is always something actionable they can do despite how they're feeling in the moment. Likewise, by concentrating on the process and activities, we create a space in which team members feel safe to discuss their struggles and accept responsibility for their failings without feeling like a failure. Accountability neither judges nor indulges excuses and, when conducted correctly, accountability creates a space in which people can have the courage to be open and honest about what got in their way.

Resource   Goal and Milestone Tracker

In the online resource appendix of this book, you will find our Goal and Milestone Tracker, as well as our Goal and Milestones Overview. The Goal and Milestones Overview provides you with an example of how to use the Tracker. You'll find both of these resources following this page for your reference. This Goal and Milestone Tracker is a fillable PDF that provides a structure for creating and tracking goals and milestones. The milestone breakdown will help keep you accountable for what you need to do to reach your goals.

All resources can be downloaded from this book's online appendix at therealestatetrainer.com/ teambook.

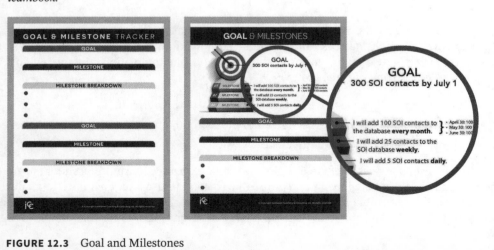

FIGURE 12.3   Goal and Milestones

No Excuses: Take Responsibility for Your Own Success

Being responsible is more than simply doing what you are told or acting upon external motivators. Responsibility is intricately linked to personal integrity. Honesty, humility, courage, and self-reflection are all characteristics of a responsible person, and the first two accountability questions are designed to both gauge and to cultivate a sense of personal responsibility.

Holding all team members accountable, asking them "How do you think you did?" and "What got in the way?" allows the team to see things from their perspective instead, and it also presents that person with a choice:

- Do they *take responsibility*, examine themselves honestly, and answer truthfully?
- Or, do they *avoid responsibility* by making excuses, responding with self-pity, or exaggerating their achievements when the data clearly tells a different story?

Excuses are a common psychological method of shifting causal attribution away from oneself (it's not my fault) and protecting our self-image (I'm not the type of person who would would . . .) when faced with negative feedback, or even the *possibility* of negative feedback.

Some excuses are more socially legitimate than others, and people will employ a range of excuses to see what they can get away with in certain situations.

Excuses that don't work, or that tend to make others feel irritated, frustrated, and less respecting of us, are:

INTERNAL → "I didn't hear you say that."

CONTROLLABLE → "I ran out of time."

INTENTIONAL → "I didn't feel like doing it,
so I did something else instead."

FIGURE 12.4 Excuses That Don't Work

Excuses that often work – in the sense that they make people feel like they want to give us a pass – are listed in Figure 12.5.

A person's particular answers to the first and second accountability questions ("How do you think you did?" and "What got in the way?") will indicate their level of personal responsibility and allow an accountability leader to gauge where certain people are at in terms of owning their choices and getting on board with the accountability process.

EXTERNAL ⟶ "My mother has arthritis and can't drive to
work, which is making me late every day."

UNCONTROLLABLE ⟶ "A winter storm knocked out
the power across the city."

UNINTENTIONAL ⟶ "I'm new to the city and I got on
the wrong train by mistake."

FIGURE 12.5   Excuses That Often Work

Again, though, the accountability leader's job isn't to confront people or evaluate their explanations or excuses. This isn't about giving people a pass based on the type of excuse they use. In almost all cases, an accountability leader should simply listen to the answers and allow people to make their own connections and come to their own realizations. On occasion, you may need to probe a little and ask additional questions that get to the heart of what's happening, but the goal is not to answer, evaluate, embarrass, or punish. Rather, the purpose of the accountability questions is to prompt team members into making connections about the type of language they're using and the pattern of their excuses.

For example, in the case of the person whose mother has arthritis and relies on a ride to work each morning, that person (who is not only your team member but perhaps a close friend) is undoubtedly experiencing a stressful and upsetting situation, and is deserving of your support and empathy. It's understandable that someone might be late for work one morning, but when something is making us late every day then an inexcusable pattern is emerging and, clearly, an alternative solution must be found.

We all have personal lives and responsibilities to take care of outside of the team, but life is also full of choices. Though sometimes challenging and often tricky, there is always something we can do to prioritize our goals and fulfill our competing commitments. If extenuating circumstances make it that a team member cannot get to work by 9 a.m., does that really mean that they cannot commit to performing their daily growth activities and hitting their weekly targets? Is that the real issue here, or is there something else that's holding them back?

When holding team members accountable, there's no need to be unsympathetic, but neither should you accept any victim language, or let people repeatedly off the hook for the same excuse. It's also crucial that accountability leaders are consistent with how they conduct accountability huddles. Tolerating an excuse one week and then lashing out about the same excuse the next week sends mixed messages about what's acceptable and unacceptable. The point is not to determine the legitimacy of the excuse, or judge whether it's a "good" or "bad" reason, but to eliminate blame and excuses all together.

On the other side, team members must be open to being held accountable. It's essential to come into the meeting with an open and honest mind-set. Team members may not feel that they are making excuses, but the line of questioning from the leader may open their eyes to issues under the surface. Remember, it is mutually beneficial to go through this process for both the leader and the team members. These dialogues are a two-way street and the more openly you approach the four key accountability questions, the better they will serve you as a team member.

TEAM LEADER	TEAM MEMBER
• be consistent in accountability huddles • be sympathetic but do not accept victim language • the goal is not to answer, evaluate, embarrass, or punish • prompt team members to make connections	• be open to being held accountable • answer questions honestly and avoid internal, controllable, and intentional excuses • make connections • recognize obstacles • learn and grow

FIGURE 12.6 Accountability Mind-Set

Of course, one could argue that you could eliminate the opportunity for excuses altogether by not asking the question "What got in the way?" in the first place. That way, team members wouldn't have a chance to offer any excuse at all. However, this question allows people to make connections about the type of language they're using, identify patterns of behavior, and recognize recurring obstacles. The point is not to censor or close our ears to excuses, but acknowledge and overcome them. Resist the temptation of identifying other people's thought processes or patterns of behaviors and allow them to reflect and self-identify whatever the challenge might be.

Oftentimes, team members who make excuses are hiding the true source of what's getting in their way. So many of us are constrained and hold back by limiting beliefs and fears that cause us to procrastinate and avoid doing what we need or want to do. We convince ourselves that we don't have the skills or ability to even *attempt* to do something. We believe that what happened in the past is what will happen in the future. As time goes on, we don't even try.

At the same time, an accountability leader is not a psychologist, and an accountability huddle is in no way a therapy session. However, it's important that accountability leaders recognize that strong emotional forces motivate our excuse making, and that responsibility and positive self-esteem are crucial in reducing the psychological pressure to make excuses in the first place.

The four key accountability questions are open-ended and reflective in nature by design. Just like a therapist or a good coach, the accountability leader is asking the questions. The team member is doing the important work of looking within themselves for honest answers. At every growth huddle, the accountability leader will ask these four questions the same way each time. Before long, everyone will have memorized the questions, and can use these inquiries to "self-coach" and guide their way through their working week with honesty, integrity, introspection, and courage.

Excuses may make us feel better or justified in the moment, but they don't change anything. Each of us can make the choice to more honestly and authentically engage in our lives by taking responsibility for our moment-to-moment decisions. Honesty means being willing to consider that there are things we need to improve upon or to change completely. In the same way that we praise the process and not the person, accountability focuses our energies on honest answers and solutions – not excuses.

Up Next: Are You in the Right Head Space?

Eliminating the use of blame applies to the accountability leader also. Don't spend your time and energy reprimanding team members for the excuse they've made, as this, too, centers your focus on a past over which you have no control. The leader must model the type of behavior they wish to exemplify and turn their attention to what the team member can do differently next time. Blame is external and keeps us stuck in the past. Responsibility is future-oriented and based on an internal locus of control – which we dive into in the next chapter.

CHAPTER 13

Make Sure You're in the Right Head Space: Cultivating an Internal Locus of Control

D o you feel like you're driving the car in your life, or are you just a passenger along for the ride? Your answer to that question is a good indicator of your *locus of control*. Locus of control is a clinical term used to define whether you believe that the things that happen in your life are largely within your control or mostly controlled by outside forces.

Internal versus External Locus of Control

While psychologists broadly categorize people as having either an internal or external locus of control, it's rarely one or the other in reality and more like a spectrum that indicates your leaning toward certain beliefs and types of behaviors.

An internal locus of control is the belief that you have the ability to consciously choose and control your destiny. An external locus of control is the belief that others control your destiny, and that your choices and actions don't make a difference.

From devising specific, achievable, and time-bound goals, to identifying influence-able activity-based indicators (ABIs), to cultivating personal responsibility, team growth is deeply dependent on measuring and focusing on that which we can control. The purpose of accountability is to cultivate an internal locus of control across the board on your real estate team and help everyone overcome the defeatism that comes with an external locus of control.

INTERNAL LOCUS OF CONTROL

- attribute success to their own efforts and actions
- believe that they have the ability to consciously choose and control their destiny
- more achievement-oriented, more successful
- take responsibility for events that happen to them
- learn from their mistakes
- take action to improve their situation

EXTERNAL LOCUS OF CONTROL

- attribute success to luck or chance
- believe that others control their destiny; their choices and actions don't make a difference
- believe that things happen "to" them
- make excuses and blame other people
- give up faster when obstacles arise
- feel anxious and helpless

FIGURE 13.1 Locus of Control

Think back for a moment to what we talked about at the beginning of Part Two, component 2 of team growth. Remember, if you focus on the activities, you can control your results. This brings up an important philosophy that team leaders must adopt: "Run your business by design, not by default." If you run your business by design, you are utilizing an internal locus of control. You are designing your business to focus on the ABIs instead of the results-based indicators (RBIs). ABIs are something that you do have control over. If instead you run your business by default, you are utilizing an external locus of control, leaving your results up to all of the external factors at play. You are not looking at your ABIs, but instead your focus is external, on your RBIs.

Psychological studies have found that people with a more *internal* locus of control tend to be more achievement-oriented, more successful, and get better-paying jobs. People with a more internal locus of control tend to take responsibility for events that happen to them (both good and bad), learn from their mistakes, and take action to improve their situation.

People with an internal locus of control use words like:

- Adapt
- Choose
- Control
- Decide
- Determine
- Influence
- Learn
- Persevere
- Resolve
- Responsibility

People with an internal locus of control are open to modifying their behavior and adjusting their strategies. They don't view failure as a sign that they are fundamentally flawed or incapable. Rather they understand that success is a process that they can control by taking ownership of their experience.

Asking all team members "What do you need to do differently next time?" makes it about each team member – what do YOU need to do – and asks individuals to take responsibility for solving their own problems, self-authoring solutions, and deciding their next course of action.

The word "differently" implies that you can't use the same excuse and solution twice. If you fail a second time, you'll need to try something new. When asking this question it's important that you place special emphasis on the word "differently." This prevents team members from having an easy out and simply saying, "I'll just keep trying." When we "just keep trying," our focus is centered on old actions that don't work. Your team should shift their focus toward taking *different* actions in the future.

For example, in the case of the person who is frequently late to their job because their mother has arthritis and needs to be driven to her job beforehand, that person might tell you that they will ask another family member to help three days a week, inquire into carpooling possibilities, or adjust their work schedule so that they stay on course with hitting their ABIs. It may take some time for the best solution to materialize and that's fine. Change is a process, and there is always a next time as long as we take ownership and are willing to adjust our approach and try another way when the existing way isn't working.

Authoring our own solutions benefits *everyone*.

FIGURE 13.2 Authoring Solutions

Authoring our own solutions benefits everybody. We come up with something that genuinely works for us, and team leaders don't have to dictate solutions that may not be compatible with that team member's lived experience. When team leaders dictate solutions, people don't have to think for themselves. External accountability is important and necessary, but it's equally important that team members go back to their desks with a sense of ownership and autonomy about how they'll do things differently next time. Everyone will be held accountable. But only each team member themselves can perform the activity. The more that team members develop an internal locus of control, the more everyone will buy into the team's goals and feel personally invested and involved in growth. At the same time, balance is key and the aim is not to completely eradicate our dependence on the outside world.

While there are few benefits to having a purely external locus of control, these people are more easily able to "let go" and move on from situations that they genuinely have no control over. People with a strong internal locus of control often take on responsibility for everything, even those things outside their power to influence. When something bad happens, they can find it difficult to let go, and may waste time trying to fix or fine-tune every little thing, even things that matter very little. People with a strong internal locus of control may put undue energy into the 80% that doesn't impact growth or find it difficult to detach from their focus on uncontrollable results.

The key, of course, is to balance our internal and external locus of control and develop an ability to rationally identify the things that legitimately are or are not within our power to change or affect. Real estate teams that focus on ABIs over RBIs instill and reinforce an internal locus of control by continuously emphasizing activities and strategies that everyone can actively do something about.

Another advantage for those with a more external locus of control is that these team members are often good team players who are open to collaboration and outside input. Again, balance is the key. While we don't want to be completely dependent on others to

Resource   Year-to-Date Check-Up Form

In the online resource appendix of this book, you will find our Year-to-Date Check-Up Form. This fillable PDF is a great way to balance your locus of control because it helps you track your current numbers throughout the year, and then points you to your sources of leads. Knowing where your leads come from will demonstrate that most of what you do as a real estate agent relies on what you do every day in the form of activities. How are you reaching out to your sphere of influence (SOI)? Are you generating leads from Expired Listings? These lead sources are within your control. Most of your business comes from the activities you consciously perform.

All resources can be downloaded from this book's online appendix at therealestatetrainer.com/ teambook.

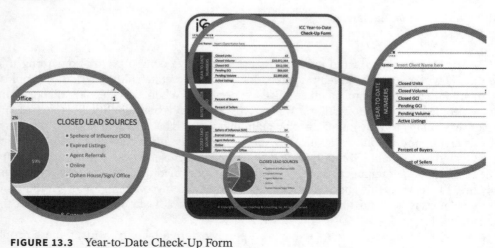

FIGURE 13.3   Year-to-Date Check-Up Form

solve our problems, we also don't want to be independent to the point of pushing others away or believing that our approach is the best and only way to do things.

When conducted correctly, using the four key accountability questions, accountability huddles create a positive, welcoming, and *interdependent* environment where everyone is in this together. Asking your team members, "What do you need to do differently next time?" fosters a sense of ownership, internal control, and self-authoring solutions. Asking your team members, "Is there any way we can help?" opens the door for collaboration and mutually beneficial participation.

Accountability Cultivates Mutually Beneficial Responsibility

Let's take a moment to reflect on the virus analogy that we first talked about at the beginning of this book. The underlying attributes that make viruses so successful in the natural world are exactly the attributes that can be harnessed to effect rapid, widespread, and lasting positive change within your real estate team, including changing the way that team members perceive accountability.

Like old-fashioned punitive approaches to accountability, there's a good reason for why viruses get a bad rap. However, as we've discussed before, many viruses are quite harmless and some provide us with significant physical benefits. This latter group are called symbionts, which comes from the word symbiosis, a biological term for a relationship or partnership based on *mutual benefit*. This advantageous collaboration has helped living creatures innovate, adapt, and expand into new niches for millennia.

Accountability is similar. A real estate team's strength is to a large degree derived from the quality of the relationship between its leader and its team members. Perhaps it's a stretch, but a functional, effective relationship between a team and its people is not unlike a mutually beneficial arrangement between a flower and a bee where each stands to benefit and each relies on the other to accomplish the goal.

Successful real estate teams are organizations where individuals take ownership, act responsibly, and hold themselves and others accountable in the interest of reaching a mutually beneficial goal.

Responsibility means taking personal ownership and operating from an internal locus of control, but accountability – true accountability – occurs when team members feel that they are a part of something bigger than themselves, and have an opportunity to make a difference in other people's lives as well as their own.

Accountability emphasizes shared goals, activities, and measures that matter for the betterment of the team. When everyone realizes that their activities and choices do not exist in a vacuum, and when everyone understands and appreciates the role and efforts of everyone on the team, they encourage each other to fulfill their part so that overall goals are met.

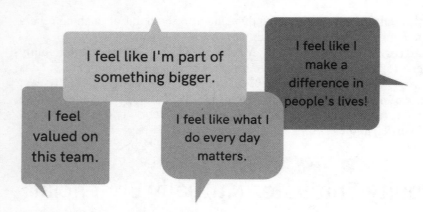

FIGURE 13.4 Ownership

It will take time for a team to build relationships and rapport and become a cohesive, collaborative unit. When properly executed, accountability causes real estate agents on a team to turn *toward* each other, rather than turning *on* each other and playing the blame game. Being honest with oneself means being open to constructive comments, alternative approaches, and substitute strategies. When approached respectfully and supportively, accountability huddles don't make it personal, and people don't take it personally when they need help. Rather, everyone understands that no man is an island, and everyone is reliant on each other to hit their ABI targets and reach the overall goal.

Everyone should listen with an open mind and remember that everyone's experience and perspective is valid.

At the same time, it's important to set the boundaries of discussion. As we previously mentioned, accountability huddles are relatively quick meetings and multiple team members may be answering the four key accountability questions. We spend Part Five of this book diving deeper on this topic. Remember that accountability is squarely focused on your team's chosen ABIs, which are measurable and within your power to influence. Focusing on ABIs ensures that any ideas and comments relate specifically to the activities, goals, and objectives in question. When conducted correctly, accountability huddles discourage negativity and promote a positive environment with the best data, information, and resources.

Collaboration and creative solutions will cause people to embrace responsibility. After an encouraging, inspiring, and imaginative accountability session, they'll return to their role with a sense of enthusiasm about putting their ideas into action. What's more, they will move through each minute of their day with a sense of ownership and control over their actions and perhaps, even, their destiny.

Case Study

Team Tami, Los Angeles, California

Team Tami is a husband and wife team, led by Chad Aronson and Tami Humphrey. They close well over $50 million in sales volume per year as the number one real estate team in the Playa Vista community of West Los Angeles near Marina Del Rey. They have been Icenhower Coaching and Consulting (ICC) clients for many years now.

When Chad and Tami started coaching with ICC, they soon started to hold weekly huddles, created a dashboard (which we will begin to do in Part Four), and began holding all team members accountable to their ABIs. Immediately, it became apparent that there were certain agents on the team that resisted this new level of increased accountability.

When most team leaders begin to implement the five components of growth on their team, the biggest fear is that agents will resist accountability and that it will destroy the team. Team leaders worry that everyone will leave because they don't want to be held accountable to doing the tough activities that everyone knows they need to do in order to get the results they want. This process is so tough because it exposes real estate agents who fake it . . . and a lot of agents fake it. They fake that they are working their sphere of influence (SOI). They fake that they are building and growing their database. They fake that they are doing all the activities. Not only do they fake out their peers, but they always end up faking themselves out, too! Without accountability, no one is checking in on them.

Accountability to the ABIs will expose team members who are motivated to do the tough activities to reach their goals. These are the people who want to ensure that they reach their goals. Ultimately, they are willing to put in the hard work to get what they want in life. The process of instituting accountability can be very revealing on a real estate team.

Expose Team Members Who Don't Want Accountability

Team Tami initially had some team members who did not want to be held accountable. The process of going through the five components of team growth exposed these team members. Of course, these agents wanted to join Team Tami because they wanted to be associated with the number one team in Playa Vista. They struggled along as solo agents prior to joining the team, and had been in the industry for quite some time. They experienced reasonable success, but they were relatively low producers and they needed to earn more income and wanted to succeed at a higher level. So, they joined Team Tami with the hopes that they would grow their business.

On a team, every team member has to do their part. The team will meet them halfway. Agents can't expect to just join a team and receive all the business they need to be successful without putting out effort themselves. Agents are expected to consistently perform certain activities to grow their own spheres of influence SOIs, regularly contact and stay in front of their SOI, conduct lead follow-up, and complete any number of other potential lead-generation activities. Each activity is tracked on the dashboard. When that happens, it exposes agents that are unwilling to be held accountable to doing those activities. They begin to show they aren't willing to do their part. Not only is this unwillingness exposed to the team leader, but more importantly it exposes it to the agents themselves. True behavioral change comes from this type of self-realization and self-awareness.

Remember, a team provides three fundamental benefits to its agents: leads, administrative support, and accountability. Agents must do their part to both generate leads and convert the leads provided to them. Teams can't hand out commission checks without any work. True team players are willing to do their part.

When Team Tami instituted the five components of growth, including accountability, with their team of agents, a minority of the agents resisted and became negative. Some even left the team because it wasn't the right "fit" for them. Team Tami went on to bring on a series of new agents who are now some of the highest-producing agents in their Multiple Listing Service (MLS).

Because Team Tami already had the five components of growth in progress and could present them to their new hires up front, Team Tami set expectations immediately. The team dashboard was used from day one and the new agents knew they were going to be held accountable. Team Tami met each week and kept track of ABIs and held team members accountable.

True talent recognizes and is not afraid of accountability. True talent embraces accountability and knows it is the pathway to success. Good team members who are willing to do their part will not hide from using systems that are put in place to keep them accountable.

Low-producing agents who are not willing to put in the work will run from accountability and the systems that promote accountability. During a recruiting appointment, a potential recruit will say that it's just not a good "fit" for them. If recruits won't commit to performing the activities required to hit their goals up front, this might be a good indicator that the recruits are not committed to becoming successful agents.

The Matching Standard

This is where one of the most essential components of an effective dashboard comes into play. We call it the "Matching Standard" for lead distribution. It's the most important results-based indicator (RBI) that you will show on your dashboard. It's there to evidence that agents on a team need to meet the team halfway. Team members must strive to generate and bring as many transactions to the team (agent-generated leads) as the team generates and provides to the agents (team-generated leads). You'll see that teams typically stay well ahead of their agents with regard to the Matching Standard, and that's ok. It's relatively rare that team members can keep up with the amount of team-generated leads provided to them.

The Matching Standard is what many ICC coaches refer to as their "secret sauce" that foundationally holds teams together. By showing agent-generated leads and team-generated leads each week on your dashboard, everyone on the team can be reminded of the benefits of being a part of the team while being motivated to do their part in helping the team reach its goals. This image shown below illustrates how the matching standard might look when displayed on a team dashboard.

Closed YTD			
	Total	**Agent Generated**	**Team Generated**
Robyn	35	26	9
Melissa	25	10	15
Kari	17	7	10
Logan	6	0	6
Jessica	8	1	7
TOTAL	**91**	**44**	**47**

FIGURE 13.5   Matching Standard on Dashboard

Most agents tend to think that just because they close a transaction or convert a lead that was given to them that they actually generated the lead. That's not true. There's a big difference between lead generation and lead conversion. Many agents can convert leads, but very few can actually do the activities to generate leads. This is where the pain comes into the real estate agent's world. Few agents are willing to go through the pain and put in the time and do the tough activities to generate enough leads. Team leaders do this, and they've put in the time and the money to generate leads for their team. They have overflow business to provide to the other agents on their team. The Matching Standard evidences that.

When Team Tami put the Matching Standard in place with this new series of agents, the new team members had an epiphany. Despite the fact that they might be on a lower commission split than they would be if they were a solo agent, the team-generated business more than doubles their income. They are getting double the leads, or more, compared to what they could generate on their own. They see and understand that they are making a lot more income because of the Matching Standard.

This is a big reason why ICC represents the majority of the top-producing agents and teams in North America and why our agents have such a high increase in production year over year. They can grow so quickly year in and year out – and it's all because ICC has teams quickly put the Matching Standard in place.

Team Tami saw the difference immediately. Team members bought in on the idea because it helped them see how much business the team was giving them and also motivated them to "match" that amount with their own lead generation. They understood the need for them to build their own SOIs. The agents also felt like the matching standard put them in charge of their own lead distribution. To receive more leads from the team, agents simply need to generate more leads themselves. It's a very simple and fair system this way. Team leaders that use the matching standard rarely have to deal with team cultural issues about who got what leads and why since it's all based on performance. In fact, the Matching Standard actually holds team leaders accountable to distributing leads in a fair way to the agents that deserve them!

Agents who don't understand the importance of building a book of business through their SOI database may say that they'd rather run around and chase leads of people who want to buy or sell now versus playing the long game of a referral-based business. Of course, there are a lot of ways to generate business, and we teach all of them here at ICC. Open houses, online leads, circle prospecting – these are all great methods for generating leads from people you don't already know. That said, these methods should never be an agent's primary way of generating business. Your SOI business should always be front and center and the core of your business. Team Tami has instilled this value in their team members.

All of Team Tami's agents are contributing to the team and they are building their own databases so they're not totally dependent on leads from the team. Some team leaders reading this may think they don't have enough leads to go around to provide that Matching Standard to their team members. Almost all of the teams we work with at ICC are able to stay well ahead on the Matching Standard. Understand that there is wiggle room and that it won't always be perfectly matched. If two-thirds of an agent's closings come from the team and only one-third comes from the agent, that's pretty normal, and that's good. Team leaders (and team members) should not obsess about requiring agents to evenly match them. Instead team leaders should treat the fact that their team-generated closings are higher than agent-generated closings as a positive thing, and that the agents still have some more work to do and goals to achieve. Leaders should never come down hard on team members for not generating enough agent-generated closings to keep up with their team-generated closings.

The Matching Standard also reminds team members that they are getting the majority of their business from the team. So if agents want more income, or even just more leads, the Matching Standard helps to refocus their concerns on their own performance.

The Matching Standard versus "Better Commission Split"

Additionally, if team members were ever to have thoughts about leaving the team, they will realize, because they are kept up to date on the dashboard from the agent- versus team-generated leads, that it would not make sense to leave. For example, suppose an agent closes 30 transactions in a year, with 10 agent-generated closings and 20 team-generated closings. If this agent were to leave the team, a quick look at the Matching Standard section of the team's dashboard would help her quickly realize that she would be giving up two-thirds or 67% of her annual income to do so!

It doesn't matter what commission split some other team or brokerage promises. When you lose two-thirds of your business, that's a lot of income to make up with a relatively insignificant commission split change. Over the years, we've seen agents leave teams and lose the vast majority of their income because they wanted a better commission split. Agents are naturally very commission-split sensitive, as we talked about in great detail in Chapter 5. An agent may leave a team just because they are having a bad week or a bad year. Often they'll say they are leaving to get a better split. They don't realize, often because they don't get to see the Matching Standard every week on the dashboard, that they are going to lose the majority of their business income by leaving! So not only does the Matching Standard hold everyone accountable, but it also provides a better understanding of where everyone's business is coming from.

No matter what the split increase may be . . . it isn't likely going to move the needle much at all. Leaving a team that uses the Matching Standard requires surrendering most of your business to do so. The blame here goes to the team leader for not keeping the Matching Standard in clear view in weekly team huddles on a team's dashboard. If the team leader does not display it on the dashboard each week, the team members will not know it. Team members will mistakenly think they generate all of their own business because they aren't regularly reminded of the difference between team lead generation versus conversion.

This is one of the most important concepts to understand in real estate. You must know the difference between lead generation (how to create a lead) and lead conversion (how to convert and close a lead). It's also the reason that agents waste so much time trying to be good at servicing business (the 80% activities) and spend relatively little time learning how to generate business (the 20% activities). Team leaders should always emphasize the importance of lead generation, and the Matching Standard helps do just that.

According to the National Association of Realtors, approximately 33% of solo real estate agents fail in the first year and don't make it to a second year. Of the agents that make it past that first year, 87% don't make it five years in the business. Those are drastic failure numbers for solo agents. By contrast, agents have a much higher chance at succeeding on a real estate team.

ICC works with many of the highest-producing real estate agents, teams, and brokerages in North America. Consequently, we have learned that agents who join teams have a success rate that's approximately 10 times higher on average than solo agents who do not join teams. We have also found that agents who joined teams typically succeeded at much higher levels because they were provided with administrative support, leads, and they had the accountability to build their SOI databases.

In recent years, if you look at any MLS in any community across North America, you'll see that typically 50% of all licensed agents have not sold one transaction in the last year. And only about 10% of the total population on the MLS does about 90% of the business in any given year. The vast majority of agents fail.

This shift to a 90/10 ratio occurred with the advent of real estate teams. We have seen real estate teams take over. The ratio was much closer to 70/30 before real estate teams widened the success gap over the past few decades.

Together We Can Achieve More

Some of you may be thinking "But maybe those agents *can* make it on their own!" It is possible for an agent to leave their team and be successful on their own. However, the odds of success are much lower. The saying, "Together we can achieve more," has never been more true with regard to real estate. Real estate teams have emerged as the true power players within the real estate industry.

These days, the agents on Team Tami are all building their SOI, hosting a plethora of successful client and community events, and are still dominating their local market as the #1 team in their area. Like a swarm of bees, Team Tami's agents are constantly making contacts, inviting all of their own SOI databases to their team's events, farming neighborhoods, holding open houses, etc. Team members benefit from the mindshare they gain from being a part of Team Tami's success. In the eyes of the public, being a team member on Team Tami equates with success, experience, and a sense of community. Even the new agents enjoy respect and admiration, simply because they are associated with Team Tami.

Team Tami's agents are hungry for success, and they show up each day feeling motivated to do more. They are all succeeding at such high levels, they are all bringing business to the team, they are all building their own SOIs, and they're also doing a great job of converting the leads provided to them by Team Tami. When you have all that success and everybody embraces accountability, the production-centric culture of the team will soar.

Of course, Team Tami did have challenges to face to get to the place they are in now. That is a natural result of working to implement the five components of team growth that we discuss in this book. Some agents will show up and realize that they don't want to do the work. Some agents will step up and realize they weren't doing the work before, and they will begin to do what they need to do. Some agents will embrace the accountability and move forward. The majority of team members will appreciate these changes, as hard as they may be, because they will make the correct choice to see accountability as a benefit – one of the most important benefits that a team provides to its agents. Team Tami discovered these truths quickly, and that's why their production has increased so dramatically year over year, and their culture continues to improve right along with it.

Next Steps

In Part Four, we turn our attention to the fourth component of team growth: Powerful Team Tools to Drive Growth.

As before, if you're reading this book as a leader of your real estate team, we advise you to continue reading each chapter from start to finish.

However, if you're reading this book as a team member, then your next step is to get ready to attend the third of your five book club sessions. The following section helps you prepare and gives you a sense of what to expect. When the first book club is over, you can then pick up where you left off and continue on to Part Four.

The Team Book Club: Part Three Discussion Guide

Remember that the purpose of the first five book club meetings is *not* to come to a particular conclusion or decide on what your team's overall growth goal or activity-based indicators (ABIs) will be. No doubt you have some ideas and are excited to get started. However, with one notable and hopefully obvious exception, it is not yet time to officially begin implementing the various components of growth.

Hold Each Other Accountable

That exception, of course, is component 3. It's never too early to cultivate personal responsibility or public accountability, so once again you will begin this week's book club by asking the group who did and didn't read Part Three. And, if necessary, book club facilitators should ask the four key accountability questions to anyone who did not manage to complete this week's chapter reading (see Figure BC.1).

Don't become overly distracted or derailed by those who haven't prepared in advance. Keep the accountability section to a minimum and keep your sight on the real purpose and subject of the book club meeting.

Distributing a Part Three summary will help refresh people's memories, or help any nonreaders get up to speed so that they can't opt out of participation. Book club facilitators can use the summary to guide the conversation in addition to, or instead of, the sample questions provided. As you read through each bullet point in the summary, ask each team member, "Did this point resonate with you?" "How?" "Why?" "Tell me more," and so forth.

1 How do you think you did?

2 What got in the way?

3 What do you need to do
differently next time?

4 Is there any way we can help?

FIGURE BC.1   Key Accountability Questions

Part Three Summary, Component 3   Cultivate Personal Responsibility Through Public Accountability

Component 3 cultivates personal responsibility by practicing public accountability. In doing so, real estate teams create a culture in which each team member feels personally responsible for their part in achieving the goal and is also held openly accountable for performing their activities and hitting their targets. When team members are instilled with a sense of personal responsibility – and when team leaders conduct respectful and responsible accountability gatherings – they will not resist or have reason to fear being held accountable. Rather they will embrace it enthusiastically with a sense of ownership, purpose, pride, and a concern for others as well as respect for themselves.

Key Points:

- Responsibility is internal; accountability is external. Being responsible involves implementing a response to designated tasks and activities. Being accountable involves providing an account or an answer of what did and did not actually happen at the time, or by the time, it was supposed to. Accountability is external, while responsibility is internal. Responsibility is a personal obligation one takes upon oneself and stems from a sense of intrinsic motivation, whereas accountability is more of a social contract or social obligation.
- Both accountability and responsibility produce action and results-oriented behavior but in different ways. When we take responsibility and act responsibly, we create or control a situation by causing something to happen. When we're held accountable for our actions, we reflect upon the efficacy and actual outcomes of those actions and address any problems with a view to doing things better or differently the next time.
- Focus accountability on activities. You can't monitor everything that happens within your real estate team. Select the core ABIs for your team and make those the focus of the four key accountability questions. Don't focus on the "trivial many" that only slightly impact growth; and don't focus on results-based indicators (RBIs) that are situated in the past and are outside your control. Shift your focus and hold your team members accountable to the most impactful activities.

(continued)

Part Three Summary, Component 3   (*continued*)

Notes:

_____

_____

_____

_____

Questions to Spark and Stoke Conversation

The following questions are simply a starting point for sparking conversation and ensuring that everyone participates. Leaders and book club facilitators are free to create questions of their own, and we highly encourage you to do so now that you're a bit more practiced in guiding your real estate team's book club.

Book Club Conversations for Component 3   Cultivate Personal Responsibility Through Public Accountability

- What ideas was the author trying to get across in Part Three?
- How do the ideas presented apply to us at _____ (insert the name of your real estate team)?
- How would you characterize our team's system of holding people accountable? Are we more authoritarian and punitive, or do we encourage people to self-author their solutions, cultivate personal responsibility, and encourage supportive and creative collaboration?
- What are some of the differences between accountability and responsibility?
- What was your attitude toward accountability before reading Part Three?
- Has your attitude or perspective changed after reading Part Three? If so, in what way?
- What is the difference between someone with an internal locus of control and someone with an external locus of control?
- If our locus of control falls on a spectrum, where would you place yourself? In other words, do you have a strong internal locus of control or is your locus of control more external?
- What new things did you learn in Part Three?
- What questions do you still have?
- Are there any quotes, passages, or ideas you found particularly compelling?
- Do you have a new perspective as a result of reading Part Three?
- Did you learn something you didn't know before?
- How has your attitude or behavior changed?
- How does Part Three relate to your role or experiences on our team?

(*continued*)

Book Club Conversations for Component 3 *(continued)*

- Did you connect with the subject matter? Did it make you nervous or excited?
- What did you like best about Part Three?
- What did you like least about Part Three?
- Which concept(s) presented in Part Three stood out to you?
- If you had the chance to ask the author one question, right now, what would it be?

No matter what questions you decide to ask team members, at the end of each book club session, you (or each book club's leader/facilitator) should ask yourself the following questions:

- Does everyone understand the materials?
- Have we discussed ways that the material relates to us?
- Are my people excited and engaged? Is there buy-in?
- Did we make the concept of accountability and responsibility *about everyone*?

If the answer to these questions is a resounding "Yes" then you are well on your way to devising a viral goal at your real estate team, identifying the activities that are most likely to drive growth and achieve success, and cultivating a sense of personal responsibility among all team members by ensuring public accountable.

PART 4

Powerful Team Tools to Drive Growth

CHAPTER 14

How a Team Dashboard Will Help You Drive Growth, Provide Focus, and Onboard New Agents

At the beginning of this book, we described the five components of team growth as a manual for metamorphosis. As you'll recall, metamorphosis signifies a fundamental change in form and structure, and when you commit to implementing Icenhower Coaching and Consulting's (ICC) manual for metamorphosis, you are committing to transforming the structural and cultural composition of your real estate team's relationship to growth.

A crucial step in starting the transformation process is reading this "manual" for yourself. The Team Book Club results in higher levels of receptivity and internalization when every member actively participates, instead of reading a summary about the five components in an email from their team leader.

Throughout the book club process this book will be your constant companion and guide. In time, however, you will internalize and apply each of the components so completely that these pages will become more of a reference, or something that you give to each new agent who joins your team.

Now, of course, there is a lot more to each component than meets the eye, but these five components provide a simple, clear, and accurate summary.

The fourth component of real estate team growth entails creating an informative but engaging dashboard (also known as business scoreboards or scorecards) that will both track your present position and steer you to your destination by motivating each team member to take action and move, continuously, forward.

Like a vehicle, your real estate team is a complex machine with many moving parts. Through a combination of visual gauges and displays, a car's dashboard gives a driver a simplified but accurate assessment of the intricate interactions and mechanisms happening under the hood. A team dashboard plays a similar role. A well-designed dashboard is

THE FIVE COMPONENTS OF TEAM GROWTH

1. Devise a viral goal.
2. Focus on activities first.
3. Cultivate personal responsibility through public accountability.
4. Drive growth with a dashboard.
5. Huddle up.

FIGURE 14.1 The Five Components

Component 4: Drive Growth with a Dashboard

FIGURE 14.2 Component 4: Drive Growth with a Dashboard

a simple visual representation of key performance metrics (activity-based indicators, ABIs, and results-based indicators, RBIs) and other crucial data points that provide the status of your goal.

A dashboard sets the agenda for your weekly huddles. A dashboard – publicly and prominently displayed – is a key component in creating peer accountability. It summarizes impactful growth activities, illustrates progress, and provides each team member with a means of keeping track of where they stand in relation to achieving the team's viral goal.

Most importantly, a dashboard *makes it about everyone*. A well-designed dashboard is a motivating and engaging tool that connects team members and drives their performance on an individual and group level. Traditional understandings of dashboards or scoreboards emphasize their ability to tap into our *competitive drive* and motivate people to pursue a "winning" performance. This is undoubtedly true, and very important – a dashboard should tell team members if they're "winning" or "losing," and inspire them to take action whether they're behind or ahead of the game.

However, not everybody is naturally competitive or driven by traditional concepts of winning. Our personality, or what's known as our *behavior profile*, profoundly impacts what motivates and drives our behavior or actions. While your real estate team will create just a single dashboard, it won't mean the same thing to everybody, nor does it need to. A dashboard engages different people in different ways, but we guarantee that it will drive growth no matter what drives each team member.

Creating Your Dashboard

This chapter focuses on the motivational principles and reasons behind a dashboard. We also guide you through the process of actually creating your own dashboard.

Remember, the implementation process will take six weeks. Once the five-week book club part of the process is over, you and your team will spend the last week "huddling up" to create a one-page Annual Business Plan. You'll learn more about this in Part Five, but as you create your business plan, you may need to edit your team dashboard. The two go hand in hand, and the goals on your business plan will determine the essential ABIs that need to be detailed on your dashboard.

For now, let's explore what a dashboard is and what it will mean for your real estate team in the future.

Before drilling down on the particular ways that a dashboard motivates each of the various behavior profiles, let's begin with an overview of what a dashboard is.

Do You See What I See?

A good dashboard is easy to understand. Yet, if a stranger were to look at your dashboard, they won't see, feel, or grasp the dashboard in the same way as you and your fellow team members.

Long after the Team Book Club has ended; long after those first few tentative steps; and long after you've hit your first annual goals and are setting your sights on a second and a third and a fourth year of growth, the dashboard will remind you of the process that started it all.

Now, let's talk about how each of the five components of team growth that we have learned about so far will factor into your growth-driving team dashboard.

Resource   Sample Dashboards

In the online resource appendix of this book, you will find these two helpful Sample Dashboards to look at as good examples of what your dashboard may look like. These are good samples to print out and use as reference as you read through this chapter. You will also find these samples displayed in the next few pages.

All resources can be downloaded from this book's online appendix at therealestatetrainer.com/teambook.

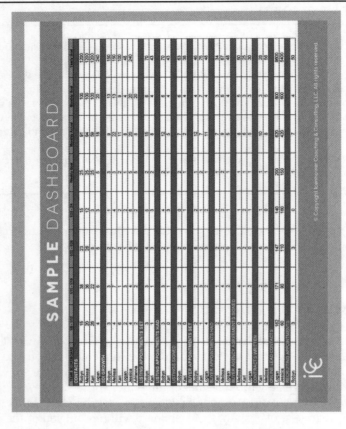

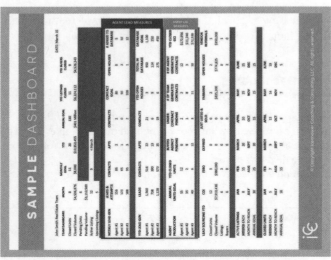

FIGURE 14.3 Sample Dashboards

Component 1: The Viral Goal

Clear and comprehensible, a dashboard prominently displays your viral goal or overall annual target and measures it against gains made through the week's growth-building activities. A dashboard can also chart activity over the months and quarters, too, but it's crucial that your dashboard boldly displays your overall viral goal and reminds team members of the ultimate purpose of all this activity.

As you'll recall from component 1, for a goal to be effective, it must be measurable if you are to stay on track, and the most efficient and straightforward way to measure something is in concrete, numeric units.

However, when team members see your team's annual growth goal displayed on the dashboard, they will not only see a number, they will also see a symbol of a different kind of goal-setting process – a process in which they were *intentionally and actively included*, a process that *made it about everyone* and was purposefully structured around everyone's *personal needs and motivations*, a process that captured everyone's curiosity, imagination, and exuberance, and which spread like wildfire throughout the real estate team.

The purpose of a dashboard is to motivate team members and drive a desire for growth. When a team dashboard is built around everyone's personal *Why*, it is an inherently motivating and inspiring device.

Component 2: Focus on Activities First

When team members see the team's ABIs displayed on the dashboard, they will not see a series of random tasks and assignments dictated to them from on high. Rather, they will see a process in which everyone collaborated and applied their energy to identifying and acting upon those activities that drive growth, and that are most likely to help the team reach its goals.

When team members see the team's ABIs displayed on the dashboard, they won't see a process that happened overnight. Whether you performed a single or a dozen Pareto analyses, or whether you spent hours in conversation discussing whose model you wanted to emulate, it took time and effort to find measurable and trackable data that quantifiably moves the needle on growth.

Though a stranger might just see a list of tasks to be performed, team members will recognize the real significance of those activities and appreciate the hours of commitment and dogged determination that went into identifying them.

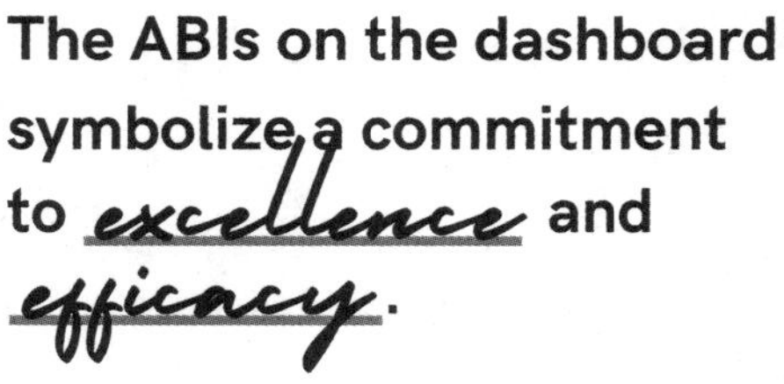

The ABIs on the dashboard symbolize a commitment to *excellence* and *efficacy*.

FIGURE 14.4   Excellence and Efficacy

The ABIs on the dashboard symbolize a commitment to excellence and efficacy. As you run through each ABI at your weekly huddle, their presence on the dashboard ensures that team members will never lose sight of what's important, and always focus on activities first.

While the day-to-day operations will and must continue, a dashboard centers your attention on that which drives growth and protects you from becoming distracted with the 80% activities that don't make much of an impact.

Team dashboards were originally modeled after the dashboard of a car. What's less known is that, originally, the word "dashboard" applied to a barrier of wood fixed at the front of a horse-drawn carriage or sleigh to protect the driver from mud or other debris thrown or "dashed up" by the horses' hooves. Traditionally, these boards did not perform any additional function, but as car design evolved, the dashboard became a panel for the placement of gauges and controls.

Team dashboards provide insight into individual people's performance relative or compared to the team's overall goal. Like the dashboard of a car, the team's dashboard will allow members to gauge individual and group performance levels and control the trajectory and acceleration of growth. Like the wooden board that protected carriage drivers from mud, the team's dashboard also has a protective purpose. No matter what gets thrown at you as you deal with the everyday tasks that keep you busy but don't make much impact, the dashboard keeps team members firmly focused on the activities that drive growth.

The dashboard will also tell you when your activities are not driving growth, or not driving it consistently or fast enough. The ability to identify risk before it becomes a major issue is especially critical to team leaders. It's far better to diagnose potential problems along the way, rather than at the end of the process when the outcome cannot be altered or reversed. A dashboard provides an easy way to identify issues, enabling team leaders and team members alike to evaluate, diagnose, and mitigate risk early on and at each step of the way. How? By keeping each team member accountable.

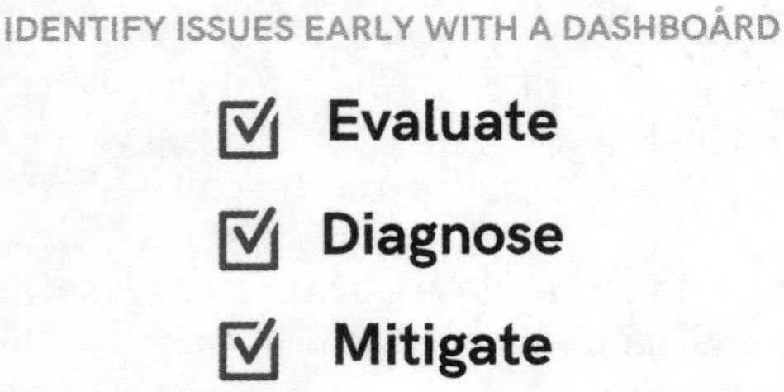

IDENTIFY ISSUES EARLY WITH A DASHBOARD

☑ **Evaluate**

☑ **Diagnose**

☑ **Mitigate**

FIGURE 14.5   Evaluate, Diagnose, Mitigate

Component 3: Accountability

At ICC, our dashboard displays the four key accountability questions. Team members will quickly memorize the questions and use them to self-coach and guide their decisions day in day out, including the accountability questions on the dashboard that send a powerful message.

Your dashboard displays what is important to your real estate team; it's a visual symbol of what matters to you. Success and growth and profitability are important, but you cannot achieve those things without accountability, and its significance should never be forgotten or undervalued.

Whether your dashboard is a physical object on a wall, a simple spreadsheet, or a software-based information-management tool, make sure to post your team's dashboard where everyone will see it or have easy and frequent access to it.

In the book *Contagious: Why Things Catch On*, Jonah Berger provides evidence that visibility is a key factor in whether a product catches on, or an idea "goes viral." Seeing others do something makes people more likely to do it or want it for themselves. Making something more public or observable makes it easier to imitate and replicate. It also promotes accountability and motivates your team members to take action.

Dashboards not only provide visibility into the activities that are being done, but also into who is doing them. Dashboards simplify complex data and provide people with at-a-glance awareness of everyone's performance at all times. When team members know that others on the team can see the status of their work, they are more likely to take responsibility for their moment-to-moment decisions and commit to doing their activities for the good of the team as well as their own benefit.

Elements of an Engaging Dashboard

When creating your real estate team's dashboard, the most important considerations are visibility, accountability, and the nature of the data displayed. Use these four key questions as a guide:

KEY QUESTIONS TO ASK

1. Is it clear and simple?
2. Is it public to everyone on the team?
3. Does it show all of your KPIs (key performance indicators), both activity-based indicators (ABIs) and results-based indicators (RBIs)?
4. Does it clearly indicate who has and has not fulfilled their ABI commitments?

FIGURE 14.6   Four Key Questions

Your team's dashboard may be simpler than the example below, but it should certainly not be much more complex. Just because you have spreadsheets full of interesting data doesn't mean it should be displayed on your dashboard. Keep it relevant to the most impactful ABIs.

Remember that the following graphic is an illustration, not an exact blueprint. When creating your own dashboard, remember that the most important purpose is to show your team members where you stand in relation to the goal, and to hold them accountable to their individual contributions and commitments.

Resource   Sample Team Dashboard

In the online resource appendix of this book, you will find this attractive Sample Team Dashboard. It's a great example of a way to make your dashboard more visually appealing and easy to read. You will also find this sample displayed on the next page, for your convenience.

All resources can be downloaded from this book's online appendix at therealestatetrainer.com/ teambook.

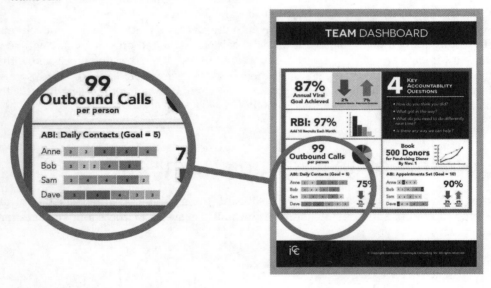

FIGURE 14.7   Sample Team Dashboard

Case Study

Larry Else, Downtown Detroit Realty, Detroit, Michigan

The Downtown Detroit Realty team, led by Larry Else, consists of about 40 agents selling over 800 homes a year. They are, by far, the number-one team in Detroit, Michigan. Larry uses his team dashboard in a unique way – for onboarding new agents.

Larry uses the ICC Agent Onboarding Training Calendar and inputs the training into the Training Measures section on his team dashboard (you can see examples of this on the sample dashboards later in the chapter). The Training Measures section of the dashboard outlines the various ICC online training programs agents are working through, and it also includes shadowing opportunities with established Buyer's Agents on the team. They shadow the Buyer's Agents showing properties, conducting open houses, writing offers, negotiating contracts, attending inspections, and so on. All of these activities are taken directly from the Agent Onboarding Training Calendar and summarized within the Training Measures section of the Dashboard to make it easy to track and keep each agent accountable at the weekly Huddle.

Every team wants high-producing agents, and Larry's team was no different. As the team leader, Larry noticed that using a dashboard dramatically increased the production of his agents, and ultimately, his team as a whole. Any time new agents come onto Larry's team, they are assured that there is structured training in place. These training measures are tracked. All of these items are prescribed via the Agent Onboarding Training Calendar, which keeps the team's training streamlined and consistent. Completion of different training events, courses, and milestones are then all recorded and displayed on the team's dashboard.

Before this procedure was implemented, Larry confessed that agents were coming to the office and getting "lost." They would start on the team, be excited, bright-eyed and bushy-tailed, ready to start the training – then suddenly, that demeanor would disappear. A mere 10% of Larry's new agents were showing up and participating in the training. Every agent, *especially* new agents, need accountability. The best accountability tool that a real estate team can use is a dashboard to hold everyone accountable to the training measures.

Once Larry started instituting the Training Measures on the dashboard via the Agent Onboarding Calendar, his agents' production dramatically increased. Particularly, the new agents that he was bringing onto the team showed an incredible uptick in training participation. All of Larry's agents were assured that they were going through a legitimate training program. Even though Larry, as the team leader, was only meeting with them once a week during the weekly huddle, each team member was empowered by being able to access their training regimen through their team dashboard.

Everything on the Agent Onboarding Calendar is self-managed. Agents take online training courses through the ICC Online Learning Center. In addition, of course, they are shadowing the experienced Buyer's Agents on the team to learn the ropes firsthand. This is no skin off the Buyer's Agents' backs because they are just going about their normal day-to-day tasks. They would be doing this anyway, and the newbie tags along to learn by observation.

In our Sample Scoreboards earlier in this chapter, you'll see that each new agent needs to perform five shadows for each activity listed. That means five inspections, five buyer consultations, five showings, and so on. Through the shadowing process, they are able to learn these key Buyer's Agent activities by shadowing experienced agents on the team.

The minute these activities and training measures were visible on the team dashboard, they were taken more seriously. At the weekly huddle, Larry's team members could see and address what needed to be done. Now, after implementing the team dashboard and the Agent Onboarding Calendar, they are up to an 80%–90% success rate for new agents joining the team.

This new agent success rate is a phenomenal result that far exceeded all expectations. Larry Else's team went from 400 to 500 transactions a year to over 800. New agents are getting onboarded, trained, and into production quickly. As a result, their agent success rate has climbed much higher.

Imagine, putting people through these training programs before they start working in production. This is possible through the use of a team dashboard and the Agent Onboarding Calendar. We are seeing teams that we coach get dramatically improved results from this revolutionary idea.

Different Metrics for Different Folks – Agent Onboarding

In addition to the Agent Onboarding Calendar, Larry Else's team also implements a unique Buyer Agent Onboarding Program to further help onboard and train new agents when they first join the team. For an agent's first six months on the team, he or she must perform two roles at once.

During the morning hours, new agents are working as an Inside Sales Agent (ISA). As a part of this role, they are learning how to make outbound telephone calls to generate business, and they are also converting inbound leads into appointments for the outside sales agents (real estate agents on the team who are in production).

Like Larry Else's team, many of our clients have started to combine the Inside Sales Agent (ISA) position and the Showing Assistant. It trains the agents to do ISA tasks every morning and Showing Assistant tasks every afternoon.

In the first six months of being a real estate agent, most new solo agents aren't able to generate much business on their own. Through this program, they can get onboarded, start training and learning right away, and be compensated at the same time as a valuable member of the team. It's usually a small base pay, and then, of course, as a Showing Assistant, if they help convert and close a lead, they are paid a small commission, too. They can get into earning income right away. It bridges the income gap for the new agent, and they learn all the habits they need to learn.

All the trainings and job shadowing tasks that they are doing are recorded on the dashboard. It motivates agents to get these tasks done because there is peer accountability. They are meeting with the entire team each week, and that is a very motivating factor. They know that these are their ABIs for this particular time in their career. They need to focus on their training and their learning activities while they are also conducting ABIs designed to grow their businesses.

New agents on Larry's team are creating amazing habits from the very beginning of their career. These agents are being held accountable to their duties, too, by being on a very tight-knit team that has all five components of team growth in place.

Resource   Agent Onboarding Training Calendar

In the online resource appendix of this book, you will find this Agent Onboarding Training Calendar. This calendar details the training activities that will take place each day as the new agent is onboarded.

All resources can be downloaded from this book's online appendix at therealestatetrainer.com/teambook.

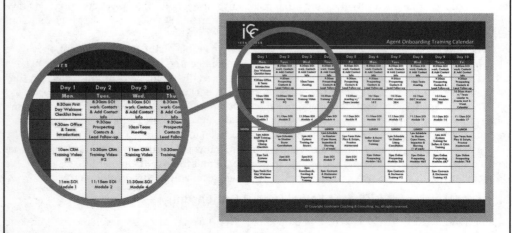

FIGURE 14.8 Agent Onboarding Training Calendar

Resource The Buyer Agent Onboarding Program

In the online resource appendix for this book, you will find the Buyer Agent Onboarding Program. You'll find the job description, expectations, and growth plan to assist you in Buyer Agent onboarding.

All resources can be downloaded from this book's online appendix at therealestatetrainer.com/teambook.

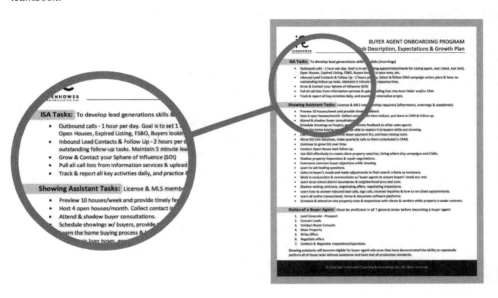

FIGURE 14.9 Buyer Agent Onboarding Program

Your Team Dashboard Will Diagnose Problems and Drive Growth

For new agent onboarding, we usually talk about the conversion measures and training measures because those are the measures that apply. The conversion measures will help diagnose problems for new agents. For example, you might be setting a lot of appointments but not getting many contracts signed. That would bring up the question, what is being said at the appointments? Or, maybe you're making a lot of contacts but not getting many appointments set. You'd want to look into the scripts that are being used to see what is being said during those phone calls. If you're talking to a lot of people, you should be setting a certain number of appointments. If you are not, are you closing fast enough to the appointment? These are problems that, if diagnosed early on, can be addressed quickly, so that good habits are formed as each team member learns and grows with the team.

Like the speedometer or odometer on a vehicle's dashboard, a real estate team dashboard gauges your progress and performance and tells you when you need to step on the gas pedal. A team dashboard tells where you are and where you should be in order to drive growth and arrive successfully at your desired destination.

Designing Your Team Dashboard

There are many ways to design and build a dashboard. While we want to provide you with inspiration, we don't want to become overly prescriptive about what your dashboard should look like.

Keep it relevant to the most impactful ABIs. When creating your own dashboard, remember that the most important purpose is to show your people where you stand in relation to the goal, and to hold them accountable to their individual contributions and commitments.

On a daily basis, your focus is on activities first and performing the actual things that will drive growth and get you where you want to be. However, focusing on activities does not mean that you should not look at results. ABI numbers tell you what was done, and where you are now. RBI numbers tell you where you are supposed to be by now.

If your team members only see what they have done each week, month, or quarter, they don't know if they are "winning" or "losing." They also need to see the numbers that they committed to meet, which should correspond to the numbers required to stay on track with meeting the overall growth goal. Knowing what we *have* done doesn't tell us much. Knowing what we *should* have done is far more informative and motivating. ICC's dashboard is a good example of this.

ICC Team Dashboard

This book includes our template as a resource. Use it as a springboard for creating your own dashboard. The dashboard is divided into weekly goals and weekly actual, monthly goals and monthly actual, yearly goals and yearly actual. The team's viral goal is clearly defined, and both ABIs and RBIs are included. It's also simple and not cluttered with inordinate amounts of data that nobody else can understand.

Resource   ICC Team Dashboard

In the online resource appendix of this book, you will find the ICC Team Dashboard. This Excel spreadsheet is editable and set up to make it easy for you to get started. On the last tab of the Excel spreadsheet, you'll also find a helpful link that will walk you through how set up and use this template for your own team.

All resources can be downloaded from this book's online appendix at therealestatetrainer.com/ teambook.

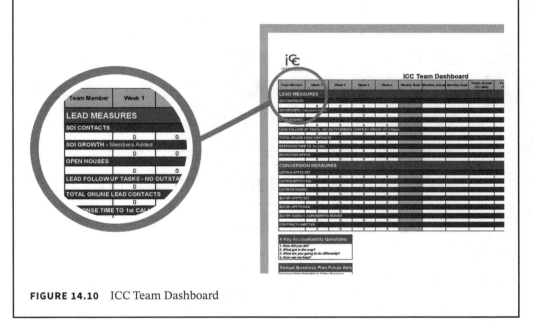

FIGURE 14.10   ICC Team Dashboard

Keep It Simple

Your dashboard and its format should fit your team. We've seen teams that use whiteboards or whatever materials they had on hand. Like we said, while you will create a *working dashboard*, you may not be able to complete every aspect of it in a single meeting. Both the ABIs that appear on the dashboard, and the appearance of the dashboard itself, may be a work in progress that you tweak and refine over time. So long as your dashboard is both easily updated and updated on a regular basis, and so long as it's displayed somewhere that your team members can see or access it, you need not concern yourself with its medium or the slickness of its appearance.

The most engaging and effective dashboards are those that are clear and simple, provide a quick, visual status update on your goals and activities, and clearly convey the results of each individual's efforts and involvement. There are several ways to achieve that, but we are going to share with you the ICC Team Dashboard spreadsheet, as well as a simple visual graphic version, that can help represent your weekly progress during team meetings.

ACTIVITY-BASED INDICATORS

LEAD MEASURES - ACTIVITY-BASED INDICATORS (ABIs)				
SOI CONTACTS				
Robyn				
Melissa				
Kari				
Logan				
Jessica				
Tasha				
SOI GROWTH - Members Added				
Robyn				
Melissa				
Kari				
Logan				
Jessica				
Adrianna				
Tasha				
OPEN HOUSES				
Kari				
Melissa				
Logan				
Jessica				
Tasha				
LEAD FOLLOW-UP TASKS - NO OUTSTANDING TASKS BY FRIDAY AT 5:00pm				
Robyn				
Kari				
Melissa				
Logan				
Jessica				
Tasha				
TOTAL ONLINE LEAD CONTACTS				
Logan				

FIGURE 14.11 Activity-Based Indicators

Activity-Based Indicators (ABIs) to Track

1. SOI Contacts – how many members of your SOI are you contacting each week?

2. SOI Growth (Members Added) – how many people are you adding to your SOI database each week?

3. Open Houses – how many open houses are you holding each week?

4. Lead Follow-Up Tasks – how many lead follow-up tasks are you doing? Part of this ABI is making sure there are no outstanding tasks by the end of the week. This applies to online leads and the follow-up (nurturing) required to make contact.

5. Total Online Lead Contacts – how many online lead contacts are you making?

6. Response Time to First Call – how long is it taking you to call a new online lead? If a brand-new online lead comes in, speed to lead is very important. Average response time should be under five minutes.

7. Recruiting Appointments – how many new recruiting appointments are you setting each week? This ABI would apply to certain people on the team who are responsible for recruiting new team members.

Remember, these ABIs are examples! We have seen teams that track many different ABIs, and these will vary depending on your team's goals. Additional ABIs that can be tracked on the dashboard include Expired Contacts, Expired Appointments, Client Event Contacts, Social Media Posts, Social Media Engagements, and so on. Work closely with your team to help determine the best ABIs and expectations in specific, measurable numbers that you should have detailed on your team scoreboard. These numbers will vary team by team and agent by agent.

Conversion Indicators

1. Listing Appointments Set
2. Listing Appointments Had
3. Listings Signed
4. Buyer Appointments Set
5. Buyer Appointments Had
6. Buyer Agency Agreements Signed
7. Contracts Written

The second section of this example dashboard is labeled "Conversion Indicators." These indicators are pretty self-explanatory, and should also be included in your dashboard spreadsheet. These indicators provide us with a tool to diagnosis problems. For an explanation of these indicators, go back and review component 2 in Chapter 6.

Let's take a close look at Conversion Indicators. If you see that a team member is setting a lot of listing appointments, but their "Buyer Consultations Had" number is low, you would

CONVERSION INDICATORS

CONVERSION INDICATORS				
LISTING APPTS SET				
Robyn				
Kari				
LISTING APPTS HAD				
Robyn				
Kari				
LISTINGS SIGNED				
Robyn				
Kari				
BUYER APPTS SET				
Kari				
Melissa				
Logan				
Jessica				
Tasha				
BUYER APPTS HAD				
Kari				
Melissa				
Logan				
Jessica				
Tasha				
BUYER AGENCY AGREEMENTS SIGNED				
Melissa				
Kari				
Logan				
Jessica				
Tasha				
CONTRACTS WRITTEN				
Kari				

FIGURE 14.12   Conversion Indicators

want to dig into the issue that is resulting in so many buyer no-shows. Now, if you are seeing a lot of "Listing Appointments Had" but very few "Listings Signed," other questions would arise. What is the team member wearing to the appointment? What does the agent's listing presentation look like? What scripts and dialogues are we using? Why are we not getting these agreements signed? We can diagnose problems much more easily when numbers like these bring the issues to the surface.

Training Indicators

1. Videos – *How should new team members be training to help them gain valuable skills and grow as an agent on your team?*

2. Shadowing Opportunities – *What hands-on experience do new team members have on a weekly basis?*

The third section of this example dashboard shows "training indicators." When we bring on new people, we are making sure that they are receiving the training they need.

TRAINING INDICATORS

TRAINING INDICATORS

VIDEOS				
	SOI	ISA	CRM, MLS & Forms	Admin Training
Robyn	Done	Done	Done	NA
Melissa	Done	Done	Done	NA
Kari	Done	Done	Done	NA
Logan	Done			NA
Jessica		Done		NA
Adrianna	Done	NA	Done	Done
Kelsey	Done	NA	Done	
Tasha				NA
LOGAN SHADOWING OPPORTUNITIES				
Showings				
Buyer Consults				
Open Houses				
Home Inspections				
Writing Offers				
Negotiating Counters				
JESSICA SHADOWING OPPORTUNITIES				
Showings				
Buyer Consults				
Open Houses				
Home Inspections				
Writing Offers				
Negotiating Counters				
TASHA SHADOWING OPPORTUNITIES				
Showings				
Buyer Consults				

FIGURE 14.13 Training Indicators

At ICC, we offer many online courses to help teams and brokerages provide this kind of valuable training to their agents. From training on how to build and grow your SOI to learning how to farm or prospect for online leads, training courses like the ones we provide at ICC are a huge asset to any team or brokerage. Having these training modules listed right on the dashboard ensures that they will be done by your agents.

Many teams and brokerages that we have worked with through the years express their exasperation at trying to get agents to complete their training. "I'm offering it to my entire team for free, and yet for some reason, nobody actually does the training!" By putting these tasks on the dashboard, it makes them essential and required. This is how team leaders can hold all team members accountable for their training!

Results-Based Indicators (RBIs) to Track

1. Under Contract
2. Pending Volume
3. Closed YTD – *divided into Agent-Generated closings and Team-Generated closings*. This shows us how much business each agent is bringing to the team from their own SOI,

RESULTS-BASED INDICATORS

LAG MEASURES - RESULTS BASED INDICATORS (RBIs)										
Under Contract		**Pending Volume**			**Closed YTD**			**Closed Volume YTD**		
Robyn	14	Robyn	$12,243,000.00		**Total**	**Agent Generated**	**Team Generated**	Robyn	$28,418,000.00	
Melissa	16	Melissa	$6,214,500.00	Robyn	35	26	9	Melissa	$17,091,275.00	
Kari (buyers)	11	Kari	$9,227,500.00	Melissa	25	10	15	Kari	$12,896,500.00	
Kari (sellers)	5	Jessica	$4,850,000.00	Kari (buyers)	17	7	10	Jessica	$4,986,250.00	
Jessica	5	Logan	$2,400,050.00	Kari (seller)	10	5	5	Logan	$2,850,000.00	
Logan	3	TOTAL	$34,935,050.00	Logan	6	0	6	TOTAL	$66,242,025.00	
TOTAL	54			Jessica	8	1	7	GOAL	$125,000,000.00	
				TOTAL	101	49	52			

4 Key Accountability Questions

1. How did you do?
2. What got in the way?
3. What are you going to do differently?
4. How can we help?

Current 1-3-5 Annual Business Plan Items

Increase Video Marketing & Online Presence
Skill Development: scripts & conversion
Hire Listing Manager

Tasks to Complete by Next Meeting

Pending Volume

Under Contract

Closed YTD

Closed Volume YTD

FIGURE 14.14   Results-Based Indicators

and how much business they are getting from the team. (We talked at greater length about the Matching Standard back in Chapter 13.)

4. Closed Volume YTD

The final section of this example dashboard contains the RBIs you should track. Under the RBIs we list out the four key accountability questions. It is helpful to have these written out explicitly on your dashboard because it makes them a required part of your weekly huddle. At the very bottom of this example dashboard, you will see the Annual Business Plan Focus Items. This is the perfect place to display these focus items because it keeps them front and center at your weekly huddle and always brings your attention back to the reason why the dashboard is so important.

ICC Team Dashboard Graphic

This ICC Team Dashboard Graphic provides a more visual representation of the dashboard spreadsheet we just created earlier. If we take a look at it, we can see most of the focus on this dashboard is all about ABIs. We have the daily contact goal (five, in this case) written out, and you can see who is hitting their numbers and who isn't. And, we can also see that we are improving our numbers over last week's numbers when it comes to daily contacts. You can also see that we have our appointments set goal here, too. On display, your team members will see the percentage of the Annual Goal that you've reached so far, as well as an important RBI (in this case, related to recruiting).

Something we love about this team dashboard graphic is that you can clearly see the four key accountability questions, which we have talked so much about throughout this book. No one likes to ask these questions, but if they are displayed on the dashboard, everyone has the understanding that these questions must be addressed. It's required because it's written out on the dashboard. It makes it less personal because it shows that the same rules and questions apply to everyone on the team.

Resource   ICC Team Dashboard Graphic

In the online resource appendix of this book, you will find the ICC Team Dashboard Graphic. This image is a great example of a visual way to display your dashboard numbers at your weekly team huddle.

All resources can be downloaded from this book's online appendix at therealestatetrainer.com/ teambook.

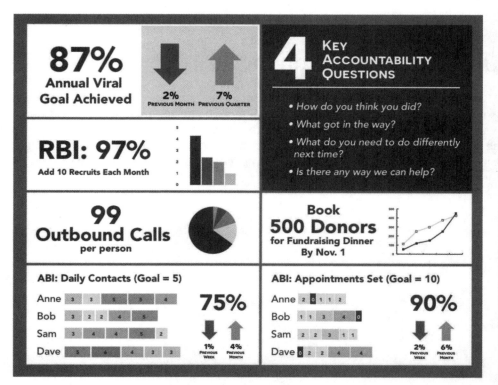

FIGURE 14.15   ICC Team Dashboard Graphic

Quick Tip   Getting Started with Your Dashboard

For those of you who are not technologically savvy or conversant in Excel, please be assured that the spreadsheet template we have provided you with as a resource will be easy to use. While we do believe in the motivating power of simple, visual data, the most important thing is that you're tracking your activities, and that your dashboard tells your team members "This is where we are now" and "This is where we should be."

The more simply and visually you can display this information, the better. Perhaps one of the five Objectives in your 1-3-5 annual plan (which you will create in week 6) could focus on developing these skills. Remember that you don't have to have everything already in place to take the first step toward growth. When you gather together to create your dashboard, you will do so on the understanding that it takes time to craft a working dashboard, and some of the most impactful things you will do this year have not yet been discovered and quantified. Growth is a process, not an XYZ formula to follow. As we mentioned at the beginning of this chapter, when creating your team's first dashboard, the only requirements are that it is:

- Clear and simple
- Easy to update
- Displays both actual results and target results
- Everyone can clearly see who has and has not fulfilled their commitments
- For every ABI and RBI displayed, you can quickly tell if you're winning or losing, ahead or behind, growing or declining

Up Next: Motivation for All

The team dashboard is an excellent motivational tool. But as you know, each team member is motivated by something different. So how can you ensure that everyone will find your team dashboard to be that driving force that pushes them toward growth? In the next chapter, we discuss the DISC behavioral model, and how you can use it to understand how each member of your team feels most motivated. And, how the team dashboard can work for any behavior type!

CHAPTER 15

Team Motivation: Using the DISC Behavioral Model to Help Team Members Understand and Adapt to Their Differing Styles and Motivations

Whether you're reading this book as a team leader or team member, you've probably learned that what engages and motivates *you* doesn't always engage and motivate *everyone on your team*. The dashboard is a motivating tool, but it engages and motivates people in different ways depending on who they are or, to be more specific, depending on their behavior type. For example, when asked about the dashboard, one of our team members explained:

> *I'm not a naturally competitive person, but the dashboard brings me into that realm by illustrating what success and winning look like. It also shows me what it looks like to fall behind. Nobody knows if they're doing well if it's not written down. Some people might not be a born go-getter, but the numbers and data on the dashboard show people like me what a go-getter achievement looks like. I understand facts and figures and seeing the numbers displayed on the dashboard helps me to make decisions*

and fix problems. Like, "If I tweaked this, I can get this," you know? But most of all, I want everyone to be happy and feel supported, and I don't want to let the team down. The dashboard helps me see my contributions to our goal and inspires me to do my best and get better for myself but also on behalf of everyone else.

Her comments revealed something that in retrospect seems so obvious. When hiring this young woman to her administrative position, her pleasant, personable, and professional demeanor was exactly what we were looking for in this role. We needed someone calm and steady who would take care of our clients and listen to their needs. We also needed someone who was able to put their head down and work steadily at tasks that might bore or frustrate more impatient or excitable people. In short, we chose this particular person because their Dominance, Influence, Steadiness, and Compliance (DISC) behavior assessment indicated that her Steadiness and Compliance (SC) behavior profile would make a very good match indeed.

Knowing what we do about the SC behavior type, it makes complete sense that someone with that profile would not engage with the dashboard competitively or in terms of winning and losing. With that in mind, we wanted to assure you that, while the exact same motivators may not drive all team members in the exact same ways, when the dashboard speaks personally to your people's behavioral motivators, it will engage them in their own unique way, and *that* is what will cause them to take action and drive growth.

The DISC Behavior Model

At Icenhower Coaching and Consulting (ICC), it is no exaggeration to say that the DISC behavior model is the backbone of almost everything we do. By far the most widely used behavioral assessment across all fast-growing industries and organizations, the DISC is valued for its affordable accessibility and its multifaceted uses, from hiring and training to improving client communication and increasing sales performance.

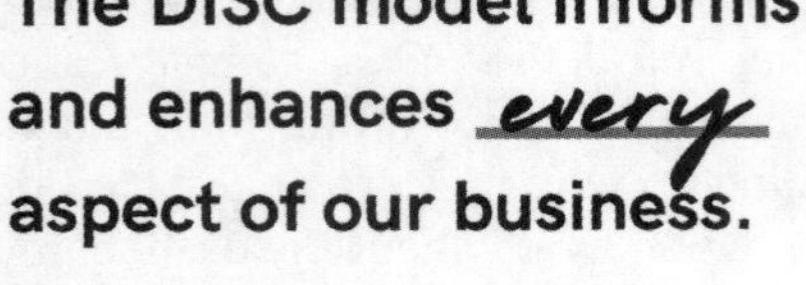

The DISC model informs and enhances *every* aspect of our business.

FIGURE 15.1 The DISC Model

The DISC model informs and enhances every aspect of our business, and it's hard to imagine what ICC would even look like without the deep knowledge and understanding we've attained over the years. Many successful organizations provide behavioral assessments for all their people, and while utilizing the DISC model is not a compulsory component of team growth, our knowledge of the DISC has informed aspects of this book – particularly our repeated emphasis to "make it about everyone." Determining the personal motivations of all team members is the first step in devising an exciting and meaningful viral goal, and tapping into those personal wants and needs is based on our understanding that everyone is motivated differently, and that a one-size-fits-all approach will not capture the imagination and enthusiasm of all team members.

As we said, utilizing the DISC model is not a requirement for realizing growth or implementing the components of growth on a real estate team, but it certainly does help. In fact, most organizations and industries prefer the DISC to other competing behavioral and personality assessments because of the DISC's many different applications. It is also much easier and cheaper to use than more sophisticated assessments.

We believe that even a basic working knowledge of behavior will help you to understand the dashboard as a motivating tool that engages different team members in different ways, depending on their behavioral profiles. The DISC model is a great tool to help you better understand yourself, your teammates, and the impact of the dashboard.

The Four DISC Behavior Profiles

DISC is an acronym for the four core behavior profiles: Dominance, Influence, Steadiness, and Compliance.

In reality, people typically don't just have a single behavior profile and, rather, tend to display a combination or blend of behaviors. If you perform an actual DISC assessment on an individual, they may assess as a DI or an IS or a CD, for example.

Our DISC profile blend reflects our strongest behaviors, tendencies, priorities, and motivators. The first letter reflects our most pronounced behaviors and priorities, and the second letter reflects those behaviors and tendencies that, while less prominent than the primary behavior type, are still very much apparent and more unmistakably "you" than the other behavior types.

At ICC, we train all of our clients on how to evaluate behavioral blends and the importance of profile percentages in much more detail than we can devote time to here. For now, simply understand that the following descriptions reflect the general characteristics of each behavior in isolation. If you recognize any of these traits in yourself or your fellow team members, chances are it's because that profile is their dominant or "lead profile" and reflects their most pronounced or unmistakable behaviors, tendencies, and motivators.

DISC profile types are classified into four primary behavior groups, shown in Figure 15.2.

When it comes to real estate teams, we know that certain behavioral profiles are better suited to better roles on a team. It makes sense, too, because we need different kinds of people with different strengths for all the varied tasks that must be done in order to successfully run a real estate team. For example, we know that administrative team members are going to be in the S and C category. That said, there are plenty of real estate agents that also fall into these categories.

One way that you can use the DISC behavior profile model on your real estate team is that it can help you figure out what kind of lead-generation methods are best for different

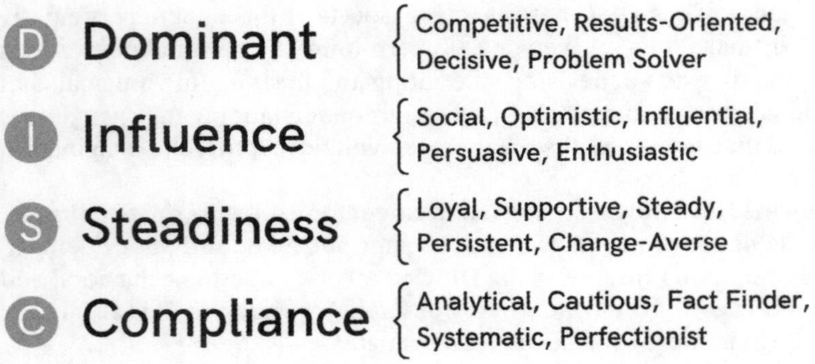

D **Dominant** { Competitive, Results-Oriented, Decisive, Problem Solver

I **Influence** { Social, Optimistic, Influential, Persuasive, Enthusiastic

S **Steadiness** { Loyal, Supportive, Steady, Persistent, Change-Averse

C **Compliance** { Analytical, Cautious, Fact Finder, Systematic, Perfectionist

FIGURE 15.2 DISC Behavioral Profiles

team members. If you know a team member's behavioral profile, it can give you insight into their preferences and their strengths, and as the team leader you can use that to the team's advantage.

Let's take a closer look at each profile in turn, paying particular attention to behavioral motivators and how each profile is likely to engage with and be motivated by the dashboard.

Dominant (D)

A typical D-behavior is fast-talking, blunt, assertive, impatient, dominant, competitive, independent, and very strong-willed.

D-behaviors are the most assertive and aggressive of all the behavior profiles. D-behaviors are primarily driven by winning and success. They are very results-oriented. They like to overcome a challenge and they are ultra-competitive. D-behaviors value personal freedom and like to do things in their own way. D-profiles strongly dislike being placed in a position where they lack the power and authority to impact results.

Regardless of our behavior profile, everyone is motivated to some degree by autonomy, but self-direction is especially important to D-behaviors who not only want to see positive results but also want to know that they personally had a hand in a successful outcome.

D-profiles tend to have a strong internal locus of control and like to take charge of their own destiny. If a D-behavior doesn't meet their target numbers, the dashboard doesn't tell them what they need to do to fix a problem; it simply tells them that there is a problem, but they have the authority and autonomy to determine how to resolve it.

The dashboard also engages the competitive nature of the D-behavior. D-profiles speak in the language of competition and winning, and they excel in ultra-competitive environments. D-profiles function best in a rapid-paced, results-oriented environment. D-behaviors are task-oriented and are motivated to achieve concrete results, but they want those results to be crystal clear. D-profiles like leaderboards and rankings and to know how they're doing at all times. D-profiles love the dashboard, because it clearly shows that their daily and weekly activities are driving concrete results.

While they don't like failure, D-profiles tend to roll with the punches more than the other behaviors. They are bottom-line people. If there's a problem, they don't take it personally: they take concrete action and move on. D-behaviors are fast movers who easily become bored, so they love the at-a-glance simplicity and clarity of the dashboard. Compared to complex and convoluted spreadsheets and analytics that overwhelm with their level of detail and granular data, a dashboard allows the fast-moving D-profile to diagnose the issue and make quick decisions about what they need to do differently or better next time. D-profiles are extremely driven and are always pushing forward.

A word of caution, however: while it's wonderful that D-behaviors are fast movers and action-oriented, they also want quick results and tend to be impatient. Though D-behaviors excel at performing activities, they also happen to be the profile that doesn't want to take the extra time to regularly track their activity-based indicators (ABIs), attend regular meetings or huddle up – or even take the time to read through this book! Sometimes, the activities your people are performing on a daily basis won't produce instant results, so D-profiles will need to overcome their tendency to be impatient and trust that the ABIs will move the needle and ultimately drive growth.

D-behaviors set high performance standards for themselves and others, and you may find that team members with strong D-profiles emerge as natural leaders that others on your team hold themselves accountable to. While those people may not be as naturally competitive as their D-profile teammates, the D-profile's drive to win will motivate others to do their best to meet the high standards of their D-profile team members.

While different behaviors will engage with the dashboard differently, you will see that every profile will impact or influence the members of your real estate team in various ways. This is especially true when we are around somebody who is an influential I-behavior.

Influencer (I)

A typical I-behavior is influential, social, optimistic, effusive, gregarious, and persuasive.

I-behaviors are social butterflies that are motivated and defined by social relationships. I-behaviors are very gregarious and outspoken, and others tend to listen to them. They are extremely positive, effusive people, and very influential.

Like the D-profile, I-profiles love seeing progress and results displayed on the dashboard. However, their motivation stems less from competitiveness and a personal desire to win, and more from a desire for social approval and to see the team achieve its goals.

I-behaviors are motivated by admiration and popularity. They fear rejection. Being sidelined on a project as the rest of the team progresses and contributes without them can be very upsetting for an I-profile, so the dashboard drives them to contribute and play a positive – and often outsized – role in meeting the goal. Like the D-behavior, I-behaviors can produce fantastic results, and often go above and beyond when it comes to hitting their daily and weekly targets. However, I-behaviors are driven less by personal competition with themselves, and more from a drive to be the center of attention or to win the praise and approval of other people.

Being so social, I-behaviors are extremely motivated by the excitement and enthusiasm of those around them. I-behaviors enjoy high energy and positivity, and they exercise a great degree of influence over their environment. The way that an I-behavior engages with the dashboard will have a knock-on effect on other team members, regardless of their behavior profile. When the performance indicators on the dashboard display growth and success, I-behaviors will act as a cheerleader and effusively celebrate positive results. And, when the dashboard indicates that the team's performance is not where it needs to be in order to meet the overall goal, I-profiles will act as influential catalysts and motivators.

I-behaviors energize and inspire others and are good at helping other team members believe in themselves and understand their role in achieving the goal. They are good at creating passion for a vision, mission, or goal, and people with this behavior profile will be key to helping your real estate team's goal go viral.

Like the D-behavior, I-profiles are also fast movers and dislike being subjected to lots of "boring" details so they, too, love the at-a-glance simplicity of the dashboard. Unlike the D-behavior, however, I-profiles are people-focused rather than task-oriented. Outside the huddle, they have a tendency to become sidetracked and may need to develop better control over their use of time. The dashboard, which is updated regularly and discussed frequently, helps I-behaviors to set realistic goals and objectives, develop strict timelines, hold themselves accountable to the team, and cultivate a sense of perseverance and follow-through.

I-profiles can become discouraged by long, drawn-out projects, so the dashboard helps to break their goals down into smaller, more manageable parts and help them to see their progress on a daily and weekly basis. When stressed, the charming and persuasive I-profile may try to talk their way out of uncomfortable situations. The data on the dashboard tells no lies, however, and will help an I-behavior overcome their tendency to overpromise and underdeliver.

Steadiness (S)

A typical S-behavior is steady, supportive, reliable, loyal, consistent, and change-averse.

As its name implies, someone with an S-profile is a very steady, stable, and dependable person. Like the I-profile, social relationships matter to an S-profile but in a different way. Whereas I-behaviors are the life and soul of a team and enjoy being the center of attention, S-behaviors prefer to work in smaller groups and build close, one-on-one relationships with people. Quiet, professional, and reserved, they are not the high-energy, effusive cheerleader that the I-behavior is, but they are similarly driven by helping other people, and excel at being good listeners and supportive team players. S-behaviors are reliable and loyal

Resource DISC Tools and Charts

In the online resource appendix of this book, you will find several DISC tools and charts available for your reference. The DISC Behavioral Assessment, DISC Profiles, and DISC Lead Gen Tendencies are included.

All resources can be downloaded from this book's online appendix at therealestatetrainer.com/ teambook.

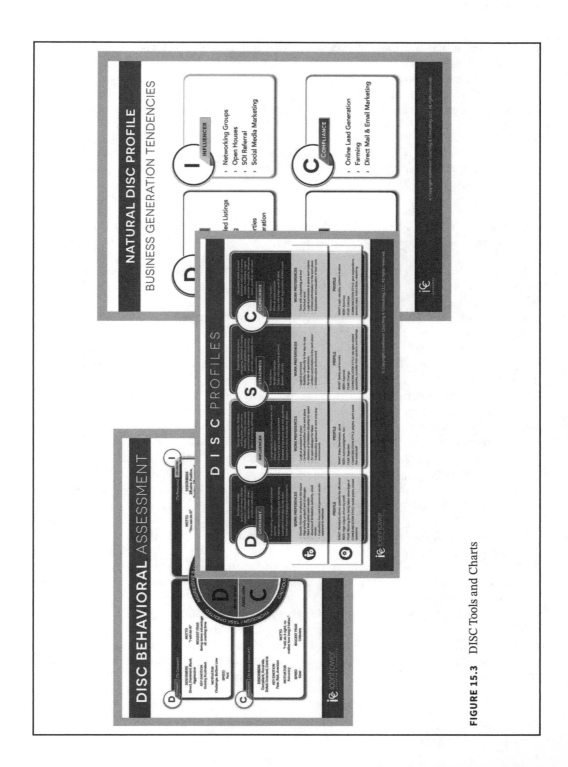

FIGURE 15.3 DISC Tools and Charts

contributors. Supporting and contributing to the team provides S-behaviors with a sense of purpose and meaning.

While everyone, no matter their behavior profile, wants to have purpose, S-behaviors who are collaborative and relationship-driven are motivated less by autonomy and independence than they are by purpose and meaning. As our administrative staff member said so clearly:

I want everyone to be happy and feel supported, and I don't want to let the team down. The dashboard helps me see my contributions to our goal and inspires me to do my best and get better.

S-behaviors love being acknowledged for their hard work, service, and loyalty. At conventional organizations, quiet and reserved S-behaviors can easily disappear into the background and become frustrated when other people receive credit for their efforts, or when they're judged unfairly for any failures. While the dashboard shows how the real estate team is collectively progressing toward its goal, it also clearly displays and delineates individual efforts, and team members with a strong S-profile will appreciate that the dashboard visibly highlights their personal contributions.

S-behaviors are not highly competitive or aggressively driven like D-behaviors. In fact, S-behaviors are discouraged by competitive situations, and overwhelmed by overly forceful people. Under pressure or stress, S-behaviors might withdraw from taking any initiatives to move forward. You may find that S-behaviors believe that they have little control over their environment or circumstances. That is: they don't naturally have a strong internal locus of control. People with strong S-profiles may be discouraged by the data displayed on the dashboard. They may become frustrated and give up, so it's important that they receive support and encouragement.

S-behaviors like stability and harmony and dislike conflict or letting people down. While they don't speak the language of "winning" and "losing," the dashboard drives S-behaviors to produce predictable and positive results. When supported by the team, they are quietly persistent and are able to put their head down and work steadily at activities that might bore or frustrate a D- or an I-behavior.

S-behaviors are highly resistant to change and they may not immediately fall in love with or appreciate the introduction of the dashboard to your real estate team (or any of the components of growth for that matter). In time, however, the dashboard will become a pleasantly familiar and reliable part of their working week. Over time, the dashboard will show them that there are good days and not so good days. Sometimes the numbers on the dashboard will say you've "won" and other times they will say you've "lost." The fact that the S-behavior doesn't speak the language of competition might be to their benefit. Rather, their steady and dependable traits and tendencies allow them to see the dashboard in a different way and understand that you always get a chance to succeed the next day. In the end, it's this daily resiliency and persistence that will make them successful in the long run.

Compliance (C)

A typical C is detailed, knowledgeable, logical, thorough, accurate, cautious, and risk-averse.

C-behaviors are conscientious, thorough, and extremely detail-oriented. They value accuracy and are deliberate, practical, and logical people. C-behaviors rely on facts, figures, and data above all else so, needless to say, they absolutely love an accurate and well-designed dashboard.

The only downside to the dashboard, from a C-profile's perspective, is that it doesn't display *enough* data. C-behaviors are the kind of people who sit down and actually read the owner's manual cover to cover before they start driving their new car! You may find that team members with strong C-profiles will come to you looking for more data and metrics to analyze, and this is totally fine, as long as they have the flexibility to understand that the dashboard is designed for *everybody* and not just them.

C-behaviors don't particularly enjoy collaborating or participating as a team. Like the S-behavior, C-behaviors are reserved, quiet, and formal in their speech and actions. They rarely express opinions or actively participate in meetings. Like the D-behavior, they value their autonomy and the ability to work independently. They prefer to isolate themselves when evaluating problems or planning strategies.

The C-profile's tendency to stick to the facts can come across as emotionless and detached, which is not super inspiring and can demotivate a team. However, it's important for leaders and other teammates to understand what's driving that behavior. A C-profile's biggest fear is criticism and being wrong. C-behaviors tend to be perfectionists, demanding extremely high standards, especially from themselves, and they can be inordinately hard on themselves.

Though they would never admit it, C-behaviors enjoy being respected for their expertise and knowledge. While everyone, no matter their behavior profile, wants to acquire knowledge and improve their skills, C-behaviors want to become absolute experts and consummate masters in everything they do. The dashboard engages the C-behavior's drive for precision and excellence for its own sake but also to demonstrate their capabilities to the team.

C-behaviors enjoy generating strategies and procedures that produce predictable and reliable outcomes. They love ABIs because they are measurable and trackable. As we explained in Part Two, when we ask you to focus on activities first, we mean that team members will not only focus on *performing* the most meaningful and impactful activities but *identifying* and *quantifying* the most meaningful and impactful activities.

When identifying your real estate team's ABIs, a particular activity or course of action must be justified by facts, figures, or other supporting data that strongly indicates its effectiveness and value. The activities you focus on must be worthy of your time and efforts, so it is crucial that you invest time and energy assessing and considering individual activities before jumping in and doing them. Of course, there will be times when you will have to jump in and do something first to know if it works (a fact that C-behaviors often struggle with), but it's nonetheless essential that you can justify an activity's value with measurable and trackable supporting data. You can't just *do*. You must *do* and *assess the effectiveness of what you do*.

Deliberate, purposeful, systematic activities produce successful and desired results, and this describes a C-profile to a T. They are driven to take initiative to ensure superior results. Though their desire for perfectionism can cause them to suffer from "analysis paralysis," if a C-behavior can overcome that tendency, then their ability to shut the door and focus on activities is an invaluable trait that will help everyone reach their goal.

A reserved and self-reliant C-behavior might not be motivated by the idea of being part of a team, but they don't necessarily need to be – so long as the dashboard confirms that their individual efforts and activities are advancing the team's goal.

Everyone is different. Each profile has their own priorities or goals, and each one tends to be driven by different things. The exact same motivators may not drive people in the exact same ways, but when the dashboard speaks personally to your team members' behavioral motivators, it will engage them in their own unique way, and *that* is what will cause them to take action and drive growth.

Next Steps

In Part Five, we turn our attention to the fifth – and final – component of team growth: growth huddles. We explain the process of a growth huddle, and get you started on your journey toward more productive (and rewarding) regular team meetings.

The Team Book Club: Part Four Discussion Guide

A quick reminder that the purpose of the first five book club meetings is *not* to come to particular conclusions, make final decisions about what your team's overall growth goal or ABIs will be, or launch into creating the dashboard. While the end of the book is drawing near, and you will soon begin implementing the five components of growth; for now, you are simply gathering to discuss and reflect upon what you have read in Part Four.

Hold Each Other Accountable

The team leader or facilitator will begin this week's book club by asking the group who did and didn't read Part Four and, if necessary, asking the four key accountability questions to anyone who did not manage to complete this week's reading (see Figure BC.1).

Again, don't become overly distracted or derailed by those who haven't prepared in advance. Keep the accountability section to a minimum and keep your sight on the real purpose and subject of the book club meeting.

Distributing a Part Four summary will help refresh people's memories, or help any nonreaders get up to speed so that they can't opt out of participation. And, as always, book club facilitators can use the provided summary to guide the conversation in addition to, or instead of, the questions below. As you read through each bullet point in the summary, ask your people, "Did this point resonate with you?" "How?" "Why?" "Tell me more," and so forth.

① How do you think you did?

② What got in the way?

③ What do you need to do differently next time?

④ Is there any way we can help?

FIGURE BC.1   Key Accountability Questions

Part Four Summary, Component 4   Drive Growth with a Dashboard

The fourth component of team growth entails creating an informative but engaging dashboard that will both track your present position and steer you to your destination by motivating your team members to take action and move, continuously, forward. A well-designed dashboard is a motivating and engaging tool that connects your team members and drives their performance on an individual and team level. Dashboards not only provide visibility into the activities that are being done, but also into who is doing them. Dashboards simplify complex data, and provide people with at-a-glance awareness of their own and others' performance at all times. When your team members know that others on the team can see the status of their work, they are more likely to take responsibility for their moment-to-moment decisions and commit to doing their activities for the good of the team as well as their own personal benefit.

Key Points:

- When creating your own dashboard you're essentially being guided by three key questions: (1) Is it public to everyone? (2) Does it show both activity-based indicators (ABIs) and results-based indicators (RBIs)? (3) Does it clearly indicate who has and has not fulfilled their ABI commitments?
- Keep it simple. Your dashboard must be simple enough to cover every element in a single meeting.
- Make it about everyone. The purpose of a dashboard is to motivate team members and drive their desire for growth. When a team dashboard is built around everyone's personal "Why," it is an inherently motivating and inspiring device.
- Everyone is different. While your real estate team will create just a single dashboard, it won't mean the same thing to everybody, nor does it need to. A dashboard engages different people in different ways, depending on their DISC behavior profile, but we guarantee that it will drive growth no matter what drives your team members.

Notes:

_____

_____

_____

_____

Questions to Spark and Stoke Conversation

The following questions are simply a starting point for sparking conversation and ensuring that everyone participates. Leaders and book club facilitators are free to create questions of their own, and we highly encourage you to do so now that you're very experienced in guiding your real estate team's book club.

Book Club Conversations for Component 4   Drive Growth
with a Dashboard

- What ideas was the author trying to get across in Part Four?
- How do the ideas presented in Part Four apply to us at _____ (insert the name of your real estate team)?
- How does a dashboard differ from the usual spreadsheets and tracking measures that conventional organizations use?
- Do you agree that a dashboard would be better than conventional data-tracking systems on our team? Why? Why not?
- What do you find most interesting or useful about a dashboard?
- Did you relate to the idea that different personality or behavior types will engage with the dashboard in different ways?
- Based on the material, do you identify with one or more of the DISC behavior profiles? How do you think someone like you would engage with and feel motivated by the dashboard?
- What new things did you learn in Part Four?
- What questions do you still have?
- Are there any quotes, passages, or ideas you found particularly compelling?
- Do you have a new perspective as a result of reading Part Four?
- Did you learn something you didn't know before?
- How has your attitude or behavior changed?
- How does Part Four relate to your role or experiences on our team?
- Did you connect with the subject matter? Did it make you nervous or excited?
- What did you like best about Part Four?
- What did you like least about Part Four?
- Which section(s) of Part Four stood out to you?
- If you had the chance to ask the author one question, right now, what would it be?

   No matter what questions you decide to ask your team members, at the end of each book club session, you (or each book club's leader/facilitator) should ask yourself the following questions:

- Does everyone understand the materials?
- Have we discussed ways that the material relates to us?

(continued)

Book Club Conversations for Component 4   *(continued)*

- Are my team members excited and engaged? Is there buy-in?
- Did we make the concept of a dashboard *about everyone*?

If the answer to these questions is a resounding "Yes" then you are well on your way to devising a viral goal on your team, identifying the activities that are most likely to drive growth and achieve success, cultivating a sense of responsibility and accountability, and using the guiding abilities of a dashboard to drive growth on your real estate team.

PART 5

Huddle Up and Make a Plan

CHAPTER 16

Growth Huddles: A Powerful Tool for Meetings Done Right

T he fifth and final component of team growth calls for team leaders and team members to cultivate their reliance on, and belief in, one another by "huddling up" and maintaining the energy, enthusiasm, motivation, and momentum you've created over the past few weeks.

First Things First

Like a sports team that gathers together on the field or court, in your daily, biweekly, or weekly huddles, the team will strategize, regroup, rally, encourage, plan your next play, and push each other to go above and beyond.

Before you can begin your daily or weekly huddles, however, you will need to go back to the beginning and implement each of the other components of growth. No doubt, the discussions and conversations that have been taking place at each of the Team Book Clubs have generated a myriad of ideas, intentions, ambitions, and objectives; but now it is time to refine those ideas, focus, prioritize, and channel your energies and efforts on the one or two goals that will make the biggest difference and have the most impact upon growth at your real estate team.

First, you will need to go back to the beginning and implement each of the other components of growth.

Component 5: Huddle Up

FIGURE 16.1 Component 5

In the next weeks, the team leaders and team members will huddle up and execute on the principles you have read, discussed, and internalized over the preceding five weeks. Specifically, you will:

- Devise a Viral Goal: Return to the first part of this book and follow our guide to devising an exciting viral goal for your team.
- Focus on Activities: Return to Part Two of this book and follow our guide for identifying and implementing activities that drive results.

In this final part of the book, we explain what happens in Week 6 when you create a one-page Annual Business Plan, and work to fine-tune your team's dashboard.

While there is much to do, and a challenging road ahead, you have already begun to implement and internalize one of the most important components of growth – cultivating personal responsibility with public accountability. By beginning each week's book club with the four key accountability questions, you have demonstrated what accountability and responsibility look like, and integrating the questions into your weekly huddles will provide an element of familiarity to a new style of gathering. Before we turn our attention to what happens in Week 6, let's take a closer look at the "growth huddle," as well as the price real estate teams pay for inefficient and outdated team meetings.

The Cost of Conventional Meetings

Making fun of meetings is the stuff of Dilbert cartoons. In one of many classics, Dilbert sits down at a conference table and asks his coworkers, "Who called this meeting?" "We thought you did," they reply in caffeine-depleted confusion, to which Dilbert wonders out loud to the group: "Maybe meetings have become a life-form capable of *calling themselves* and thus reproducing human hosts. . . ."

The idea that meetings are a type of virus that use humans as hosts to replicate might strike you as absurd, but you have to admit that most meetings have the capability of turning us into unthinking automatons or zombie-like sleepwalkers. It's not just Dilbert. Nobody enjoys meetings. They're too long, they lack structure and focus, they're rarely productive, and half the time the bagels aren't even fresh! Inevitably, the same people dominate the conversation, no one else gets a word in edgewise, the meeting gets derailed with irrelevant discussion or petty debates, and the result is a group of disengaged and irritated people zoning out.

Not only are these meetings tedious and dull, but they are also costly. Conventional meetings waste time that could be spent focusing on high-value activities and moving the needle. Yet most people spend an inordinate amount of their working lives sitting in meetings, focusing simply on staying awake, when they should be focusing on tasks and activities that drive growth.

An average 15% of an organization's time is spent in meetings, according to research collected by telecommunications company Fuze. Bad meetings cause professionals to lose about 31 hours every month (approximately four work days), and another study calculated that the United States wastes more than $37 billion to ineffective, unproductive meetings annually.

Research by Wolf Management Consultants on professionals who meet frequently shows that 95% of meeting attendees miss parts of meetings, 73% take other work to meetings, and 39% admitted that they have dozed off at meetings.

The author of *Death By Meeting*, Patrick Lencioni says: "Bad meetings not only exact a toll on the attendees as they suffer through them, but also cause real human anguish in the form of anger, lethargy, cynicism, and even in the form of lower self-esteem."

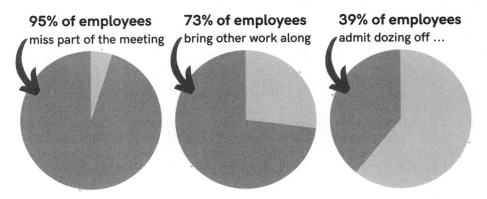

FIGURE 16.2   Wolf Management Consultants Graph

According to the *HR Digest*, ineffective meetings:

- Prolong action and decision cycles
- Lower employee engagement and morale
- Interrupt workflow

- Promote even more meetings and re-work
- Disengage and obfuscate responsibility
- Steal employees' productivity

"Huddling up" preserves the camaraderie and utility of meetings but does away with their irrelevancies and inefficiencies. Camaraderie and utility are at the core of huddling up. Like a sport's team that gathers together on the field or court, huddles are a space in which team leaders and team members will gather. But, like a sport's team that briefly huddles together to plot their next play, you will never forget that you're still in the game, and the clock is about to start ticking again. You need to take swift, decisive action and get back out there and play. Team huddles inspire amazing plays.

The Surprising Secret of Team Effectiveness

Over the years Google has spent considerable time, energy, and money trying to understand its people and how they work. One of their most interesting undertakings was "Project Aristotle," which set out to collect and codify the secrets to team effectiveness. Specifically, Google wanted to determine why some teams excelled and thrived while others failed or fell behind.

As described in an article in Inc.com, over a period of two years, Project Aristotle studied 180 teams, conducted 200-plus interviews, and analyzed over 250 different team attributes, but "there was still no clear pattern that could be plugged into a dream-team generating algorithm. . . . It wasn't until Google started considering some intangibles that things began to fall into place."

As they grappled with identifying what made a team successful, Google turned their attention to what psychologists and sociologists describe as "group norms" – the traditions, behavioral standards, and unwritten rules that govern how groups function when they gather. They reanalyzed their data and identified the following five key dynamics that set successful teams apart from the rest.

Five Key Dynamics on Successful Teams

1. **Psychological Safety:** Can we take risks on this team without feeling insecure or embarrassed?
2. **Dependability:** Can we count on each other to do high-quality work on time?
3. **Structure and Clarity:** Are the goals, roles, and execution plans on our team clear to everybody?
4. **Meaning of Work:** Are we working on something that is personally important for each of us?
5. **Impact of Work:** Do we fundamentally believe that the work we're doing matters?

① **Psychological Safety**

② **Dependability**

③ **Structure and Clarity**

④ **Meaning of Work**

⑤ **Impact of Work**

FIGURE 16.3   Five Key Dynamics

Google's study confirmed many of the things we, at Icenhower Coaching and Consulting (ICC), have known for years to be true. Top-performing real estate teams have clear goals and well-defined roles within the group. There is a clear sense that the goal, and the work they do, is "about everyone." On the best real estate teams, the work or role has personal significance to each member. They believe that their work or role is purposeful, positively impacts the good of the group, and creates change. On the best real estate teams, people get things done on time and meet high expectations and commitments. And, on dream real estate teams, people don't hold back from a fear of seeming stupid or incompetent. Rather, everyone feels safe to voice their opinions, ask questions, and look for help and guidance when they need it.

Having said that, it is important to understand that huddling in and of itself might not be of benefit. While it's important to create a safe space in which team members are free to take risks or voice their opinions without fear of a backlash, if a huddle is not performed well, or if the "players" don't discuss something of value, then huddling up is not necessarily effective and veers dangerously into the territory of conventional organizational meetings that get sidetracked with irrelevancies and inefficiencies. With that in mind, in the next chapter, we drill down on some best practices for holding successful growth huddles.

How to Hold a Growth Huddle

Huddles communicate vision, foster camaraderie, and provide clarity. Follow these five best practices to set your growth huddles apart from conventional team meetings.

1.   Keep the Growth Huddle Brief

All effective huddles are brief and to the point. Start on time and end on time. Put a strict 20- to 30-minute time limit on the growth huddle (less if you are holding daily growth huddles), and also put a time limit on how long each individual can speak. Of course, this may depend on what arises during the four key accountability questions. If team members have fulfilled their commitments, the huddle will be very brief indeed. Remember that only the person answering the accountability questions is allowed to speak. Not only does this allow them to express themselves, but it also keeps everyone accountable to the time limit and upholding the "brief but intense" spirit of the huddle.

2. Huddle Up Frequently

The only things worse than long meetings are irregular, sporadic, and nonexistent meetings. On a football team, players huddle every 24 seconds to plot their next play/offensive attack. Though the leader and team members won't be gathering together quite as much as that, huddles are most impactful when they are frequent and occur at a regularly scheduled part of the day. At a minimum, your growth huddles should be held weekly, though many real estate teams love the momentum and energy of a daily or every-other-day huddle.

3. Growth Huddles Are Sacred

No excuses: you can never ever, ever skip a weekly growth huddle. Huddles are not just another meeting. They can't be. Not when you're discussing such high-level matters. Growth won't happen when you postpone huddles under pressure from day-to-day activities. Try to hold your huddles at the same time each day, or on the same day each week. Consistency makes the huddle habitual, ensuring those on your real estate team are more accepting of it. Huddles are generally most effective first thing in the morning, centering everyone's focus on the coming day. Alternatively, huddling up halfway through the day allows you to regroup. If things haven't been going so well, a midday huddle allows team members to regroup and remind everyone that it's never too late to take action. No matter what time of the day or week they happen, the most important thing is that they happen. So, refrain from canceling, missing, rescheduling, or showing up late to your team's meetings.

4. Skip the Coffee and the Doughnuts

Instead of meetings where everyone gets comfortable and inevitably gets off topic, reflect the importance and difference of huddling up by eliminating anything distracting or irrelevant. Some teams implement a standing huddle to encourage people to stay on topic and

Resource   **Sample Weekly Calendar**

In the online resource appendix of this book, you will find the Sample Weekly Calendar. This calendar is a great guide on how to infuse your Weekly Huddle into your team calendar. Keeping it brief and consistent each week is key!

All resources can be downloaded from this book's online appendix at therealestatetrainer.com/ teambook.

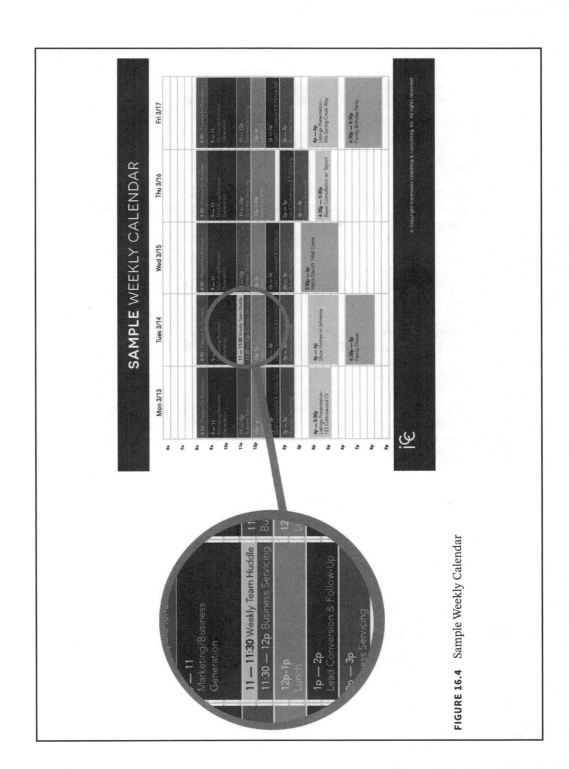

FIGURE 16.4 Sample Weekly Calendar

not get overly comfortable before heading back out "on the field." If possible, this is an excellent tactic, but remember that your real estate team members are not elite-level athletes – different people have different abilities and there's nothing wrong with providing a comfortable place to sit, so long as you don't settle in for hours on end and everyone understands that the huddle is a place to focus and galvanize action.

5.   Take the Lead, Then Take a Backseat

Every growth huddle needs a leader to keep the huddle on track and hold team members accountable when needed. On a sports team, the best coaches instruct their team as to what is to be emphasized during this brief period of refocusing. An example of this might be for only the Point Guard to speak initially during the huddle before any other player can contribute. As players become more experienced, the discussion can be more directed by the players' own analysis of what is happening on the court.

As the head of the real estate team, team leaders will be the ones to lead the weekly growth huddle; and on larger teams, individual departments can conduct separate or smaller huddles. Either way, we recommend that you engage everybody and ensure that all team members take an active part in participating in the huddle. In time, allowing different team members to lead the huddle will foster a sense of ownership and shared responsibility, not to mention cultivating leadership skills.

Remember, at each growth huddle, an accountability leader will ask the rest of the team to provide an "account" of their activities. For those who have hit their weekly activity-based indicator (ABI) targets, the data on the dashboard will speak for itself. There is no need to hold those people accountable or ask them the four accountability questions, as they have clearly taken responsibility and achieved their daily and weekly goals.

Four Key Accountability Questions

When an individual has not met their ABI commitments, the accountability leader will not react negatively or punitively. In fact, they will take a back seat, refrain from comment, and simply run through the four key accountability questions.

① **How do you think you did?**
② **What got in the way?**
③ **What do you need to do differently next time?**
④ **Is there any way we can help?**

FIGURE 16.5 Four Key Accountability Questions

These questions are designed to keep everyone at the meeting thinking and talking about the ABIs and eliminating irrelevant or unproductive discussion. Each question plays a particular part in cultivating both a sense of personal responsibility and of collective and collaborative accountability. They are designed to lead team members through a process of self-discovery where they think for themselves, identify their stumbling blocks, and author their own solutions.

At the end of the growth huddle, individuals will have a clear picture of the problem, its roots, and a clear picture of how to proceed. Their solutions will have come from within and be further strengthened by the support and feedback of an increasingly bonded team. When conducted correctly, accountability produces a harmonious state where people feel that they have personal control over their life and choices, while also knowing that you're all in this together.

Growth Sets the Agenda

A growth huddle is typically divided into two parts: the dashboard and the annual business plan. Though slightly different, both are focused on growth.

Growth-focused real estate teams protect their huddles from operational issues that divert their focus. A huddle is not the place for the 80% that doesn't make much impact. This valuable time can be destroyed by updates and reports about how existing business is coming along or how new systems are being implemented. Although these items are always somewhat important, if they are not in direct alignment with a team's growth goals they must be kept off of the agenda.

In the same vein, while the huddle is designed to help team members author solutions, don't mistake that for a need to find problems. This desire might dominate the team leader's thinking, leading them to become a "problem solver" and not an innovative, growth-oriented leader. As you veer off-course, toward problems, and away from growth, so will the entire team.

If team members are supposed to take the weekly growth huddle seriously, it needs to be focused on serious, productive things, and nothing is more serious or important to a real estate team than ABIs. ABIs demand to be taken seriously because they're directly tied to the growth and success of both the leader and the team. For those 20 to 30 minutes, forget about everything else and use your ABI-focused dashboard and your annual plan to set the agenda.

In the first half of your growth huddle, your dashboard and the ABIs displayed on it will set the agenda. Guided by the four key accountability questions, the team leader and the team members will run through the dashboard, from side to side or top to bottom, and cultivate some meaningful, productive conversations around the ABIs.

It's worth noting that some of the most productive and generative discussions and solutions happen when people have *not* hit their target numbers and fulfilled their commitments. Leaders should not waste time and energy reprimanding people for excuses or approach accountability from a place of frustration. The best brainstorming arises from the third and fourth questions: "*What are you going to do differently next time?*" and "*Is there any way we can help?*" Just imagine your team discussing productive issues like how to write stronger offers that get accepted, or how to motivate sellers that lack urgency to list their home, or maybe even what scripts everyone is using to call past clients to invite them to the team's client appreciation event.

Like a sport's huddle, a real estate team growth huddle is focused on tactics and strategies. However, huddles are also a place to identify and talk through problems, not necessarily solve them in their entirety. Not everything gets completely resolved in the huddle, but everyone should walk away with creative solutions to a common challenge and be bolstered by a sense of support, determination, and capability.

Huddles are a place to
***identify* & talk through problems, not solve them in their entirety.**

FIGURE 16.6   Huddles Quote

The second half of a growth huddle is typically focused on your annual business plan, which we'll describe in more detail shortly. As you'll soon see, in addition to the most impactful activities (i.e. the ABIs), further tasks and objectives will need to be accomplished in order to achieve your annual goal. Once you've discussed the week's ABIs and walked through the four key accountability questions, you can then turn your attention to the objectives and focus areas on your one-page annual plan. Over the course of the year, the team leader and team members will slowly chip away at each of these objectives, checking them off as they're completed and displaying them as achievements to be proud of and celebrated.

Speak in Commitments, Not in Numbers

When you celebrate, it should be because the people on your team have fulfilled their commitments. Commitments carry more weight and meaning than simply hitting targets or meeting the numbers. Commitments are about responsibility and intentionality. Commitments are sacred. We make commitments to our children, friends, and partners. When we *commit* to our team, we infuse that familial support and dedication into our work.

Commitments made at the weekly huddle represent the things that must happen, beyond the day-to-day operations, to move the ABIs forward. The commitments made by those at the huddle matter because, when kept, these commitments drive the ABIs and thus they drive achievement of the viral goal. Your team members should feel as though ABIs are commitments that they cannot renege on without letting other people down.

Make It About Everyone

Huddles are engaging and effective for many reasons. Needless to say, human-to-human contact where individuals look each other in the eyes and account for their actions and responsibilities is a powerful way to unite a group of people. And if one person gives up or reneges on their commitments, he or she is held accountable by a "face to face" in the next huddle.

Everyone on the real estate team should be in attendance at the weekly huddle. The huddle is not only *about* them, it is *for* them: to celebrate achievements, identify problems, and make adjustments, while also challenging and encouraging each other. This focus is what produces wins – on the court, on the field, and for your growing real estate team.

Make Your Growth Huddles Dynamic by Making Your ABIs Exciting

When we talk about what a huddle is versus a conventional meeting, one of the distinguishing factors is that a huddle is not boring. It is dynamic. The team leader runs through important tasks and activities that each team member should be doing.

You may be thinking – that still sounds boring. Well, what are your activities? Sure, some activities are boring, but maybe the leader needs to put a better plan in place to make them more engaging for the whole team.

For example, client events make the activities part of the real estate agent's job more positive, more exciting, and less daunting.

At ICC, we coach our clients to create an Annual Database Contact Plan by which a structure is developed for contacting sphere of influence (SOI) database members 40 times a year. Most of these "touches" will be digital, like emails and social media messages – very

Resource   Client Appreciation Events Packet

In the online resource appendix of this book, you will find the Client Appreciation Events Packet. This packet will help you brainstorm, plan, and execute your next client appreciation event. With ideas for all kinds of events, including virtual events and social-distancing-friendly events, you'll be sure to find some ideas that fit your needs. This packet also provides you with a Client Event Contact Plan, so you'll know a good cadence for reaching out to your SOI members, from the initial save-the-date to follow-up thank-you notes. Also included in this bundle are Client Appreciation Event social media invitation templates, making it easy for you to start your client event campaign.

All resources can be downloaded from this book's online appendix at therealestatetrainer.com/ teambook.

FIGURE 16.7 Client Event Packet

subtle and easy contacts. You will have a couple of phone calls in there, too, and some text messages. The whole point of the Annual Database Contact Plan is to stay in front of your SOI, but at the same time, you don't want to harass them. You must always come from contribution and add value when you are reaching out to your SOI, never annoying them. These are our SOIs, so we want them to like us and refer us business.

With client events, it makes this 40 touches a year concept easy. It takes the weary task of reaching out to people we know and puts some meaning behind it. This way, you are simply inviting your SOI members to a party, or to pick up a free pie at Thanksgiving, or to a Photos with Santa event. The possibilities are endless.

So, you're going to be reaching out to your SOI members about your client event. That's way more fun than just a random phone call to see if they know anyone interested in buying or selling their home. Suddenly, your tasks become positive and upbeat.

Now, you must plan out your client event contact plan ahead of time. For example, say you are on a big team and you plan to have six client events per year. That means you will host an event every two months, which means you have two months leading up to each event where you can make anywhere from 10 to 15 contacts to each of your SOI members. With each of these contacts, you are always inviting and never being annoying. And all the while, you are staying in front of your SOI members and staying first in mind.

So, how does this relate to your weekly growth huddle? Well, you're on a team, and teams have the ability to host larger-scale client events than solo agents. Typically, solo agents are unable to spend a large enough amount of money to put any sizeable event on. Often, they just don't have the dollars for marketing, and they also won't attract as many contributions from their preferred vendors because they typically don't generate a huge amount of business for those vendors.

Most of the teams we coach at ICC are able to get sizeable contributions from affiliates like mortgage lenders, title companies, escrow companies, home warrantee companies, homeowners insurance companies, etc. to help put forth some marketing dollars.

The team generates all this income and this marketing budget from its combined production. Truly, together, as a team, we achieve more. Team members band together to generate a better result as a group as opposed to a solo agent. So, when you're huddling up, guess what you're talking about each week? The super awesome client event that you have planned for next month. Your activities? Booking the face painter. Reaching out to a local taco truck. This is what client events can do for your team. Not only are client events excellent for generating more business, but they are also excellent for team spirit.

Case Study

The Rick Fuller Team in the San Francisco Bay Area, California

Rick Fuller is a long-time ICC coaching client and is also now an ICC coach himself. Rick definitely knows a thing or two about conducting weekly huddles from his experience coaching other teams, and more importantly, from implementing growth huddles with his own team.

The Rick Fuller Team is the number-one-producing real estate team in the San Francisco Bay Area, and we've had the pleasure of watching their team triple in size and sell over 500 homes per year since working with ICC. He has a relatively large team, with over 20 agents. Rick will tell you, once he led his team to start huddling up on a weekly basis, they found that they were able to accomplish so much more. And, an added benefit was how good it was for their team culture. Providing a weekly huddle made each team member more productive because they were being held more accountable. When we initially started working with Rick, his team's production was just a mere fraction of what it is now. However, their numbers climbed rapidly once these principles of a successful team growth huddle were put in place.

The Rick Fuller Team boasts a strong administrative staff with a Marketing Director on his team. His Marketing Director is responsible for organizing, planning, and marketing these events with dynamic promotional material. Then, the Marketing Director distributes those materials to all the members of the team. This is where the magic happens. Now, the team members are encouraged to build their own SOIs by marketing the events – and they've been handed the tools with which to do so. All the contacts that are tracked on the dashboard during the weekly huddles are often just save-the-dates, reminders, and invitations to a party. When the Rick Fuller Team members are marketing to their SOI members, they are always inviting, always giving, always coming from contribution, over and over again. They would not likely be able to do this on their own.

Now you can imagine in a weekly huddle everyone getting together sitting down and having a conversation about "Okay, let's look at the client event contact plan. It is the third week of the month, everyone should be sending out our marketing image in a direct/personal message to SOI members on Facebook and other social media networks. You all already have this in your inbox, created by our Marketing Director. We have to make these touches this week, everybody can continue to make their calls to their SOI, remember, that's three per day. Let's see how we all did last week." This is actually what the weekly huddle is all about. We have our client contact plan as an agenda item under our annual business plan. We are working on our client events and so we must hold everyone accountable to the activities around the contact plan. And guess what? It's exciting! We're not "working." We are planning a party! The huddle should not be about spreadsheets and CRMs – it should be about fun, too! That's why building and working your SOI database by way of client events is a great way to do this.

At ICC we typically encourage agents to use their SOI referral databases as the core pillar of a team's production. This way, agents are able to build a big, robust, referral-based business. Just for clarification, there are many other methods for generating business, and teams rarely limit themselves to just one. However, we typically recommend that building a strong SOI be the foundation of a team's marketing plan, and depending on each team's characteristics, a few additional lead-generation sources as well.

This is how the Rick Fuller Team has risen to success. It takes a team of this magnitude to do more and more events, better and better each year. This is the key to their huddles each week. They are exciting, chipping away at the annual business plan. This is progressive leadership where everyone gets involved, and it creates an amazing real estate team culture.

FIGURE 16.8 Client Event Ideas

215

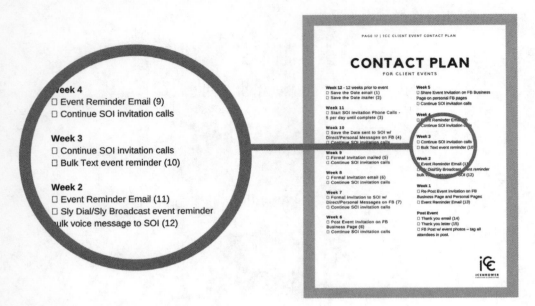

FIGURE 16.9 Client Event Contact Plan

The Implementation Process Continues

Now that you have a clear sense of what we mean by huddling up, let's turn our attention to the next phase in implementing growth on your real estate team.

Growth huddles are goal-oriented, ABI-focused, and to a certain extent guided by the numbers and data on your team's dashboard. Therefore, before you can begin your daily or weekly growth huddle as described earlier, you will need to implement each of the other components of growth. Begin by returning to the first chapter of this book and follow our guide to devising an exciting viral goal at your real estate team. Then, return to the second chapter of this book and begin the process of identifying your team's most impactful ABIs.

Notice that we say, "begin" the process. Understand that this is, very much, a process. Identifying the most effective growth activities that drive your team forward is no easy feat, and it won't happen overnight or in a single meeting.

Nevertheless, a journey of a thousand miles begins with a single step, and you can certainly begin creating and implementing a dashboard. To that end, there will be a lot of things that you need to do to support you and your team members in discovering, implementing, and honing ABIs. To achieve your overall, annual, viral goal, there will be many more things that you need to accomplish in addition to identifying ABIs, creating a dashboard, and holding a huddle. For that reason, in addition to devising a viral goal and focusing on ABIs, we strongly advise taking a high-level approach and creating a one-page team business plan.

Up Next: Creating Your One-Page Annual Team Business Plan

Once the book club part of the implementation process is over, everyone will spend Week 6 "huddling up" to create a one-page annual team business plan. Through the creation of this business plan, you will also need to fine-tune your dashboard, as the two go hand-in-hand. This gathering will resemble a traditional team meeting in the sense that it will be longer than a brief, 20-minute growth huddle. However, this is not an excuse to sit back on your phone while someone else drones on and on for two hours. Though this meeting will be longer in length, its growth-building purpose remains the same, and the strategic, collaborative, and powerful spirit of the huddle still applies.

CHAPTER 17

Create Your Annual Goals and One-Page Team Business Plan . . . and Focus Your Growth Huddles on Them

As we said way back in the introduction, we're assuming you picked up this book because, like so many others, your real estate team or brokerage is stuck in the status quo, has reached a point of stasis, or is at a significant turning point.

You are reading this book as the leader of your team, managing broker at your brokerage, or as the team member or agent at your brokerage. Whether you find yourself in a place of leadership or in a place to be led, we wrote this book with you in mind.

When you picked up this book, we offered you a chance to begin anew. Whatever your real estate team's growth goals may be, this book was designed to help you achieve *your team's* definition and vision of growth.

We have covered a lot of ground, from devising a viral goal to the process of identifying activity-based indicators (ABIs), holding team members accountable, and creating an engaging and motivating dashboard.

The One-Page Plan

Along with the five components of growth, creating an annual plan is a crucial element in your team's winning, growth-building strategy.

Successful real estate teams utilize a simple *one-page plan* to organize *everything* they want to accomplish in a single year. The annual plan will consolidate everything you need to do in the course of a year into a simple one-page document.

Some aspects of the annual plan will overlap or interrelate with the five components of growth, but please understand that they are not one and the same thing. While the annual plan doesn't tie in directly with the five components of growth, *everything on this plan should be in alignment with achieving your viral goal.*

Sometimes, real estate teams will hold an annual one-day retreat to focus on creating and developing their annual team business plan. We've also seen this done biannually where teams hold a second mid-year retreat to assess where they are in reaching their goals and making needed modifications before finishing out the second half of the year. This can help reenergize and refocus the team. Whether you implement a formal retreat or not, real estate teams that are committed to going above and beyond are always looking for ways to reinvigorate and motivate their team.

A single-page plan is easier to refer to than a multipage document and allows everyone to follow its action steps. Include or display your team's plan in your weekly huddles as a regular reminder of your goals and to foster accountability as well as encouragement. As each item on the plan is crossed off throughout the year, team members will be assured that the team is growing and improving in direct alignment with your annual goals.

A tidy 1-3-5 format allows you to focus on the key actions that specifically lead to the results you desire without having to endure the tiresome process of drafting more formalized plans.

Focus on the *key actions* that specifically lead to the results you desire.

FIGURE 17.1   Focus on the Key Actions

Determine Your One Big Annual Goal

Begin by determining your one big annual goal. In other words: devise and determine your viral goal (refer to Part One). While the one-page annual plan and the five components of growth are not one and the same thing, your viral goal is the "1" in your 1-3-5 plan, and everything on this plan should be in alignment with achieving your viral goal.

As previously discussed, start by establishing a specific, measurable, and time-bound goal for your real estate team to achieve by next year.

Additionally, whether your goal is conceived as total sales volume, gross commission income, number of properties sold, net income, number of new team members, etc., make sure it has a numeric value associated with it so that it can be broken down into quarterly, monthly, and weekly components for measuring progress throughout the year. Knowing these numbers makes it easy to determine if you are ahead or behind your target.

Most importantly, this number-one goal must be about each person on your team. Leaders, the best way to inspire your team members about team growth on a personal level is to include them in the process. Team members, the best way to feel invested in team growth is to feel included in the business planning process!

Establish Three Key Focus Areas to Reach the Main Goal

To achieve the overall, annual, viral goal, there will be many more things that you need to accomplish in addition to identifying ABIs, creating a growth-driving dashboard, and huddling up. Just because the most important thing you can do is fulfill your daily and weekly ABI commitments doesn't mean that your team doesn't need excellent customer service for your clients, or human resources and operations systems for your team members.

While these things are not the highest-impact 20%, neither are they the 80% that don't much matter. Remember that Juran (who coined the concept of the Pareto Principle) adjusted his definition over time. While he originally referred to the principle as "the vital few and the trivial many," on realizing that no effect is truly trivial, he later preferred to think of it as "the vital few and the useful many," signaling that the remaining 80% of the causes should not be *completely* ignored.

A great deal of your day-to-day tasks will fit the strict definition of the trivial 80% that doesn't move the needle on growth. However, within that 80% there will be many useful and much-needed things that must be achieved to facilitate and support you and your team members in performing your ABIs and achieving your greater goals. Some of these things might start to show up in part "3" of your 1-3-5 annual plan.

Resource   **ICC Single-Page Business Plan and Business Planning Guide**

> In the online resource appendix of this book, you will find the ICC Single-Page Business Plan, which is a fillable form PDF, as well as a Business Planning Guide. In this chapter, we dive in on how to use this business plan for your real estate team.
>
> *All resources can be downloaded from this book's online appendix at therealestatetrainer.com/teambook.*

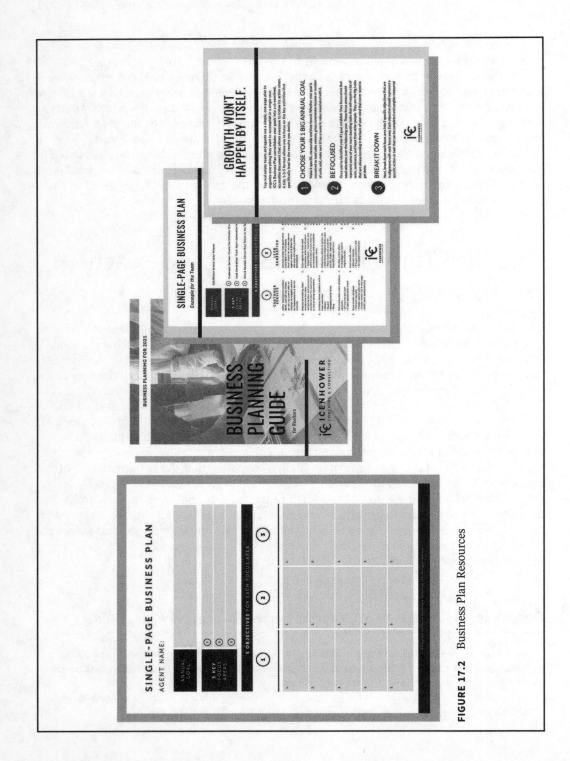

FIGURE 17.2 Business Plan Resources

For a business plan to be effective, it must be focused. Once you've identified your number-one viral goal, establish three key focus areas that need attention over the following year. These focus areas should represent some of your more daunting tasks that will require a lot of work, assistance, and input from other people. They are the big tasks that are always looming in the back of your mind that never seem to get done.

Your key focus areas will depend on the size of your team and where you're at in terms of growth and development. A few examples of key focus areas for real estate teams include customer service, team culture, online presence, social media, recruiting, hiring a coach, or developing a lead-generation plan or system. Here at ICC, working on identifying the best key focus areas for a team is something we do regularly with our clients.

Stretch your imagination and think of everything you need to do in order to hit your goals this year; then, whittle those down to the three most important focus areas.

In the first year, a great focus area would be the creation of your team's dashboard. While you already created a working dashboard in Week 4, you may need to take several meetings to adjust and fine-tune every aspect of it. Identifying ABIs can take time, so a dashboard is inevitably a work in progress that you will tweak and refine, especially throughout the first year.

Remember what you learned from component 2. When you break it down and take things back to basics, *making contact and engaging other people is the primary activity that underlies most every team's strategy or model.* On some level, making contact and engaging other people will tie into every single ABI that you implement on your real estate team.

With that in mind, another focus area might be "Skill Development" where you're teaching team members how to grow their sphere of influence (SOI), how to prepare for and conduct listing appointments, how to memorize scripts, or how to modify their behavior profile and communicate more effectively with other behavior types.

Identifying ABIs is one thing, but you also must learn how to execute them effectively. A certain lead-generation activity might be completely new to agents on the team, or maybe they just need more skill development to improve on activity they've already been doing. Anything different that you need to do to be able to successfully implement and/or hit the ABIs should be included on the plan. Certain ABIs may explicitly appear on the plan, but understand that identifying the 20% ABIs is a separate and additional process that you will need to perform, in accordance with the practices and strategies we discussed in Part Two.

No matter what three focus areas you ultimately decide upon, ensure that they are in direct alignment with achieving your #1 viral goal.

Plan Five Objectives for Each Key Focus Area

Next, break down each focus area into five specific objectives that are in alignment with each focus area. Each objective should represent a specific action or task that can be completed and tangibly measured.

The key to developing effective objectives is to ensure that they effectively correlate to each key focus area. Otherwise, you will just have a scattered to-do list that is unlikely to ever be completed.

Resource   Action Steps

In the online resource appendix of this book, you will find Action Steps, which is a fillable form PDF, as well as Sample Action Steps. We're also going to show you the Sample Action Steps on the following page, followed by the blank Action Steps form. The Action Steps form will help you devise the Action Steps that will follow each of your five objectives that you create based on your three key focus areas. See how it breaks down into a concise list of things your team must accomplish. Think of the Action Steps forms as a way to exponentially accelerate the implementation of your 1-3-5 business plan!

All resources can be downloaded from this book's online appendix at therealestatetrainer.com/ teambook.

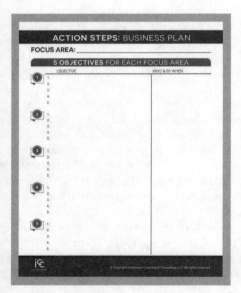
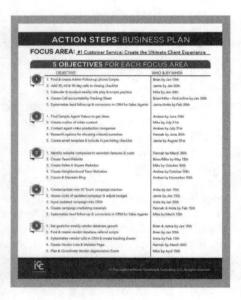

FIGURE 17.3   Action Steps

More importantly, each of the objectives – all 15 of them – must be in direct alignment with hitting that #1 goal up top. That is: they should not and must not be an assortment of random things that you've been meaning to get done forever. Rather, when establishing objectives, your question should be: "Does *this* objective help us to reach *this* goal up there?" If it has a significant enough impact toward assisting you in reaching the goal, then it belongs on the "1-3-5" plan. If it does not have a significant enough impact on reaching your goal, or is not in alignment with one of the three key focus areas, then it does not belong on your annual plan.

Specific ABIs might fall under the umbrella of a particular focus area and form one of the five objectives, but there are other things that need to be done outside the ABIs. You're not going to track *everything* you do on the dashboard, but a lot of other things will nonetheless need to happen to achieve your viral goal. You might need to increase your marketing. There might be systems you need to set up, or people you need to hire.

There are a lot of different ways to grow your SOI. There are a lot of different ways to market your real estate team or secure listing appointments. In fact, there are a lot of different ways to accomplish just about anything in real estate. So, there are a lot of different things you are going to need to do in order to be effective at all of those things. You will need systems to support your increased efforts. ABIs will be some of the objectives, but they won't be all of the objectives. Simply put: there are other things you will need to do as well, so your five objectives are not necessarily ABIs, though they certainly can be because, just like the ABIs, your objectives should be highly actionable and measurable in nature.

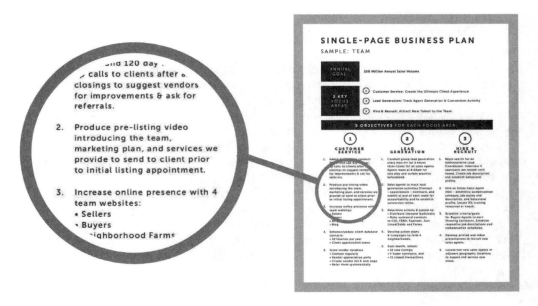

FIGURE 17.4 Sample Team Business Plan

One example, based on the earlier sample team business plan, is the second objective under the key focus area of Customer Service. You can reference this sample within the Business Planning Guide provided at the beginning of this chapter. The objective states, "Produce prelisting video introducing the team, marketing plan, and services we provide to send to client prior to initial listing appointment." This is a solid objective because it directly feeds into the key focus area of "Customer Service: To Create the Ultimate Customer Experience," which also contributes to the overarching annual goal, or viral goal, of reaching $50 million annual sales volume.

To take it a step further, you can consider how you would break down each objective you've listed within your weekly huddles. For example, the second objective of "creating a prelisting video" could be broken down into multiple tasks, the first being finding a videographer. This task could be brought up at a weekly huddle, as each team member brings their own ideas to the table and you decide on the best videographer for the job. From each chosen objective, many tasks and topics to discuss are generated for your weekly growth huddles. The key is to break each of the 1-3-5 business plan's objectives down into these little baby steps so that we continuously move forward toward our goals each week. More importantly, everyone on the team is involved in the process.

We have seen teams use a 1:4:6 format or a 1:5:5 format with great success. However, it can ultimately be discouraging and counterproductive if you bite off more than you can chew. A 1:3:5 format allows you to be ambitious, but pragmatic, about creating exciting, ambitious, but humanly attainable goals!

The Power of Crossing Off Objectives

As you and your team work through objectives during your weekly huddles, there is something very powerful about crossing them off once they have been completed. This is an important step that you should do as a team. As you refer to your Team Business Plan during your huddle each week, cross off the objectives once they have been completed, signifying a milestone in reaching your annual goal.

It is important to remember to not work through too many objectives at once. We recommend working on two or three at once, at the most. If you are working on too many of your objectives at the same time, it can feel overwhelming to your team members and also very disorganized. To maintain a clear focus and to keep your huddles less scattered, make sure you hone in on a few at a time.

Some of the teams we coach at ICC complete all of the objectives on their business plans by late summer. This is not uncommon! When this happens, take a moment to pat yourselves on the back! Then, huddle up and create a team business plan for the remaining months of the year.

Next Steps

Congrats! The end of this book marks the beginning of your journey toward implementing everything you've learned and creating a high-performing real estate team.

If you're reading this book for the first time as a team leader of your real estate team, it is now, at long last, time to introduce this book and the five components of team growth to your people.

Remember, once the team leader has finished reading this book and digested its principles, everyone on the real estate team should also receive a copy of *The High-Performing Real Estate Team*. At that point, the entire team will embark on a five-week journey through the book together. Each week, for five consecutive weeks, everyone will read one part from the book and then meet to discuss it. At the end of the five weeks, your team will have a clear understanding of each of the five components of team growth and will be ready to take what they have learned and apply it directly to your real estate team.

If you are the team leader or broker of a larger real estate team or office with different departments, we recommend first holding a book club with the leadership team. The exact same reading schedule and book club process will occur, but among the team's leaders/managers only. After the leadership team has read this book and conducted their own book club, they will then branch out to conduct *simultaneous* book clubs within the different departments of the team or brokerage.

Of course, if you're reading this book as a team member, that means that the implantation process is already well under way and your next step is to get ready to attend your weekly book club session – in this case, the final book club session. As always, the following section will help you prepare and give you a sense of what to expect. When the fifth and final book club is over, you will maintain the momentum and enthusiasm of the past five weeks and huddle up with your team to take the next steps on your mutually beneficial and rewarding journey into growth.

The Team Book Club: Part Five Discussion Guide

Welcome to the final book club meeting! Congratulations on making it through each of the five parts of *The High-Performing Real Estate Team*. We applaud your willingness to not only participate in the process, but also to push yourself to grow, learn, adapt, and challenge your perspectives. We sincerely hope that the Team Book Club has been a positive, productive, and inspiring experience for you, and that the process has brought you closer to the people who've joined you in conversation and exploration. Though this week will be the final week that you come together as a "book club," we trust that you've enjoyed these weekly gatherings and are eagerly looking forward to huddling up together on a regular basis!

Hold Each Other Accountable

The team leader or facilitator will begin the final book club by asking the group who did and didn't read Part Five and, if necessary, asking the four key accountability questions to anyone who did not manage to complete this week's reading (see Figure BC.1).

At this stage, it's highly unlikely that anyone has not completed the reading, so we trust that little time will be taken up with the accountability questions at your final book club. Having said that, cultivating personal responsibility takes time. Don't become overly distracted or derailed by those who haven't prepared in advance. Keep the accountability section to a minimum and keep your sight on the real purpose and subject of the book club meeting.

1 How do you think you did?

2 What got in the way?

3 What do you need to do differently next time?

4 Is there any way we can help?

FIGURE BC.1   Key Accountability Questions

Part Five Summary, Component 5   Huddle Up

The fifth and final component of team growth calls for you and your team members to cultivate your reliance on, and belief in, one another by "huddling up" and maintaining the energy, enthusiasm, motivation, and momentum you've created over the past few weeks. Huddling up preserves the camaraderie and utility of meetings but does away with their irrelevancies and inefficiencies. Camaraderie and utility is at the core of huddling up. Like a sports team that gathers together on the field or court, growth huddles are a space in which leaders and team members will gather together to strategize, plan, rally, encourage, motivate, and support each other. But, like a sports team that briefly huddles together to plot their next play, you will never forget that you're still in the game, and the clock is about to start ticking again. You can't spend too much time talking about what you've done and what you're going to do. You need to take swift, decisive action and get back out there and play. Team huddles inspire amazing plays.

Key Points:

- Best practices for holding growth huddles: Keep the growth huddle brief; huddle up frequently; speak in "commitments," not in numbers; make it about them.
- Growth huddles are sacred: Never skip a weekly growth huddle. No excuses.
- Growth sets the agenda: Just as a huddle allows players to tune out the deafening noise of the crowd, your weekly growth huddles allow you and your team members to tune out the distractions of the day-to-day and focus your attention on what is most important: ABIs and the 20% activities that drive growth. A growth huddle is typically divided into two parts: the dashboard and the "1-3-5 annual plan." Though slightly different, both of these things are focused on growth.

Notes:

_____

_____

_____

_____

Distributing a Part Five summary will help refresh people's memories, or help any non-readers get up to speed so that they can't opt out of participation. Book club facilitators can use the provided summary to guide the conversation in addition to, or instead of, the questions below. As you read through each bullet point in the summary, ask everyone, "Did this point resonate with you?" "How?" "Why?" "Tell me more," and so forth.

Questions to Spark and Stoke Conversation

The following questions are simply a starting point for sparking conversation and ensuring that everyone participates.

Book Club Conversations for Component 5   Huddle Up

- What ideas was the author trying to get across in Part Five?
- How do the ideas presented in Part Five apply to us at _____ (insert the name of your real estate team)?
- How does a growth huddle differ from conventional team meetings?
- How has Part Five influenced your perception of meetings?
- What excites you about the growth huddle? What are your concerns, if any?
- What did you think about Google's research into team effectiveness?
- Does our real estate team demonstrate the five key dynamics of successful teams? (Psychological safety, dependability, structure and clarity, meaning of work, and impact of work.)
- In particular, how can our team create a culture that promotes psychological safety and allows our team members to take risks and express ideas without fear of dismissal or judgment?
- In the section about growth huddle best practices, what stood out the most? What did you think, specifically, about the idea of speaking in terms of "commitments" rather than numbers?
- What is a 1-3-5 annual plan? How does the annual plan interrelate with the five components of team growth? How does the annual plan differ from the five components of team growth?
- What are the most important factors to bear in mind when creating our team's dashboard?
- What new things did you learn in Part Five?
- What questions do you still have?
- Are there any quotes, passages, or ideas you found particularly compelling?
- Do you have a new perspective as a result of reading Part Five?
- Did you learn something you didn't know before?
- How has your attitude or behavior changed?
- How does Part Five relate to your role or experiences on our team?
- Did you connect with the subject matter? Did it make you nervous or excited?
- What did you like best about Part Five?
- What did you like least about Part Five?

(continued)

Book Club Conversations for Component 5   (*continued*)

- Which section(s) of Part Five stood out to you?
- If you had the chance to ask the author one question, right now, what would it be?

No matter what questions are brought up in the meeting, you (or each book club's leader/facilitator) should ask yourself the following questions:

- Does everyone understand the materials?
- Have we discussed ways that the material relates to us?
- Are my team members excited and engaged? Is there buy-in?
- Did we make the concept of "huddling up" *about everyone*?

If the answer to these questions is a resounding "Yes," then you are well on your way to (1) devising a viral goal at your real estate team, (2) identifying the activities that are most likely to drive growth and achieve success, (3) cultivating a sense of responsibility and accountability, (4) using the guiding abilities of a dashboard to drive growth at your real estate team, and (5) huddling up to strategize, organize, light a fire under each other, keep the momentum going, prepare for the next play and, most importantly, break and get on with the game of growth.

Index

Page numbers in *italics* denote figures.